When a

MAN

Turns

FORTY

When a
MAN
Turns
FORTY

THE ULTIMATE
MIDLIFE MANUAL

By Curtis Pesmen

Rodale Press, Inc.
Emmaus, Pennsylvania

Copyright © 1999 by Curtis Pesmen
Illustrations copyright © 1999 by Molly Babich

All rights reserved. No part of this publication may be reproduced or transmitted in any form or by any means, electronic or mechanical, including photocopying, recording, or any other information storage and retrieval system, without the written permission of the publisher.

Men's Health Books is a registered trademark of Rodale Press, Inc.

Printed in the United States of America on acid-free ∞, recycled paper ♻

Cover Designer: Christopher Rhoads
Cover Photographer: Mitch Mandel
Author Portrait: Puliatti Photographic

The excerpt on page 43 from *The Country of Marriage,* copyright © by Anthony Giardina, 1998, Random House, is reprinted by permission.

The excerpt in "Changes in Attitudes" on page 223 from *A Pirate Looks at Fifty,* copyright © by Jimmy Buffett, 1998, Random House, is reprinted by permission.

Library of Congress Cataloging-in-Publication Data

Pesmen, Curtis.
    When a man turns forty : the ultimate midlife manual / by Curtis
Pesmen.
       p.   cm.
    Includes index.
    ISBN 1–57954–022–8   hardcover
    1. Middle-aged men—United States—Life skills guides.   2. Midlife
crisis.   I. Title.
HQ1090.3.P47   1999
305.244—dc21   99–12006

Distributed to the book trade by St. Martin's Press

2 4 6 8 10 9 7 5 3 1   hardcover

Visit us on the Web at www.menshealthbooks.com or call us toll-free at (800) 848-4735

OUR PURPOSE

"We inspire and enable people to improve their lives and the world around them."

Foreword

Men, by and large, are doers, not talkers. That's great if you need a bridge built or a car engine repaired. It's not so great if you're plunging into the vortex of midlife, wondering whatever happened to the young stud you used to see in the mirror. Age creeps up on you and one day—wham—you're on the other side of life, and you don't even know how you got there.

Worst of all, you feel like it's your duty to go through this rite of passage alone. The ones who know the most about what's going on—other guys who are tumbling through the vortex—usually don't talk about it. At least not with other guys. When a man turns 40, he can expect a large cardboard cutout of the Grim Reaper to mysteriously appear on his office door. Or someone gives him black balloons. Or a lame card that reminds him that he's so far over the hill that. . . . At 40, we men do what we often do when we're confused and maybe even a little scared. We crack wise. We laugh it off. What we really need is help and camaraderie as we hurtle through the vortex.

That's what this book is all about. Curtis Pesmen talked at length with more than 100 men and dozens of leading health, nutrition, and fitness experts about what their lives are like at this crucial turning point. *When a Man Turns Forty* is filled with their voices—and their wisdom. It's not a bunch of shrinks telling you how you should feel. It's a bunch of other guys, real men, giving you the straight dope on how to get through this time, reinvent yourself, and come out of the vortex as the strong, confident man that you always wanted to be. I guarantee you this: You'll recognize the men in this book. You work with them. You live next door to them. You see them at the gym or at the bar. You may even recognize yourself in some of them. I certainly did.

After you hit 40, every birthday is cause for reflection and an alarming realization of how quickly the past 12 months have swept by. All in all, I feel pretty lucky. I have a great family, a fun job, and a snappy new suit. I don't have any regrets about where I find myself. Well, maybe one. I wish I'd taken better care of myself when I was young. I spent the early half of my twenties driving a truck for a living. Not the world's healthiest occupation. I smoked too much, was 20 pounds underweight, and the only exercise I got was lifting bottles of beer in one roadhouse or another. I worked sick a lot because I got sick a lot. I finally wised up at 30, quit smoking, started exercising, and stopped treating beef jerky and pickled eggs as major food groups. I've challenged myself physically a little more every year, and every year I've been able to meet that challenge.

You'll meet plenty of guys in this book who have set—and met—their own challenges. Whether it's climbing a mountain or retiring young and rich, they have come through the vortex of midlife changed for the better. Healthier. Happier. More financially secure. They feel better about themselves and about their lives. Hell, they just flat-out feel better.

And that's really the key point that too many doctors and health experts miss. The best motivation to exercise, eat right, control stress, and get your priorities straight isn't to avoid disease or some other health problem down the road. The best reason is how great it makes you feel every day.

Like many of the men in this book, I find myself feeling better at middle age than I've ever felt. So can you.

Michael Lafavore
Editor-in-Chief, *Men's Health* Magazine

Contents

Introduction

Welcome to the "Country of 40." For a guy who's always been young for my age—having skipped kindergarten, entered high school while playing Little League baseball, and started college at age 16—I arrived at 39 with a simple mission. I wanted to find out what is normal for a man to feel when he turns 40 and to offer him some reasonable ways in which to make this year a memorable one.

I wasn't about to promise eternal youth nor proffer some 10-step untested regimen of longevity drugs or other substances. No, that would be a task for other authors; indeed, a number of them have hungrily staked out that turf. Focusing on the "normal," I believed, with a nod to the leading lights of anti-aging medicine, would be a more appropriate and worthy mission. Part of the reason is sheer numbers: More than two million men will turn 40 each year from 1999 through 2003, according to the U.S. Census Bureau. In five years, that adds up to more than 10 million guys—a decent-size country.

Having learned what I've learned about men over the years (and having written three other books for and about them), I knew that at least a sizable minority of those millions could use a little help with such a big birthday. Even though, it turns out, there's a lot less to fret about at 40 than you might have thought. I first thought about it, in fleeting terms, some 15 years ago. . . .

It was only a moment in time—a TV moment, at that—but it felt a lot longer. It was a summer morning in 1984 when Bryant Gumbel, older and wiser, came at me, and suddenly I thought, "Look out— he's going off the script." It was my first time on the *Today* show, and Gumbel was ditching the rehearsed Q and A so he could score a nice little segue. I was 26 and had been invited on to talk about how men age. Gumbel, then 34, was smirking, probably thinking, "What does this guy know about aging?" Maybe I'd written a new book about it but he was going to have some fun. He was going to finish our segment by leaning in toward me, closer than he had a right to, and asking, "You looking forward to turning 30?"

"Yes," I said, lying to an audience of 4.6 million people.

"Forty?" he asked, remaining in my face.

"Yeah," I lied.

"Fifty?"

"Yep," I said. It was on cue and untrue. Bryant now had his moment, Willard Scott had a chicken hat on, it was 8:18 A.M., and I was looking forward to getting off the damn set.

Thinking back, it was an unkind thing for Gumbel to do, and so, as he's long since left *Today* and since CBS has long since canceled his prime time show *Public Eye*, I need to ask, "Are you, Bryant, looking forward to being 50? To 60? What about turning 70?" I'm curious.

For the record, I don't usually look forward to birthdays, especially the milestone ones. Most other guys, including the 19 million American men in their forties, don't either, despite a host of good news about diet, exercise, and possible hormone replacement for both sexes in order to delay expected effects of aging. Let's face it: We spend our whole lives getting older.

Thirty means goatees (for those who haven't grown them already). Forty means sex-and-Viagra jokes. Fifty means prostates, as in, "Have you had yours checked?" These are the big ones for a man, even if the first so-called biological clock typically doesn't kick in until one's forties. Meantime, men at 30 usually are less concerned about aging than about the fact that their bodies don't process alcohol as efficiently as they did in their Jägermeister-shot-'n'-a-beer college years.

"Midlife is a time for changing the ways we think about and honor our physical bodies, for understanding their importance to the quality of the rest of our lives and their relationship to spirit," says

Kathleen Brehony, Ph.D., a Virginia psychotherapist who specializes in life transitions and development. There's much we can control from age 40 on, but increasingly, there will be much beyond our control, Dr. Brehony and other experts believe. Indeed, I was surprised to find how much emphasis was placed on spirituality and religion by the subjects I interviewed. This included an old college roommate of mine, who had told me he was seeing a "spiritual counselor" to help him navigate some stressful times during his second marriage. (I wasn't even aware of the existence of spiritual counselors, at the time. I thought everybody went to therapists or social workers for this kind of "work.")

When I asked other men: "Has your life changed in a major way since your 40th birthday?" or "Have you changed your church- or temple-going habits at all since your 40th birthday?" I got wide and varied responses, but a strong contingent of positives in the changes related to career, love lives, and religion. "I just broke up with my girlfriend of two years," said Matt, 42, of Oklahoma, "and if I wanted to say one thing, it's that I've gone through a spiritual revival. For the first time, I'm finding spirituality. And I'm talking to a therapist now. Breaking up with her is what pushed me. You might say I've used the relationship as a tool for growth.

"You know, in life," Matt added, "most people's relationships with God are that they don't really need him until they have traumatic experiences like I did. What's that expression? 'There are no atheists in foxholes.' I'm in a position now to be able to do some stuff. I'm self-employed now. I have time to do some soul-searching, if you will. This breakup came at a time when my mom had died. My girlfriend had just wanted to get married. I felt that, too. But I felt that if we're going to be spending the next 40 years together, we've got some things to work out."

At first, when I asked Jared, a 40-year-old lawyer from Phoenix, about his recent entry into the Country of 40, he denied its significance. Then he seemed to think about what he was saying: "For all practical purposes, I could be 38 or 39 again," he said. "For me, birthdays are just a date. You get a few cards. You turn another year older. But if a bunch of 19-year-old nymphets had come over to my house on my birthday, that would be different." Just another birthday? I'll bet he wasn't talking 19-year-old-nymphets on his 21st birthday. Or even his 30th. He also seemed to make excuses for having not worked on maintaining his friendships with other men as he neared midlife: "There's less time for them," he said. "You're more focused on family. The time necessary to pursue it and let it develop—it's just not there. I guess I have to assume some responsibility for that."

As for the more corporeal pursuits, we now know that the peak years of biological functioning for men are roughly 20 to 40, no matter how you measure it. "The youth of 20 is at the height of his bodily vigor and is getting ready to take his place as a man in the society of adults," the late author and life-cycle scholar Daniel J. Levinson says in *The Seasons of a Man's Life*. At the other end of young adulthood, about the time a man hits age 38 or 39, he starts to realize that his summer of life is winding down . . . and here comes fall. That's the mindful part, Levinson states, when he takes his "place as a man," thinking about mortality for perhaps the first time.

That's largely what this book is about—taking your place as a man. In getting to know many of the more than 100 men who were interviewed for these pages, you'll learn a lot more about how to be 40 than you will about how to live to 100. Longevity itself is a worthy goal. It's just not the primary one of *When a Man Turns Forty*.

That said, the news for 40- to 50-year-olds today is that there are more ways than ever to slow the aging process—some proven, some close to being proven, and some that won't be a lock for 10 to 15 years. This is the promise of the new longevity medicine we'll look at, briefly, in chapters 1, 4, 6, and 8, without going so far as to make risky prescriptions. Hell, we face enough medical risk already, some of which is due to our own failings.

"American women make 130 million more doctor visits per year than men," says Ken Goldberg, M.D., a urologist and director of the Male Health Institute near Dallas. When I asked him why the numbers were so out of whack, he said it was part ignorance, part arrogance: Guys believe "they're bulletproof." Goldberg, 50 and trim (and a self-described former "fatty"), believes that if men practiced more preventive health, particularly in their forties, they would soon shrink the seven-year edge in life expectancy that women still hold over men. The ignorance, he adds, is probably easier to change than the arrogance.

So a secondary purpose of writing this book, if my instincts and research served me correctly, was to help reduce this ignorance among men, about men. In so doing, I hoped to be able to reframe the concept of midlife crisis and possibly set it aside. (I believe you'll believe I was able to do that, if you stick around for the rest of the book.)

Among my most garrulous of interviewees, you'll see that many couldn't seem to wait to tell me about their most recent accomplishments (there's an unmistakable urge to break away from the big firms and start one's own business and entrepreneurial efforts at this age). Others, who spoke more haltingly, felt as stuck as industrial-strength Velcro in their staid careers—and in lifestyles they can't even think of leaving. At least for a while. . . .

But the most telling thing I learned was that, at 40, most of them truly believed they were "younger" than their fathers were at that same age. Even if they weren't regulars at the gym or out on the jogging trail, they simply had this belief. And so perhaps this pushed back the notion of midlife crisis further into the future. Perhaps. For if it indeed turns out to be true for men that, as Gloria Steinem has said of modern women, "Fifty is what 40 used to be," then there's more to look forward to in your forties than you probably imagined. But don't take my word for it. I've just recently taken stock of my 40th year. Listen instead to our "elders"—the 41- and 42-year-olds who make up the bulk of this book's chapters and who are thriving.

Certainly there are midlife crises that involve divorce, death, and downsizing. Certainly there are hair loss, puffy eyes, and changes of pants sizes to contend with and prioritize. But when I wound up my research, I was left with the distinct feeling that *midlife crisis* is an overused term. For that reason, you won't find it overused in these pages. Instead, you'll find dozens of stories of midlife pauses as well as scores of fortyish solutions to problems you may not have seen coming. At least, not yet. And so welcome, again, to the Country of 40. Contrary to what you may have heard or read elsewhere, you may just find you'll enjoy your stay.

Boulder, Colorado
April 1999

What 40 Means to Men

*We don't understand life any better at 40 than at 20, but we know it
and admit it.*

—JULES RENARD (1864–1910)

I t wasn't just another birthday party. Not at all. For the 15 Chicago
men ages 39 to 41, who gathered in midsummer and headed 140
miles west to the Mississippi River town of Galena by sedan,
minivan, and sport-utility vehicle, it was a 40th birthday weekend they
wouldn't soon forget. For starters, there would be no women. Not in
the house they had rented. Nor in any of the nightly activities they had
planned. Not even in the swimming pool they commandeered, slipping
their clothes off to celebrate like teenagers for perhaps one last time.
(Only this time, they left their boxers on.)

Over the long haul, this sports-themed road trip to commemorate
all the 40th birthdays of the group at once would become more important to its participants than they had grasped at the time. They weren't
sure what turning 40 was all about, yet they knew enough to know

when they set out that wives, strippers, and girlfriends would only get in the way. Instead the men—most of whom had met each other in college—had golf and softball, beer and barbecue on their minds when they rolled west on I-90, away from city traffic on a Friday afternoon in July. When they returned on Sunday night, they were a little bit older and sadder than when they set out. Still, they made sure to tell me later, in small groups and solo interviews, that they had laughed their asses off through many of the 48-plus hours of celebration. By most accounts, this was the best birthday party they had been to in 10 years.

"What I remember most is the softball game," said Bob C., 42, a health care analyst and father of two toddlers, a year after the event. "What struck me was that it was all about feeling free, confident. I didn't feel that I had to prove anything to these guys—even though a lot of them were good athletes.

"We all run around and have our busy lives," he continued, "and here were just two hours of carving out, on a vacant lot in some subdivision, time to play just a pastoral game. We had a softball that I had saved on my desk at work—from a softball company, I think—and I guess I had saved it for too long. It lost its moisture or something . . . because here comes Brian up to bat late in the game, who nobody thinks of as *the* athlete, and he knocks the damn cover off the ball. It actually came off. It was hilarious." It was also, if you want to get high-concept-cinematic about it, *City Slickers* meets *Field of Dreams* meets . . .

"Oh my God, it was like *The Natural*," said Brian B., 41, an illustrator and the most recently married member of the crew. "I still have the ball, signed by everybody." (He sounded like a Little Leaguer retelling the tale.) But that same hit pretty much ended the game because it was the only softball any of them had thought to bring to Galena.

Taking the Field at 40

For Bob and Brian, the sports were symbolic of other things as well, starting with "in" and "out" cliques in high school, which is where their friendship started. (They were borderline "in-crowd" guys.) They didn't have a mission in mind when they decided to make the trip, other than to party with a group of men they had remained friends with for two decades. Brian did tell me later, though, that he hoped they would make new memories, instead of just rehashing old ones. "Long term" was the operative phrase for the group, as time has a way of testing things and, often, teasing them out. At 40, there's been enough time to look back.

A few weeks before my interviews with the traveling revelers, I huddled with a therapist in Boulder, Colorado, who over the years has run a number of men's groups, offering a modern twist on standard group therapy. I wanted to know what kinds of issues men typically talk about—and don't talk about—when they hit their forties and get a bit introspective. Tom Fiester, Ph.D., 55, who helped found the Boulder Men's Center in the mid-1980s, clued me in instantly. "Feelings and emotions," he says. "We're not allowed to have them."

Men at midlife often feel that they have to dig themselves out of a hole because they've somehow found themselves feeling alone and burrowed in by demands—you know, family, job, money . . . the big ones. Yet, eventually, we do open up to our feelings, at least those of us fortunate enough to have had them drawn from us by our partners, family members, or—once in a while—friends. To work through a life's worth of issues and goals by oneself takes a little time, to put it generously. Perhaps more time than a raucous 40th birthday and a few months' follow-up can provide.

In Bob's case, he believes his running and finishing the New York Marathon in his thirties meant a lot more to him than mere toned calves and quads and aerobic conditioning. From the vantage point of his early forties, he considers the race and preparation for it a meaningful life lesson (especially as he hasn't been back to that starting line since).

"I was 32," he told me. "It was a stage-of-life thing I did, partly because I was feeling like I needed something else besides work. It was the last time I really had a significant running experience." He went on to explain that he started running two years out of college, after his first marriage broke up. "It was my way of allowing myself to think and find myself." He continued running, off and on, through a stint in graduate school and into his early thirties. "I sort of made a connection that I needed more," he said of his marathon quest, "even though I was moving up the ladder pretty quickly at work."

And in taking the time to "find himself" after an early divorce, averaging 15 to 20 miles of weekly running, he literally laid the ground-work for a more healthful future. "I remember telling myself I should run the marathon that year because 'I've got some time'; and I had some things to address—whether to stay in New York or move back to Chicago, that kind of thinking." (He moved, having recently met in Chicago the woman who would become his second wife.) And he took a new job there, more for the love-life possibilities than for any short-term career potential. In short, he did some of his early-forties ground-work in his thirties.

So when he headed out to Galena, he felt in tune with his friends, not competitive with them. "It was just so great to take this stop point in life and still have all these guys I still feel close to," he said. "And we didn't spend much of the weekend catching up on the chronology of each other's lives. It wasn't, 'Tell me what you've done since we last saw each other.' It was just comfortable feeling that you didn't feel the need to catch up on everything." They did, obviously, talk about their mates, jobs, and families on the rides out and back; and they did so to the accompaniment of apropos 1970s sounds, including the Rolling Stones, Marvin Gaye, and whatever else they could get their hands on.

Unlike many men at midlife, Bob contended that he didn't have in mind any specific goals to be accomplished before he turned 40. "I thought instead, by the time I'm 40, here's what my life ought to look like. But I did think 40 is a time to think my life ought to be in some sort of a flow—as opposed to when you're 25 and you're putting your sense of values against what others might call the real world." He added, "I never felt that 40 was a supercharged number. When I was 40, I felt like I was still in my thirties; 41 hit me harder."

That was mostly because he and his wife were having trouble having children. They had been married five years and had been trying, unsuccessfully, to have a child for three of them. At 40, he said, he still had a flicker of hope that their baby "would come through our own biology." But by 41, they had agreed to turn toward adoption. He felt as if they were shedding a piece of their identity—which hit me hard when I heard it. (Perhaps because I was 40 and childless at the time.) "You can set yourself up for disappointment or artificial deadlines," Bob said, although he and his wife were overjoyed to have adopted two children while they were still 41.

"By the time I was 42, I had this incredible turnaround." Part of it, he explained, was that he had set himself up, career-wise, to be able to devote large amounts of time to being a dad at a relatively advanced age. "I did a lot of my hard work in terms of my career back in my thirties," he said. The implication was that these kids weren't going to be struggling to see their father during their infancy, or struggling to be happy and loved, for that matter.

"I think that all of us, particularly guys, want to have some comfort level by that age," he added. "I don't mean we should stop taking chances, but everybody likes to think that he's got a few things under his feet. I mean, I got the house when I was 39. It was important for us. I had never owned a piece of property before; this place gave us sort of equal footing. Because before we got it, we had lived in my wife, Mary's, old place for a few years."

As for the state of his psyche at midlife, after taking a few hard hits in his personal life and career in his twenties and mid-thirties, Bob signed up for his first yoga class when he was 37. He found it more than relaxing—worlds apart from the high-contact, frenzied pace of soccer and ice hockey that he had had played as a youth. That same year, he visited an ashram with Mary. "One of the things I realized there was that when I was younger, I tried to reassure myself through friendships and jovial times," Bob said. "Although, as I get older, I find that I get that through being a partner to someone. We all are part of a greater and more magnificent good, which doesn't mean that I can't go to the golf course and have a beer. It's that I just don't try to fill emptiness with it any more. I know very few people who are our age who would say, 'I drink just as much now as I did then.'"

After 18 holes of golf (it was a bring-your-own-cooler public course) and before the Sunday softball game, the 15 Chicago boys barbecued burgers and steaks and sipped cold bottles of beer on Saturday night, talking about what they'd been doing lately and what they hoped to do next. (They even chomped a birthday cake—nice *adult* planning, guys.) Yet by design or happenstance, they didn't end up focusing too heavily on job talk. It just didn't seem to fit, Bob and a few of the others said. Other things were more important that weekend. Softball, for instance.

"That was just so wonderful," Bob said. "Things like getting three or four hits. Some of the guys just kept spraying hits all over the field. On a personal level, it was just spontaneous. You wanted to get a hit, beat out a grounder, catch a ball. It was one of those seesaw moments."

It was a moment in which the nonjocks played like all-stars and the ex-jocks seemed to feel their age. For a few days or a few hours, at least, the playing field was level. For them, this was one of the unexpected findings of being 40.

Leaving Youthful Things Behind

Patrick M., 42, another of the "Chicago 15" set, is always in a hurry. And he's just about always late. But to hear him tell it, the single, never-married business consultant, formerly from Virginia, has good reason for never seeming too mellow. After all, he almost died, at age 25, in a violent car crash. In a way, he's been making up for that ever since. "My favorite toast comes from *Breaker Morant*," he said, referring to the 1980 film about the Boer War. "'Live each day as if it were your last, for if you do, one day you will surely be correct.'" He added, for effect, "It's not the kind of quote married guys end up quoting very often."

On the day his life almost ended, September 29, 1981, Patrick was on his way back to Notre Dame after rooting for the Fighting Irish at an away game in Ann Arbor, Michigan. (He was in graduate school at the time.) Under a late-afternoon sun, and without warning, a full-size sedan cut into his lane and collided head-on with his frisky MGB convertible, sending him through the windshield and onto the side of the two-lane highway.

"I woke up in an ambulance with an oxygen mask on and with faces peering over me," he said. "They were trying to interview me to find out what had happened." His head and torso were pretty much okay, save for severe bruising, but his left ankle was fractured and had to be reset in the emergency room.

The ironic part of the accident was that, because of the cool fall weather, Patrick had stopped the car less than an hour before the accident, popped the trunk, and grabbed a motorcycle helmet. He kept one there, alongside his roller skates, for the times at which he skated too fast for conditions. He then strapped the helmet onto his head before driving on, because, for one thing, it would cover his ears and keep them warm, and, for another, it was a hell of a lot quicker to put on the helmet than to put the top of the convertible up by hand. Also, it must be said, the helmet looked a little rakish, which Patrick didn't mind. He had no idea that it would soon save his life when his body was flung headfirst through the flimsy windshield.

"I always expected to die young," he said, when I asked him how his accident affected his view of turning 40. "I just did, I don't know why. A lot of my heroes died young . . . Jack Kennedy, Abe Lincoln. I've always tried to live my life as if my thirties would be my last decade." He sounded so matter of fact as he spoke that I found it chilling. I also knew that he had a sister who had died in her twenties, from a long illness, back when he was in college.

"I feel like I'm having a midlife crisis in reverse," he said. "Ironically, I recognize that, at 42, some of my friends are asking the questions, 'Should I leave my wife? To take up with a 25-year-old?' They are buying their convertibles, and it does not bode well. I say to them, 'I'm finding myself with a real estate broker now, for the first time in my life, looking to buy property. I'm in a place I think I'll be in for a while.' This is the first job I've had that could last the rest of my life. And I'm dating a single mom—the first time I've dated a contemporary of mine (age-wise) in a long time. She's 39." Over the past 10 years or so, he had gone the younger-woman route on dates and relationships, though usually within about 10 years of his own age. "Remember," he added, "I was engaged at 29, and I thought I'd be a dad soon after that." (It's the only time he's been engaged, and he said he still feels some pain 13 years later.)

"The most profound thought I have about this is that the 40th birthday has come to mean what the 30th once did. It is the entry point to total manhood. In 1910, 1940, 1965, the issues of marriage, home, children, and career were all settled for men by 30. You had your periods of experimentation, but 30 was a little bit dreaded because it was the end of your 'youthful period.'

"But we now live in a world," Patrick said, with more gravitas than perhaps this insight deserved, "with *Melrose Place* and *Friends*, where people are so wealthy and comfortable, there's no shortage of eligible candidates. It is now 40 when your youthfulness should have passed. You should be well-entrenched in long-term things by then."

So now he's getting entrenched, more slowly and surely than most of his peers. But, as he allowed, with a pretty good reason for the delay: "Every year, on September 29, I pause and take stock of the last year. And I realize my time should have run out 17 years ago. This is religious, but I don't believe God saved my life. That's not my claim. What

I do believe is that each year has been a gift from God. And I have tried to live each year as if it were the last year of my life." And so he celebrated 40, with the rest of the guys on the golf course and ball field, with perhaps a bit more appreciation than anyone else who had come, in part, to play.

The Measure of a Man

Despite the millions of men entering midlife in America today, there's not always security in numbers. In fact there is an undercurrent of worry among many that things for them are simply too serious too often. There's also an explanation for these feelings, rooted in much of our recent masculine history. Consider how we measure our lives at midlife today: careers, cars, 401(k) plans, homes, leisure pursuits, and, of course, family—or the lack of same.

But we don't often reflect on the fact that as recently as the start of the nineteenth century, American manhood was rooted in land ownership or in a self-image defined by being an independent artisan or farmer. You were your land, in a sense, or, alternately, what you made with your hands. Within a few decades, and certainly by 1850 (after the effects of the Industrial Revolution had taken hold), that all changed, according to author Michael Kimmel in *Manhood in America: A Cultural History*. Suddenly, American men began to assess their self-worth by their positions in the evolving marketplace—a shift from a gauge made of fields of grain to one by which others could only guess at one's overall economic standing. It was an exciting time, to be sure, but not nearly so stable as it was for the generations of farmers and artisans who'd come before. In Kimmel's words, "Now, manhood had to be proved." In other words, it was no longer inherited.

Manhood can be "proved" any number of ways today, but it's unsettling when what you've chosen as a proving ground doesn't jibe with your needs as a man entering middle age. That's when a distinct malaise, tinged with fear and unease, settles in. Just when your job or career is about to "judge" you, you may be looking elsewhere—from the tavern to the gym—for sustenance of other kinds.

As a way to hark back to the lives their macho forebears lived (and especially in view of "Casual Fridays" at the office, I might add), Kimmel says modern desk jockeys wear such "masculinizing" accessories as Timberland or cowboy boots, aviator sunglasses, and colognes with such monikers as "Aspen," "Stetson," or "Safari."

"If masculinity cannot be achieved at work," Kimmel adds, "perhaps it can be achieved by working out. Men's bodies provide another masculine testing ground. . . . When our real work fails to confirm manhood, we 'work out,'"

Reading this pop analysis, I thought back to Bob the marathon runner, who had admitted to me, almost defensively, that when he ran his big race, he had "only" a runner's body. No definition. No upper-body muscularity. No flexibility, he said. I, on the other hand, felt sort of proud of my nonrunner's body and the fact that, at 40½, it was able to send me around a 10K race, held at a high altitude, in less than 54 minutes. But who's counting?

John M., 42, a single professional from Baltimore (who wasn't part of the Chicago group), has also over the past couple of years opened up his idea of what manhood at the age of 40 means. Yet he still can't help but use money as an overarching measure: "I'm not satisfied with my income," he said, "which should be twice as high as it is today. Everybody I went to school with is much more advanced professionally than I am.

"As of the late thirties, early forties, one feels a satisfying sense of substantiality and a comfort in one's own skin, especially if you've always been a late bloomer, as I have." (He made a point of telling me about his sex life post-40, saying that it's been "much more active. I've become a prodigious sexual performer—much in demand. Now I understand the attractions of promiscuity.") But, again, who's counting?

At the same time, however, John mentioned that he had a growing sense of "the fragility of human life and how quickly it can be snuffed out." After boasting of his enlivened sexuality, he conceded that, "At 42, I am closer to death than to birth, and that starts to influence one's thinking."

A Playboy Looks at 40

With old times as his primary influence, Brian's eyes were bigger than his barely there gullet. When Brian, the newly married slugger of the Chicago 15 who smashed the cover off the softball with one mighty swing, went to buy beer for the big birthday weekend, he expected the suds to fly. The reality? "We bought a lot, but didn't drink a lot. It was not like the old days. We're definitely more temperate. And instead of a keg, we stuck to bottles pretty much." He added, "Everybody's a little more particular about the beer they drink these days."

Maturity, I wondered? Sophisticated palates when it comes to brew? Or simply the effects of 20-some years of advertising taking hold of a group of men who can't help but be influenced by it (especially during a time in their lives when "manliness" takes on new meanings)? Along with the overbuy of beer, Brian and his cohorts overstocked on food, too, as if they were hunkering down for a 10-day stay in the prairie. "We stopped at a kind-of-like supermarket and filled up at least 1½ carts," Brian said. "We thought it was going to be enough food for 20 of us over the weekend; ended up we bought for 40. The people working the store were kind of scared."

In terms of Brian's own fears, more than a few of the crew had wondered over the years if he was afraid of getting married. Or why he had let a couple of stellar-looking women get away. His answer was more weighty than might have been expected from a longtime bachelor who admits that in the past he dated largely for looks. He also was the only man in attendance to have dated (no one-handed fantasy here) a *Playboy* Playmate. That didn't last, however.

"I wasn't consciously putting off getting married," he said. "But I enjoyed prolonging being a bachelor. I had blown a couple of relationships or let them get away. And I remember parking in the back of my mind, in my mid-thirties, that after those ended, I kind of had my feelers out for marriage. As I approached 40, I knew that if I was going to have a happy rest-of-my-life, I didn't want to have another missed opportunity. I knew there weren't going to be a lot of Pams out there."

And this time, he didn't let it slip away. At 39, Brian married Pam. When he was younger, he was more pliable with women, more willing to go with the flow and adapt his own lifestyle to their particular ways. It wasn't until he had a stronger sense of who he was that Brian was ready for marriage. He came to understand that bending or changing for your partner isn't always the answer. In fact, it can be part of the problem, as he learned from his two sisters and a brother, who shared with him marital troubles they had had over the years. Many of the problems stemmed from their unsuccessful attempts to change or to "fix things" in their marriages.

For a time, Brian incorporated their words and lessons and worked more on himself than on any partnership that he was 50-percent vested in. "I just wanted to be more mature about things," he said, "and more mature when I finally got married. A successful marriage, they always say, is when you merge two separate identities into a greater whole. I had a hard time with that for a long time. It frightened me. Now I believe. Back then, I thought I might make smarter judgments if I waited." And, by extension, he hoped to not fall into the traps whereby a partner makes you feel penned in, not fully yourself.

The reality for Brian, however, is that part of what he does for a living—drawing and illustrating for print and electronic media—doesn't lend itself to him being "a good provider." In fact, "I was always the great Bohemian of the group," he said, "just scraping by. I was always the 'and guest' guy at weddings. And always the floating guy for sports events, because my hours were flexible." Translation: If four tickets to the Bulls game landed on your desk at 5:30—because the losers with the Frito-Lay account who were supposed to go suddenly couldn't make it—you'd call Brian and have him meet you near the stadium at 7:00. Chances are, he'd show. When he looks back at his friends who got married at age 30 or so, he doesn't see them as having given up great things, like freedom. He thinks instead that they simply came to terms with some of the standard lifetime partnership issues a lot sooner than he did.

"I had a relationship break up once because a woman said to me, 'At the rate you're going, you're not going to amount to anything, to be able to provide. And that's been a nagging problem with me . . . ' I've had this box I feel that I've created for myself," Brian said, "that once I get the work, I'm great. But going to get the work is different. It's not me. It was also probably the most driving force preventing me from committing and settling down. I thought of it this way: I've made my whole living, basically, out of being a kid. Doing illustration, cartoons, creating art for Web sites." He's done it by relying on his own imagination, by doing things children do. The only difference is that he gets paid for it.

The Power of 40

The major difference between how Brian felt at 40 and how he felt at 30 has to do with companionship—his need for it and the value he places on it. "I can spend days alone, not talking to anybody, and still have a great time," he told me. "But the fear of growing old alone creeps in . . . and at some point you realize that you can only sustain yourself so long. You have to create an emotional legacy. I used to think about stuff I can do, stuff I've made that has sprung from my imagination. These are things I should be passing along to my own kids. I don't care if they're adopted, if they have three noses. It's just important to have some kind of legacy, to have some kind of mark of your existence. And I didn't used to feel that way."

These days, he talks more about learning a new set of rules than about how he used to pride himself in not going with the flow. The rules are those made for couples, for families, for men and women looking for a deeper kind of connection than they may have had in their twenties. "I still have to slough off that armor, that costume, that I aspired to for so long," he said. "I enjoyed it—the arsenal of arrows in your quiver. Now it's not so much shooting arrows; it's letting arrows hit you—letting partners' puzzle pieces fit you. It's inviting, opening up yourself to be part of something bigger.

"You want to leave a few footprints out there," Brian concluded. "I would suspect that my group of friends is somewhat special. Now I'm having a different perspective through my dad, who turned 80 this year. All his friends are gone, and he's thinking, 'What am I doing here?' I learned early on what that's about, when I went away to live in St. Thomas for a year." He was 28 at the time. "I left these guys and didn't know what I was leaving." He found out in due time; in due time he got it back. For longer, I might add, than a simple summer weekend.

When I asked Michael Perelman, Ph.D., co-director of the marital and sex therapy clinic at New York Hospital–Cornell Medical School in New York City, what he thought 40 meant to men today, he didn't mention lifelong friends as a leading indicator of accomplishment. On the other hand, he didn't discount their value, either. Instead, Dr. Perelman takes a broader view. To get at the notion of 40, you need to look at 42 and 45 and 47, he says. It's the entire decade that tells you more about the man. "I think the forties are a period of tremendous personal power, in which one has a tremendous opportunity to make one's mark on the world. An opportunity to actualize oneself in a way that very few younger people would be able to do," Dr. Perelman said. "It's definitely something to look forward to."

FULFILLED AT 40? FOUR REAL-LIFE ANSWERS

Forget about having made your first million. (That's in chapter 11.) For now, you may simply want to ask yourself the question I asked men ages 40 to 44 in trying to gauge the meaning of 40: "In your opinion, would you say you are satisfied with your life at this stage of life?"

• "Absolutely not," said Steve, 41, of Texas. "I've made the most out of difficult situations, but the best years are yet to come." He went on to say he has much left to accomplish, mostly in the world of music. "I expect to have three finished works by the year 2000. I'm just starting to get pretty good. . . . To get 10 pages of music, I had to write 60. Even 25 percent of the Beatles' music never got recorded. Or something like that. For me, being able to write music all day and play it is the thing. Anything else is icing on the cake."

• "Yes. Because I have a wonderful marriage and a wonderful family. I have good health. I have been moderately successful in my occupation and business," said Rick, 44, of Florida. "At midlife, you've lost friends and relatives. It's important to have friendships intact and prospering.

"As for what's left . . . on a personal basis, besides raising the kids, I'm seeking more of a spiritual connection—a mental development. Like, now I'm meditating more.

This, of course, is a professional view. And with all due respect, I honor it, as I've learned to do in talking with more than 15 therapists over the course of writing this book. But sometimes, I've also found, truth is stronger in—not stranger than—fiction. In fact, one novel, *The Arrangement*, which is some 30 years old, comes immediately to mind. Written by the noted film director Elia Kazan, the book has a remarkable passage that is particularly relevant to countless middle-aged men even today. You can almost envision it as a scene from a movie. In it, a family-court judge is deciding the fate of 40-ish Eddie Anderson, after he has acted irresponsibly, severed his marriage, and burned down a family home.

"I sold out my damned life day by day, all the years of it," Eddie says. "But now I'm going to start a second life, and I don't want any of

It's like, 'Water the roots so the plant will grow,' so to speak. And I want to accomplish financial security."

• "No. I think I've been slow to learn certain things about work and career stuff," said Mark, 40, of New York. "There's a lot I should have learned and done earlier. I'm playing catch-up now."

A builder in a competitive time, he went on, "I'm working on a couple houses right now, in the country, plus a couple of remodeling jobs. I'm getting my name out more. Like being in a home builders' show." He added, "I printed some pamphlets," pointing out a business strategy he had never used before. "Word of mouth is not enough. I'm working on creating a more secure situation and solidifying that."

• "Going from married for 10 years to single has been interesting," said Scott, 40, of Illinois, "and with my ex-wife and child out-of-state, it's very much like being 28 or 29 and single again—only everyone's older. I've worked for large companies for the last 10 years, and I'm ready to run my own show.

"I've done a lot and accomplished a good percentage of what I set out to do," Scott, now a vice president/engineer, added. "If I died today, I know I've made at least a small positive impact on the world. This is a good thing to feel."

the possessions that cost me so dear. That is my way of saying that all is not over for me, that I'm not giving up anything, except that which almost killed me."

Eddie, it must also be said, had bungled his career as an adman and had carried on a hot affair for months before the judge rendered his ruling.

"Now, now," says the judge. "I just want to make sure you mean it. . . . No one can live completely as he'd wish. We all pay something in time and in disgust for rent and for groceries. It's an arrangement you make with society. . . ." The judge went on, restating his feelings to Eddie that a man may give up a piece of his soul in order to feed his family. Yes, it may sound old-fashioned, the judge said in the time of the 1960s, but we all end up doing things that we pretend to like though we may in fact abhor them. "[D]espite all this, it is a civilization of sorts, isn't it?"

Without saying it exactly, the judge in Kazan's work has summed up much of contemporary thought about what it means for a man to be 40 today. It's about desire and about tampened desire. It's about work and about work we wish could be more fulfilling. It's about responsibility and about responsibilities we sometimes wish we didn't have. And it's about, most of all, the degree to which we make peace with—or challenge—the compromises we face at midlife.

In the words of Carl Jung, the famed Swiss psychologist who figured most of this out post-Freud and pre–John Gray, "We spend the first half of our span of years . . . finding our place in the world, finding our sexual orientation, finding our appointed work, finding what things can serve us and what we must avoid or abjure. But by the age of 40 or so, we take a change of direction, and henceforth seek knowledge of the world and of mankind, and above all knowledge of ourselves."

Above all . . . knowledge of ourselves. That sounds like quite a road trip.

What 40 Means to Women

When the artist formerly known—and, okay, still known—as Madonna turned 40, perhaps the only shocking thing about her birthday was that she didn't try to shock people anymore. Not her fans, not her detractors, not the overly respectful television journalists who scored the big interview with her that ran on *Entertainment Tonight*. If you didn't know better, you would have sworn she had settled down, sworn that she had reinvented herself once more. "I think it was more traumatic for everyone else," she said of turning 40. "I guess it's supposed to be a milestone birthday, the age of wisdom. I feel a lot smarter than I was when I was 30 . . . I feel a sense of accomplishment."

On television, the rock star/dancer/actress/author/ex-wife of Sean Penn appeared comfortable in her role as down-to-earth new mom. Her hair was wavy and long and dyed a decidedly unflashy shade of brown. Her demeanor was confident and quiet; much less giddy than it was during *Truth or Dare*, the revelatory 1991 rock-tour documentary in which she starred and in which she performed faux fellatio on a soda pop bottle in front of her roadies and show crew.

(Of course, that was then.) This night on national TV, if you didn't know too much about her, you might have thought she'd lately been studying the Bible or something. In a way, she had been. The Kabbalah, to be precise—the study of certain esoteric, secretive interpretations of Jewish scripture that in recent years had caught on among a small subset of Jews and non-Jews in Hollywood and other creative communities. Along with yoga, of which she is quite fond, the interest in Kabbalah and spirituality helped mark the Madonna-at-midlife era more firmly than any CD or any starring role in an underperforming motion picture. Who among America's 138 million females would follow her now? It used to be dance-club divas and gum-snapping teenagers; perhaps now it would be the next wave of soccer moms.

To me, the fact that Madonna was looking back thousands of years for answers to her modern midlife problems seemed a bit precious at first. (So did the fact that she said she got both diamonds and a yoga mat for her birthday.) And although I've never been a big fan, I paid $8 to see her in *Evita*, and I once followed her around a magazine store on the Upper West Side of New York City just to see what she would flip through (fashion books) and what she would buy (*British Vogue*). Now, after using the better part of two decades to sell herself as a wildly sexual being, here she was at 40 with a little daughter, Lourdes. And she was looking for more. Could a 41-year-old Madonna be sexy? Did she need to be? By inventing yet another Madonna—one who is maternal and quietly content rather than overtly sexual—she was either being precious or prescient.

The more I looked into how women feel about age 40, the more I came to believe that once again Madonna was doing the right thing at the right time, for herself. Women, it seems, don't face 40 obliquely, as men tend to do. In many ways, much as men find this difficult to admit, they are ahead of us. Perhaps it has something to do with female biological clocks that kick in during their thirties. Perhaps it's because of upbringing and gender-oriented social skills (women often tend to be networkers; men tend to be emotional loners). Whatever the reason, it seemed to me that Madonna's public airing of her private feelings toward God and motherhood, in the long run, may have meant more to women than selling zillions of CDs or setting funky fashion trends ever did.

The Sexually Invisible American Wife

Women face 40 sooner than men do, which doesn't mean they are any happier about doing so. It's just that they don't tend to skirt the issue as long as we do. Blame it on motherhood, for starters—even if biolog ical clocks are not the whole story. In broader terms, you could blame it on pregnancy, hormones, weight gain, and child rearing; but whatever you choose to blame it on, a 40-ish mother in America these days finds that it's simply not as easy to feel sexy as it should be. At least that's the view of Elena K., 39, a health care worker and married mother of two, from suburban St. Louis, who was not at all shy when talking about bodies, including her own. (Maybe that's why she ended up in the medical field.)

"When I get concerned about turning 40," Elena said, "I think, 'If humans had 12 fingers instead of 10, then [age] 48 would be a big deal. It's a quirk of the base 10 system.'" She added, "There's a lot to be said for being a grown-up, and I find it very tedious when people say, 'Oh, I'm really a kid. I'm not a grown-up. I just wear grown-up clothes. Ha, ha.' I've spent 40 years working very hard to be a grown-up and that pleases me tremendously. To me, being a grown-up means that you can get the big picture, weather the storms." In other words, "Forty is a nice mile marker at which to say, 'After this point, there will be no family-of-origin complaints.' After 40 it's *your* problem."

In particular, there were two problems Elena mentioned that concerned her (and by extension, her friends' and cohorts') apparent lack of erotic spark. "I feel myself becoming sexually invisible," she said. "Most days, I walk around looking like I'm between carpools—and I am. I realize that the torch is being passed to a new generation.

"Among men my own age, I feel that I remain a vital woman," she added. "I'm married. I'm not trolling for a new conquest. But part of my identity—and part of most women's identities—is how men respond to them. And 10 years ago, when I walked down the street, I got a different response than I get today. And I got it a lot more effortlessly than I get it today."

In her twenties and thirties, Elena allowed, she was actually uncomfortable with the attention that she garnered from men, especially when it was uninvited. She also believes that she responded to these overtures, in part, by gaining weight. Though she doesn't put all the

FERTILITY AT 40

For many women over the age of 40, fertility might seem an exercise in futility. Here's why: The "quality" of a typical woman's fertility dips somewhat around the age of 30, but changes remain merely subtle until 37 or 38, according to Nancy Klein, M.D., assistant professor in the division of reproductive endocrinology at the University of Washington in Seattle. After 40, experts say, the decline becomes pretty steep: The quality of women's eggs at that age is the main problem, not the hormones per se (which is apparently why many 40-ish mothers can bear children using donor eggs from younger women, but not with their own eggs.)

It is also worth noting that, while men's sex hormone levels also appear to drop in our thirties and forties, men typically remain fertile well into our forties and often into our sixties—and beyond. Remember, it's in part a numbers game: As a result of hormone cycles and ovulation, women release one egg every month or so—just 12 eggs or so a year to be fertilized. Men, meanwhile, release millions of sperm each month, each week, each time that we ejaculate.

blame on men and their comments, she does believe that they contributed to her building a buffer zone between her and the guys. A buffer zone of perhaps 20 extra pounds.

"It's funny," she went on, "because I never really thought of myself as a particularly dazzling woman or as an incredibly attractive woman. But I realize that by just being the age that I am, there are a lot of men who no longer consider me alive." Curiously, it was a connection she had that helped her focus on the lack of connections she's been experiencing in recent years. "I kind of had one of those moments," she said, "when I was talking to someone for work. I had called a man whom I don't know personally; we just got on like a house on fire. . . .

"Sometimes you meet people of whatever gender and you connect," she related. "They speak your language. At that time, he was 20 and I just turned 39, and I realized that difference was [insurmountable] on any nonprofessional level. And that was a little reminder to me: I've never been professionally hip, but I've always been fluent in every age's language. I could have a conversation with my peers—20 and 30 and older. Now, I'm losing my fluency in 20 and 30, especially where men are concerned. There is a portion of the population that I no longer interact with. Let me stress to people who say, 'She can [still] go to a rave' that I don't want to do it to feel falsely young. I went out and enjoyed my twenties and thirties and expect to enjoy my forties. But I'm wistful because I've reached a point of no return."

Tied into all these realizations about a less sexy midlife, or at least a less flirtatious one, Elena also touched on parenthood traps that kick in at around 40. She has two daughters, ages 13 and 6, and doesn't believe she'll have any more kids. (This is partly due to medical history, not mere age; she and her husband had trouble conceiving their second child.) She also pointed out that by marrying young (at 21), she believed she was looking more for a playmate to go to movies and parties with than for a true partner. At this point in her life, she said doesn't just "want to date" her husband—and she doesn't want to continue having the same basic arguments (about home, parenting, and money issues) they have had for 15 years. She wants a true partner. And, "I want a lover, but not just a lover."

Balancing Family and Work

For women who married relatively young, like Elena, this is not the easiest time to try to reconnect, or connect for the first time, with a husband. For he, too, may be feeling pressed during his move through age 40, for a variety of reasons, including career-related ones. "We are currently working on it," Elena said of her and her husband. "And my feeling at this point is, I don't want to be an independent person sharing living quarters. I want to connect, and that's something we're working on. I want to be really married."

On a brighter note, being a parent of two children of such varying ages gives these parents a wide perspective on how well they are doing. At this, Elena and her husband give themselves high marks. While both have had success professionally, she said, proudly, "I'm better at parenting than at anything in my life. I came to it with a lot of thought, a humility, and a certainty. I looked at what my friends did and what I thought worked. Then, I consciously made choices about how I wanted to behave to my children. I'm reaping the fruits of conscious and conscientious parenting. It's incredibly moving and heart-filling.

"To a reach a point with a child who is old enough to give you some idea of how you are doing is a great thing about this age. I'm no longer trying to keep them from killing themselves," Elena said, "and I am moving into a relationship that's not necessarily equal, but is more mutual."

As for her career, in the midst of a massive, decade-long push toward HMOs as our nation's leading health providers, Elena has seen her share of women come and go from the workforce, during and after pregnancy, during and after downsizing. She is college-educated and confident, but not cocky, about her prospects at 40. Everyone is replaceable in health care these days (even doctors—as nurse practitioners in some cities have become primary care providers). "I graduated in the middle of a severe economic downturn," she explained, "and finding a job was a huge problem. Most of the time, I managed to find a job that I wanted, but I was also working at department stores or at jobs I didn't like. In general, I think I'm better at getting the big picture at work: When something went wrong in my twenties and thirties, I'd prove it was not my fault. Now I accept the blame—even when it's not entirely justified—if I think that's the best way to get past the problem.

"I also realize that, at 40, I'm not going to be the child prodigy that I thought I would be," she said. "In my thirties, nothing seemed serious. I had a lot of fun professionally and based decisions on what sounded like fun. Now, however, if I want to meet career goals that I set in my twenties, I have a finite amount of time. And my task over the past year or so was to figure out what I really want.

"The thing that I think is different for me than for a lot of my women friends is that I'm approaching 40 like my male friends [have done]. I'm involved in my career, not worrying how to get into the work force. And I'm not having the same crisis of, 'I'm 10 years behind my class.' And that's a part of turning 40 that a lot of women are undergoing. I have a lot of sympathy, but it's not happening to me: My whole life, I've been acutely aware that nobody lives forever. When I was in my twenties, I was planning for 40. And now I'm planning for 60."

As she inches closer to that postmenopausal, pre-retirement milestone, Elena is in no hurry to finish that plan. Just to get a handle on it would be enough for now. Just to get a sense of order mixed in with her accomplishments. (Any rekindling of sensuality, with a touch of eroticism, would be a bonus.)

"I like people who take their fences cleanly. And 40 is a fence," she said. "I think it's a good time to examine choices and how you make decisions. If they're not working, if plan B isn't working, try plan A one more time. To reach to the calendar with desperation is not an issue of 40. It's an issue of character."

Single and Sexually Confident

If only, if only. . . . Gina R., 38, a hotshot, headstrong, never-married television producer from Boston, had a few things on her mind about men at 40—and wasted no time in spitting out sound bites. When I reached her for our appointed interview, I was hoping she (being in the mass media and all) would be able to speak for millions of women. I'm not sure she did that, yet by speaking as frankly as any of the women I interviewed for this chapter, she produced enough audio "footage" to resonate with midlife men for a long time.

"It'd be nice if they had it together by then," she said, speaking of the big birthday. "But I find guys around age 40 who haven't been married yet to be agitated. They want to 'fix' everything with themselves quickly, and so they tend to be much more in a hurry to get a relationship going, much more judgmental about other people." It sounded to me as if Gina had been burned by a few of these guys, or at least uncomfortably bemused by them.

"There's a certain kind of neurosis that 40-ish guys have," she added, "which is why" I tend to have relationships with guys who are in their thirties." Most of the 40-ish guys intent on fixing things in a hurry, she noted, have been divorced, which likely grates on their self-images. "One guy I went out with, Mark, was a geneticist who was attached to staying young. He was like others who've said, 'I'm 40, and I can still go all night,' or 'I'm 40, but I don't look it.' Or, 'I bench 240 and do StairMaster.'" Overkill, in other words.

"Actually," Gina added, "I don't mind the age. And I did kind of have a little bit of a relationship with a guy who was 41 or 42—not that

SOUNDING THE RETREAT

Someone gave Madonna a yoga mat as a 40th birthday present, so get ready for a "trendlet" to take hold: Yoga mats may well replace the black balloons and fake caskets that show up at so many surprise 40th birthday parties—for both sexes. Taking a cue from the former Material Girl, I sought some womanly (and spiritually tinged) advice from Susannah W., a 40-year-old female yoga instructor from Boulder, Colorado. I approached her because I heard, through a friend, that she had celebrated her 40th birthday in some dense Rocky Mountain forests with a dozen other women on a body/mind retreat of sorts. (Naturally, I couldn't help thinking back and comparing this to the 15 Chicago guys in chapter 1 who headed to a golf course for their weekend 40th birthday retreat.) And although I've only taken one yoga class in my life, Susannah, a divorced mother of one son, seemed a lot more grounded than I expected. Her focus was precise, no matter how far away she may at times feel in classes or sessions.

"I've never felt as physically strong as I feel now," she told me. "And I think 40 is a real marker of choice—as to how you will be in relation to your life force." You can choose, she said, whether you will allow yourself to deteriorate or whether you will somehow "tune in to a more subtle goal of energy that takes experience and wisdom to appreciate." When she talked about being strong at 40, Susannah explained that it has to do with physical and emotional endurance.

A little later, when I asked her to elaborate a bit about body/mind endurance, I was thinking a lot about patience. She was thinking about much more: "We have a greater capacity to experience it," she said. "And I have more than I've ever had in my life. With the biological clock and all, our value is grounded in physical appeal and sex appeal. Maybe it's because women are more reflective, and it may be why more women come into their own at this age. They're not as burnt out."

long ago. But he was so excited to be involved that I was grossed out. He was a good-looking guy, a TV producer. Problem is, these guys have dated so much, it's hard to get to know them beyond the dating shtick. They just don't know how to get real."

Gina has no patience for other late-thirties and early-forties women who don't have the same take on men that she has. "I tend to avoid women . . . who sit around and talk about how there are no men," she said. "I mean, it's a total misnomer out there that men are commitment-phobic. To me, it seems that, at 40, that's all they want to do. Commit."

True to my gender, however, I couldn't resist asking her about the more sensual parts of the women-in-the-woods retreat (a Lilith Fair "lite"?). "It was very Tantric," Susannah said, using the yoga buzzword that is, in the minds of Western followers, most often linked with sex. She continued, "To be with all these women, talking about sexual energy; it wasn't directly sexual, but it was about learning to activate that energy for healing." More, I thought. "It was not genital, not nude," she offered, "but we were doing erotic dance, partner yoga poses, and reading erotic poetry. We were learning about energy that is normally generated through the pelvis during orgasm and how that is [often] held up through the spine."

Okay, then. Energy through the pelvis. Another key gender difference: While so many young adult and midlife men often search for a "button" or a sexual spot to touch in order to please their partners anew, here were adult women, out in the woods, dancing erotically and learning to "let go of" sexual energy that may have been crimped somewhere amid the nerves and vertebrae of the spine. We want to push; they want to unleash.

So what does 40, finally, mean to Susannah and other soulful women like her? "One of my students said to me," she related, not taking credit for the thought, "that turning 40 is great because it's when you stop taking [crap] from people. We've had so much of our self-esteem based on taking care of others. But at 40, we give ourselves permission to take care of each other . . . to live in a way that's authentically expressing who we are."

In not-so-many words, many women learn to drop their guard even further, at 40, just as it seems many men learn to drop their guard for perhaps the first time. And you don't necessarily need to retreat to the mountains to find this out.

It's surface, surface, surface at first; three dates and maybe some safe sex; and then the talk about . . . getting . . . serious. Too fast for conditions, this solidly urban single says.

"I have two very close friends," she related, "who were already in long-term relationships. They just got married. I swear, there was this sense of, 'I'm 40, I'm 40, I'm 40. It's time to get married.'"

And what of Gina's love life of late? I wondered, not so innocently. "My most recent boyfriend," she said of the 35-year-old specimen, "I'm not with anymore—we can call him Peter Pan. But how's my year

been? Well, there's been a lot of good sex, but like I said, we're not together anymore." After she slapped the unfortunate "Pan" label on the
good man, I soon found out that she had good reason. He bikes and in-
line skates everywhere, she said, citing the belittling chapter *Bicycle Boys*
from the Candace Bushnell book turned HBO series, entitled *Sex and
the City*. And this trait, while cute and perhaps invigorating at first, got
tiresome after a while. Gina recalls, "This year, he picked up a skateboard, and I said, 'Listen, Randy, I'm really going to start worrying
when you get a tricycle.' He said, 'I don't want to be 40 and doing the
same things I was doing when I was 25.'" The dude had a point, no?

There's something about men turning 40 that makes Gina wonder
at times, "Do you think people know when they are in a crisis?"
Looking back, she said of two-wheeled, four-wheeled Randy, "The
skateboard didn't bother me, until it bothered me that it didn't bother
me. Because there's something about me that wants to remain ever
young—it was sort of a joie de vivre. But I started thinking, 'Why
doesn't he attack life in the same way he attacks sports?'" To his credit,
Gina allowed that he got her much more involved in physical pursuits
than she had been through most of her twenties.

In fact, before she began to brag a bit about her body at age 38, she
said that when she was growing up, she was "heavy . . . more like
chubby." As she got older, though, she went through phases where she
attracted a lot of men; then she went through phases as a loner of sorts.
"When I turned 30," she recounted, "I said, 'I have to act like 30.' I
couldn't wear—wouldn't wear—a bikini anymore.

"Also in that time, I lost weight. Then I turned 35, got fit, looked in
the mirror, and thought, 'You look good.' I was waiting for the aging to
happen. Till it does, I've turned into a 16-year-old slut. Right now, I'm
wearing cutoffs and a midriff top. I'm a size six, and I still have tits. I
have good skin—I even got a piercing on my upper ear. Sexually, too,
I know who I am and what turns me on. Plus, I know how to kiss
someone like I mean it."

Isn't there any downside, I wondered, to being 38, female, professionally secure, sexually confident, single, and impatient with the 40-
year-old men who haven't figured all this out themselves—and who
aren't "size sixes" anymore? Truth be told, too many of these men have
just traded in their size 36 "relaxed fit" khakis for size 38s. The only
downside Gina would cough up is that the older guys—in their mid-

to late-forties, say—would look at her "and think I'm a chippie. But I'm not.

"I don't know if that's an age thing," she said, "but when it comes to sex, after having really been involved with someone, it is so different. I mean, you have an idea of what sex is when you're younger—from movies or love songs. Later on, you think you're having an orgasm just about any time you're having sex and breathing hard—I don't know if I appeared self-conscious, but for a while I had a little yelp at the end. Then, when I dated this guy on and off for six years, I felt I was really there. And I had a really nice sex life—it changed." The yelp faded. Or, at least, Gina wasn't conscious of it any more. And that was not a bad thing. "Was it because I was 34? All I know is that [until then] I never felt so much as a woman. I was able to be more sexy, alluring, experimental. In control. And at 24, I wasn't thinking that way."

On the cusp of 39, she is all but on a mission. "I'm very proud to prove that you don't have to be washed up at 40," she told me. "I think that is a function of taking up skating in my thirties and of riding my bike." Before a woman can have great sex, she believes, she needs to have a healthy body image. "I used to feel this pressure to go to the gym, build up my arms. But I don't feel pressure to be ultra-skinny anymore. Used to be, if I wore tighter clothes, people said I was showing off. But when I wore baggy clothes, I would look fat. Now I don't [care]. If my boobs get me in the door, fine. Something else will keep me in the room." At 40, chances are, it won't be timidity.

The Role of Female Body Image

At 41, Lisa R., a married mother of two from Portland, Oregon, can't help but think about the future. In particular, about age 50. "Part of my situation is that I'm the youngest in my family," she said. "I have an older brother and sister. And even though I'm married to someone five years younger, the trauma of turning 40 was mitigated by my sister turning 50. I didn't really have any issues about it, though. My mother had me when she was about 40 and I always thought I was raised by senior citizens. To me, 40 was old."

To be sure, her mother smoked, didn't exercise, used gobs of butter in cooking, and favored a bouffant hairstyle. She certainly didn't try to hang on to her thirties, according to her daughter's memories. And yet Lisa, who never felt she was a fashion slave, has noticed a change in her own body and body image of late: "I've gone through all the stages of being health-oriented," she said. "But since I have two young children, I've forgotten all about it for a while. (It's less a health/age thing than a time thing.) But I am trying to get more serious about grooming: I've never been one to shave my legs regularly or try very hard. And now I realize that when you look 'together'—your toenails are polished—you look like you have more control of your life, like you have it together. I spent many years looking like I was fresh out of the asylum. Plus, I also think that women see this from magazines—that after 45 or 46 there's a downward slide toward 50 with the menopause issue."

So for five years, at least, she is back in the grooming game, albeit with reservations. "I spent most of my youth fighting my weight," she related, "and something happened to my metabolism when I was pregnant. Plus, I breast-fed for a long period of time, which may have had an effect on my physiology. Something about my body and food changed and I don't have a problem with my weight now." Looking at her, many men might say she looks healthful, earthy, sensual, and comfortable in her own skin. That's no accident. She does and she is.

By contrast, when *Self* magazine surveyed thousands of its readers about body image in the early 1990s, some 5,000 women who responded weren't nearly so comfortable in their own skins. (I was working there at the time, and I remember thinking that you couldn't get 5,000 guys to respond to a survey on body image. . .) Although readers of the magazine, on average, are more body conscious than the average woman and much younger than 40 (the median age of its 1.1 million readers is 31), the results were telling in their depiction of body image problems among American females: Only 7 percent of the respondents said they were "satisfied" with the way their bodies looked, and 94 percent said they thought about their bodies frequently or constantly. A stunning 84 percent said that they considered themselves to be overweight.

"Even though I know it's not true," wrote 40-something author Gwenda Blair in the *Self* article that related the survey findings, "a part of me believes that if I could look right, I'd be right, which is a problem, because although I'm attractive, I don't stop traffic. As an adult, I'm never going to look like Madonna." As part of her body image "makeover," then, Blair vowed to spend more time staring at herself without looking for Madonna. (Interesting that even Madonna herself came to the same realization when she later hit 40.) And Blair swore that she liked what she saw in the mirror—she gave herself permission to feel good. Not a big deal by many men's standards, but to women around the age of 40, it was a noticeable alteration.

One alternative for women who no longer feel comfortable in their own skins is plastic surgery. Lisa simply said she wouldn't even consider it. She described the effect of cosmetic surgery on the faces of some celebrities she's seen as "a wax face that's melted. It's scary." And not a pretty sight. If she were divorced or in a business in which people looked at her all the time (she used to be in the health club industry), she said she might feel differently. "But I feel like, 'Let it go,'" she said. "Be glad that you're alive, and leave it alone."

Perhaps not surprisingly, she feels the same way about a decision she doesn't really need to make for another 7, 8, 10 years: the decision of whether to take hormones as supplements during and after menopause. "I would never in a million years do hormone-replacement therapy," she said. "I think—even though I know there have been improvements in [women's long-term] health with it—if your body were still meant to have it, it would have it." Forget that hormone-replacement therapy apparently results in reduced heart disease risk and potentially reduces breast cancer rates. "I certainly worry about cancer," she said. "But I'd never do it in a million years."

Female Hormones and Sex Drive at 40

Forget a million years. That's too many. The news about women's bodies at midlife is that we may know a heck of a lot more about hormone-replacement therapy in 10 years than we know now. And we, as caring, sensitive, sexually interested men, are already paying attention to reports that link women's hormone fluctuations to mood changes and alterations in libido. It's a new area of interest for many men who thought they'd heard the last about PMS a decade ago—an interest

BOX SCORE

WOMEN: THE VIEW FROM 40

First, the good news:

- On average, working women report that they are more confident about their careers than they were at 30.
- On average, they report that they are more confident about their body images—an important component of how they feel about their total selves.
- There is less chance of unintended pregnancy at 40 than at 20 or 30 in cases of faulty or forgotten contraception.
- Women in their forties consistently have more satisfying sexual responses than they did at 20.

The not-so-good news:

- Fertility at 38 to 42 is more problematic, on average, for women contemplating midlife pregnancy.
- Cellulite is more prevalent, even among women who work out regularly.
- Women are more demanding sexually, on average, than they were at 20. (That's not-so-good news?)
- At 40, mood swings and recurrent PMS may arise among a minority of women due to perimenopausal hormone changes.

that's both selfless and a bit selfish. Much as we've seen gains in research about other kinds of hormone supplementation (including DHEA, human growth hormone, and testosterone for men), women who find their hormones changing in their early and mid-forties may soon be able to control their flow of them more precisely. Here's a short course in what you may need to know, hormonally speaking.

Just as testosterone is the leading male sex hormone, estrogen is the leading female sex hormone—even though, as it is not widely enough known, both sexes produce both hormones. (Women in their thirties, however, produce just $\frac{1}{20}$ the amount of testosterone that men of the same age do.) At the same time, it's worth noting that estrogen helps the skin, blood vessels, urinary tract, and breasts remain flexible, toned, or both. Yet, in general, doctors just don't know enough about what happens to women's hormones to have a complete and accurate picture of a typical woman of 40, according to Carol Petersen, managing pharmacist at Women's International Pharmacy in Madison, Wisconsin. They know a lot more about the role that hormones play at 50.

That said, there are a few things we do know about how hormones affect behavior, fertility, and sex drive. "In the early forties, it turns out that hormone levels have become almost normal—more predictable, less variable," says Nancy Klein, M.D., assistant professor in the division of reproductive endocrinology at the University of Washington in Seattle. "Estrogen becomes a little higher around ovulation (when a ripe egg is released during the middle of the menstrual cycle). And progesterone (another key female hormone) is the same or a little higher during a cycle and when a woman ovulates. That goes against popular belief. Popular belief is that [females'] hormones are in decline."

So while this new information takes time to settle in, over the short term, most doctors and female patients will continue to hold to facts that are reasonable and predictable: A woman's hormones—and fertility—begin to slowly decline in the early thirties and tend to decline as she nears menopause (which is when estrogen production all but ceases, around age 50). In a woman's mid- or, in some instances, early forties, she enters the so-called climacteric, which is the time period in which estrogen, progesterone, and testosterone fluctuate markedly.

The interesting aside is that a woman in her forties who is "losing" estrogen is "gaining" a higher proportion of testosterone in her bloodstream and tissues. This may well be why many reports indicate a heightened interest in sex among midlife women. (We'll wait for the scientific proof; for now, the theory is merely enticing.)

Perimenopause Alert

While sex-hormone levels may not tell the whole story about female hormones and the premenopausal years known as perimenopause, they do tell enough. For instance, although the median age of a woman at menopause is 51.3, the spread ranges from 45 to 55. In addition, peri-menopause typically lasts from a few months to a few years. Yet if you count the earliest symptoms, the average time for perimenopause is three to four years. Up to 50 percent of women may not exhibit any symptoms of perimenopause at all, according to David F. Archer, M.D., director of clinical research in the department of obstetrics and gyne-cology at Eastern Virginia Medical School of the Medical College of Hampton Roads in Norfolk and president of the Northern American Menopause Society.

So what are the signs or symptoms of perimenopause? "Instead of regular periods with normal hormone production, [women may] skip or have extra periods or bleeding between periods," Dr. Klein says. There are symptoms of low estrogen such as hot flashes, headaches, dif-ficulty sleeping, fatigue, and sometimes anxiety—a lot more of the typ-ical symptoms that you hear from women during their menopausal transition. There are also sexual signs, such as a possible loss of libido, associated mood swings, and more sparse pubic hair.

But symptoms don't tell the whole story either, because symptoms are most often associated with sickness and disease. And peri-menopause is a stage of life, not a disease. In fact, over the past decade or more, researchers have gathered intriguing evidence to show how women can counteract some of the early hormonal effects of the ear-liest premenopausal changes—by having more sex. (Try that with a disease.) Winnifred Cutler, Ph.D., a biologist and behavioral endocri-nologist, conducted rigorous, profound studies of women at Stanford and the University of Pennsylvania over 10 years or more, which led her to an arresting conclusion: Both undergraduate women and those approaching menopause who had weekly (except during menstrua-tion) sexual activity with men tended to be more fertile and revealed estrogen levels about twice as high as their contemporaries'.

As an aside (and I didn't ask her specifically how she studied this aspect), Dr. Cutler and her teams also found that while "weekly sexu-ally active women" recorded "optimal fertile" cycles of 29.5 days, mas-turbation was not effective in producing those same regular, optimally timed cycles. The effect on the females' bodies was not triggered by penetration, per se, or orgasm, but a man needed to be present and gen-ital stimulation was required. Just another reason for 40-something guys to consider their partners weekly—at *least*.

Hollywood and Hormones—Susan Sarandon–Style

It was big news in Hollywood, but not for the usual reasons. In the mid-1980s, word got out that Susan Sarandon, serious, comic, sexy actress who has shored up such movies as *The Rocky Horror Picture Show*, *Atlantic City*, *Bull Durham*, and more recently, *Stepmom*, was pregnant with her first child at age 38. Her second child, conceived with her current partner, actor Tim Robbins, 12 years her junior, followed a few years later, and her third arrived when she was 45 years old.

Say what you want about cookie-cutter starlets and the lack of roles for 40-ish actresses. Women across the country, especially those who had delayed childbearing until their late thirties, were inspired by Sarandon's medical (and "unmarital") history, which had more to do with her prolonged fertility than with perfectly smooth skin. (She certainly didn't seem to mind ditching the glamour look in *Dead Man Walking*.) This was a victory of sorts for 40-ish women everywhere because not only was a feminist icon giving birth right smack in the throes of midlife, she was doing it with a much younger man, and she was doing it while retaining her image as a libidinous leading lady. Could it be that Sarandon even made motherhood at 40 seem, well, sexy? Maybe so. At the least, she got women (and men) in midlife thinking about some key notions of aging and allure and fertility. And thinking about them in a positive light.

Marriage: Do the Ties Still Bind?

C an you know your wife too well?

After 5, 10, or 15 years of marriage, can you know her so well that you believe there's nothing more to learn, little more for which to yearn? Is that possible? Or is it laziness? Either way, a discomforting thought. . . . From favorite clothes and scents to body hangups and how she prefers her orgasms, you have them down pat. From frustrations with her family and friends to unfulfilled aspirations, you've heard them. From just how soft she likes the volume on the living room CD player to just how ticked she gets when you bring home the cheap shampoo (again), you know these things.

When I initially approached this question about levels of intimacy in my fourth year of marriage, I thought the answer was, in a word, no. I was 40 at the time; 40½ when I felt qualified to answer it more completely. The main reason I answered no at first was that my marriage seemed young. My wife, Paula, then 36, and I had never believed that our marriage was typical. Due to our highly mobile careers (mine, writing/editing; hers, on the production side of the movie business), we travel at least twice each month and often live apart from each other for weeks or months at a time—except for long weekends. In our six-plus years of being and living "together," we have counted only one year in which we spent more than eight straight months under the same roof.

Our marriage has more stops and starts than most, more days and hours of reconnoitering and reconnection than we care to admit. We're still learning a lot about each other because if you add it all up, the time we've spent together barely exceeds three years. Practically new-lyweds, some would say. Yet, mindful of what middle age means, we are behind the curve when we realize we are still planning to have a family; still planning to be more normal as a married couple than we've been so far. "Enough career," we've said at least half a dozen times, smiling, en route to the airport once more. . . . Then comes a half-hug and a kiss outside the west wing of the terminal, with one of us casting a wary eye over the other's shoulder, checking for airport cops looking to shoo us from the drop-off lane.

I don't know my wife "too" well. In fact, I don't believe I know her well enough. (To this day, I'm not certain of her favorite scent.)

Having said that, I've been forced to think time and again about millions of other couples and what they may be going through at midlife. One fact I've uncovered is this: Before marriages crumble or grow, there's bound to be talk about talking. Yet despite the conventional wisdom, talking alone isn't always enough.

For decades now, the top pop-psychology books have told us that we need to get to know each other better in order to make marriages stronger, to become better partners. Communication is the byword, the key. Or at least it used to be.

It sounds reasonable, after all. "Many of us seem to believe that being in an intimate relationship endows us with mental telepathy and we expect to be mind readers," state therapists Jennifer Knopf, Ph.D., and Michael Seiler, Ph.D., in their book *Inhibited Sexual Desire*. "But no matter how close you feel to your partner, you can still guess wrong—and often do. Likewise, if you expect your partner to know how you feel and to act on that knowledge, doing precisely what you wish, you will be disappointed, no ifs, ands, or buts about it." State the goals, ladies and gents. Before you can be close, you have to be clear. Or so experts say.

Remember *You Just Don't Understand*, by Deborah Tannen, Ph.D., in

THE CHEATING GAME

Ever since questions about adultery spilled out beyond pop culture to envelope the Clinton presidency, answers about what constitutes the very act have become more murky than ever. In Colin Harrison's deftly written novel *Manhattan Nocturne*, the protagonist, Porter Wren, says of his first act of adultery, "I was wrong to have [had sex with] her, but I had not been wrong to have *wanted* to; no, that was very right."

This kind of illicit thinking brings to mind a modern-men's infidelity quiz I've devised—with answers graciously provided by Tom Fiester, Ph.D., a Boulder, Colorado, therapist who specializes in men's issues. These are not definitive answers, just one respected expert's opinion. As they say at Wrigley Field, "Get your pencils and scorecards ready. . . ."

Q: Is discussing a sexy Internet site with a colleague, then visiting it (separately) at a mutually agreed upon time, adultery?

A: For me, adultery implies a relationship. It's difficult to construe that as a relationship. It's pornography but it's not infidelity.

Q: Is thinking about another person during sex adultery? (Some therapists actually advise clients to try this.)

A: No, it's not. Again, because the standard for me is "relationship." If my wife comes back from a high school reunion and says she was attracted to an old boyfriend, I don't consider that adultery.

the early 1990s? How can we forget the *Men Are from Mars, Women Are from Venus* series by John Gray, which still flourishes, even though it seemed to borrow so heavily from Tannen's more scholarly work? Here's the revised marital news, men, as you'll soon see: Being from different planets can sometimes help your marriage. It can help over the long term, especially if you've hit a rut at or around age 40.

How so? Well, explains Neil Rosenthal, Ph.D., 50, a Denver marital and family therapist and syndicated newspaper columnist, being in a rut means first acknowledging the rut. "It's about taking responsibility for your behavior," he says. "And that's not saying you're innocent and she's guilty—it's about making an accurate assessment of what you have done that leads to things you might do to change. That's the be-

Q: Is visiting a topless bar adultery? What about going to a topless bar with your wife? (It's something I once did on a whim in Las Vegas and wish, in retrospect, that I hadn't. My wife didn't exactly consider the chest-jutting, butt-swinging, pole gymnastics "erotic.")

A: No, it's not an erotic event. I also don't believe that one to three random visits equals adulterous behavior. I have clients in my practice who are fighting over that very thing. The women consider it adultery. . . . The issue is intimacy. The healing issue for each of these women will come only with time and when her man develops an intimate relationship with her. It's just real important to women that they feel sex is special with them.

The real question is: If you go to a strip club where there's dancing and you masturbate behind a glass window while watching, is that adultery? Yeah, because it means you've left your partner as a sexual being.

Q: Is kissing another woman adultery? What about slightly open-mouthed kissing while hugging? Is it the fine line of saliva exchange?

A: Well, I don't know. Certainly a kiss on the cheek isn't. And you can't even go to the Bible for a clear-cut answer to this one.

Q: Is receiving oral sex near the White House Oval Office adultery? (For most of us, the question may be more appropriate if set in a business-convention hotel room.)

A: A one-night fling? It certainly is, because it's a relationship (a sexual one).

ginning of a healthy self-assessment." In short, it's about looking inward first, before trying to oh-so-connect with your partner the way TV talk shows always proselytize.

The potent message of the late 1990s and beyond is that even clear-headed communication, after 5 or 15 years of marriage, may not be enough to bolster a yawning marriage in midlife. One couples therapist told me that there comes a point in time at which most men, whether or not they'll admit it to their wives, wonder: Will I ever wander? That thought and the related thoughts of perhaps knowing a partner too well are the kinds of messages that gnaw at a longtime-married man's psyche.

For if he knows his partner too well, he fears, the excitement that brought him and his wife together in the first place may forever have vanished. It may be time to look around, he may think. Or, if and when his thoughts are not about infidelity, it may be high time for him to look at his partner a little bit differently. "Exchanging glances, gazing into one another's eyes, are the routes through which we make emotional contact with someone we love," says Bonnie Maslin, Ph.D., author of *The Angry Marriage.* "If you are unable or uninterested in having such an intimate exchange, it may be indicative of anger with your spouse." In other words, not necessarily boredom, nor apathy.

One 39-year-old interviewee from suburban New York told me that after he had read a story about a man's incredibly casual infidelity, "it convinced me that adultery's role in our culture is changing." He said this more than a year before the President Clinton/Monica Lewinsky scandal broke in early 1998, and added, "Aside from that, I know at least two men in their forties whose wives have encouraged them to [sleep with] someone else."

Obviously, this is not the norm. But it does raise an interesting question: Do these wives, perhaps, know their husbands *just well enough*?

As for looking inward, instead of outside, a marriage, Gary A., 40, a public relations specialist in Chicago, said to me, "At 30, we had been married for 4 years. At 40, it was 14. Over time, we've grown closer, given up on changing each other, and become kinder and gentler to each other. Having children, now three and five years old, has made us more a family than the weakly linked individuals we had been. The kids, for me at least, have opened my heart. Whereas before, I was more or less a hard-hearted careerist."

In short, Gary seems to have grown as a person and also as a partner. He went on to explain that he and his wife had separated once, long ago, in their first years of marriage, "to get some space" and help figure things out. It wasn't as complicated as it was both frustrating and necessary for his much younger psyche, he said. Yet in reviewing his comments, which were made during a rough year for him career-wise, I found myself focusing on his use of the phrase "given up on changing each other." While at first that may sound defeatist, it is anything but. By rethinking his role as husband, father, and provider, he has done the work necessary to effect change in his marriage. It's just that it may not yet feel that way to him.

For Craig S., 41, an engineer from Austin, Texas, questions about connecting and disconnecting riffled all through his 40th-birthday year. "At 40, my life profoundly changed because I went through a divorce, I got a new job, then a promotion," he said. His marriage wasn't the anchor that he long ago had believed it would be. Now it gets lumped into a series of things that "just happened" to have happened around 40. When I later asked about his sex life after the big birthday, he added, "I get to have it now." Apparently, Craig and his wife hadn't known each other too well in that regard. Thankfully, though, they hadn't had children, either.

Intimacy That's Not

Jokes about sex, or the lack of it, are of course coin of the realm for men at around 40. On a more serious note, in Anthony Giardina's powerful book of short stories, *The Country of Marriage*, the author parts these unsettling waters expertly, almost chillingly. In one story, "Days with Cecelia," the narrator is at one point on a couch with his wife, who may or may not be having an affair with someone she's met at work. He recalls:

> *And the two of us . . . lay there watching a Michael Caine spy movie from the sixties. . . . My bathrobe happened to be open, unintentionally, and at the point where Michael Caine was about to be tortured, my wife reached over and lifted my penis. It is quite a long one (or so I've been told), and as she held it there, limp but extended upward by her grasp, it bisected the image of Michael Caine's grimacing face. She held it for the length of time it took for the torture to be completed and then put it back in place. A commercial came on and we lay there in a kind of awed silence.*

Fictional or not, brutal or brutally honest, this is the kind of story that says, Yes, you can know your partner too well. In this story, the spot of "awed silence" remained in force a long while. It was, for better but mostly for worse, a sign of desperate communication from a bored, frustrated wife. On a personal note, I had never before read about, or witnessed, a soft, exposed penis being used as a utilitarian screening device to shield a spouse's viewing of action-movie torture. You might call it torture in itself—torture of the midlife male psyche.

You couldn't really call the aforementioned fictional Caine-screening a sex scene. But the absence of any thought of sex between these partners speaks directly to how sex may be used as currency in a relationship that has gone stale. This is a case memorable for its stark imagery, for its ability to encapsulate how much can (and does) go un-said between two people who have taken vows to love, honor, cherish, and support each other.

Even for 40-year-olds in not-so-dire straits, a few unsettling questions may arise, including: How do you navigate the scary waters of the unsaid? How do you even begin to know whether your marriage will outlast the many temptations and severe marital tests that occur in the years from 40 to 50? Despite the lulls, don't you have it better than single or divorced peers?

"When you ask them [midlife marrieds] about changes, you're really asking them about crises," says David Schnarch, Ph.D., co-founder of the Marriage and Family Health Center in Evergreen, Colorado, and author of *Passionate Marriage*. "People usually mark their lives by crises—and don't pay attention to processes unless they become acute." Dr. Schnarch is a staunch believer in dissecting the processes of marriage as well as forcing longtime married couples to confront their partners up close and personally. Dr. Schnarch explained in an interview that, using this method, he often sees profound changes in three days or less between couples who visit his counseling and workshop center. An example of how he helps them accomplish this: He teaches couples to have "eyes-open" orgasms. "It's hard to describe the impact of looking into the eyes of someone you love as you reach orgasm. . . . Looking into each other and climaxing can be electric, tender, forceful, and nurturant, all at once." (Notice that he goes further with the concept of looking into one another's eyes than Dr. Maslin does.)

If this kind of lovemaking makes partners uncomfortable or self-conscious, it also all but forces them to ask, Why is that so? Self-awareness, however, Dr. Schnarch goes on to say, is inherent to intimacy. "You can't be carrying a lot of anxiety or a load of unresolved issues to bed," he adds. "You have to feel pretty good about yourself to let your life mate look inside you."

IRONING JOHN

Forget, for a moment, those titillating ads for instructional sex videos in the back pages of men's magazines like *Men's Health, Playboy, Esquire,* and *GQ.* Before you ponder carnal secrets and tantric sex skills to spark a marriage that's too full of lulls, consider the case of Jim Thornton.

I met Mr. Thornton years ago in New York City, and I soon learned that the man could write about quirky things: lingerie, the biology of brains, even male multiple orgasms. But little did I know that he could also mend marriages. Not long ago, he sent me a copy of a book he had written, *Chore Wars: How Households Can Share the Work and Keep the Peace.* Yes, it's about cleaning bathrooms and ironing shirts. But in it, he also describes one hell of a valuable tip for husbands.

If you're in a marriage for the long haul and you know you lack skill in the cleaning arena, think about a maid. No, not to come and simply clean. Pay her in part to not clean. Pay the maid, instead, to walk you through your home, room by room, and teach you how she cleans each surface, cabinet, toilet, and molding. And blinds. Don't forget the pesky miniblinds. It's bound to be a well-spent $50 to $75. Every bit as valuable, for some, as a dozen roses.

Note: Thornton has now been (mostly happily) married for more than 15 years.

What intrigued me about Dr. Schnarch's approach to intimacy and surmounting blocks is that he is not afraid to challenge the commonly accepted wisdom of his peers and the so-called leading thinkers in marital therapy. He doesn't say you must have eyes-open orgasm to be as close as a longtime married couple; he merely points to a path along which you might choose to travel. Similarly, when I asked him about 40-ish men who complained to me about marriages gone stale—as their romantic times have been replaced by duties of jobs or homes—he again cut to the crux: "We like to focus on situational events," he says, "because it's easier. It gives people a simple handle on and way of looking at things, but at the same time, it immobilizes people when the crisis hits." In short, couples often talk their way around troubles, blaming job changes or the children's demands, even as they believe they are confronting those troubles. Dr. Schnarch's comments are wise words, especially for harried fathers and overextended, aging business types who all too often hear themselves spouting what sound like slogans.

Married and 40

Terry P., 42, a happily married man from Ogden, Utah, could be classified as a harried father and businessman—even if he doesn't see himself that way. He travels, on average, two weeks each month as a leading corporate-planning consultant, and leaves most (but not all) of the household responsibilities in his wife's care. Married more than 17 years at the time of our interview, Terry sounded absolutely in love with his wife and with his life, despite the increasing pressures he was feeling as three of his five children—three girls and two boys—entered or moved through their teens at the same time that his business approached a critical stage of growth.

"I consider Robin to be the center of my life," he said of his wife, who recently turned 40, not worrying whether that sounded at all harsh in regard to his children. In explaining it further, he said, "It's unique. There aren't many people who can say, 'My best buddy is my wife.'" His best buddy simply is. When they first met on a blind date, Terry tried to impress her by taking her to a movie in downtown Chicago at a theater for which he had finagled a free pass from a friend (he wasn't going to fool her into thinking he was a spendthrift). The movie was *Mandingo*, which was pretty racy—no pun intended—as it dealt with interracial sex and slavery; the two felt more than a bit out of their element as two suburban white kids in a theater populated by nearly all black patrons. (Of course, black kids in the 1970s may have felt similar vibes in barely integrated suburban movie houses, too.) And while they say love is blind, first dates aren't. More than 20 years later, both Terry and Robin share vivid memories (the traffic, the neon, the hairstyles) of that date.

When they met up again a couple of years later, on a school trip to London during college, things were different—more settled, somehow. "I got to know Robin really well that summer," Terry said. "We'd go to places like the British Museum, and I would say something, anything; then she would ask me a question about what I'd just said—as if she was truly interested. I asked about her interests, her hobbies, and she seemed thrilled to answer. For anybody whom that happens to [at that age], it's kind of magnetic.

"I found out later on," Terry added, "that she came from a family with eight kids where nobody really listened to her. So when

Robin and I would take a walk in Regent's Park or somewhere, and I would ask her about herself, I remember that she would love it. You could see it in her face." To this day, one secret of their marriage is their day-to-day patter and how it has been built, like a foundation, into the framework of their marriage. They question and listen to each other not as relationship exercises but as ways to connect and prod each other a bit as each of them matures. They remain truly interested in the nuances of how the other person is changing, growing, and actually dealing with success and frustrations. Things like the kids' activities and fears; the fears that corporate takeovers sometimes evoke in susceptible parents, especially among midlife men; and how to make the most of what now seems like precious little time together as an entire family.

When they had their last child, a daughter, Terry was 40, Robin, 38. It was a "surprise," as Terry put it, but one that was totally welcomed into the family. Just as Robin began to recover from the delivery (her physical drain was marked, as it was a cesarean birth), she and Terry noticed a surprising change among the other children: The girls were actually fighting over who got to take care of baby Hannah, which went a long way, Robin found, toward muting some expected postpartum depression.

For his part, Terry got more involved in his youngest child's daily life than he did for his first son and daughter. "Fatherhood at 40," he said, "is defined by the age of your kids and how many there are in the family. For me, being a father at 40 was a lot more comfortable than when I was younger, even though I was thinking about costs of college educations and weddings. It's easier in a way, but there aren't the 'firsts' you experience—not as many discoveries—as compared to the earlier kids.

"At 30, when our first child was born, I remember taking time to be with him, but not nearly as much as I do now. And being self-employed, I hear about these guys who have paternity leave with their jobs; I thought, 'Great,' but I can't do it." Thinking back, Terry said he and his wife didn't feel "defined" by their children when they had one or two. But now, in their forties with a basketball team–size brood, as much as they try to keep their selves centered, that's changed. "You become defined by your kids," according to Terry. "When you have several kids, your life starts to revolve around what they are doing, plus their challenges and problems."

Still, Terry makes a point of getting away with Robin on a regular basis, as a couple, even if just for a spot of time. "We try and take 'date nights,'" he said, "just the two of us. We don't take the cell phone; sometimes we just go to Target—not shopping for anything; we walk the aisles. That's it."

At this stage of life and marriage, "there is a growing clarity about what will be and not be—in terms of his achievement, productivity, career stability, and recognition," says Dr. Schnarch. It is a "matter of process," he adds. The process, in short, is one of coming together. At 25, a "man is in the process of defining who he is, who he wants to be, and what he wants to do with his life." By the time he reaches 40, a man is in the process of redefining who he is as a husband, father, and provider.

Gary, introduced earlier in this chapter, doesn't come from the Beaver Cleaver background that Terry and Robin did. Growing up in Detroit without an at-home father (his dad left when he was six), Gary noticed how hard his mother seemed to work to keep him and his family together and contented as kids in a single-parent household. Gary, who is African-American, doesn't quote rates of black-versus-white single-parent families when discussing his own upbringing and marriage; he merely speaks, as a modern husband and father, about the facts: those of his life, his wife's, and those of their upper-middle class family.

"I'm kinder and gentler at 40," Gary said, in describing himself as a husband. "At this station in life, going on 15 years married, I'd say that although it was pretty difficult at first, you figure it out and get better at it. People grow up with this sort of idyllic view of marriage and what to expect, and that's not always helpful. I came from a single-parent household, and before it was that, it was a dysfunctional marriage. I didn't have a real understanding of what [a good marriage] looks like. That can contribute to your having an idyllic view of what these things are supposed to look like.

"I pretty much grew up—or didn't—by the time I was 30, 31," Gary added. "And yet I know a lot of guys in their early thirties who have no intention of marrying. This is not to say marriage is a litmus test for adulthood. But it does require a maturity of a person, I think. It requires you to be perhaps less self-absorbed, less self-centered, and fairer. And it requires interdependence, something men are not usually drawn to. From boyhood on, men grow up thinking of themselves [first], and that they must be self-reliant."

As if to emphasize this point, Gary confessed to a time in his 14-year marriage when he and his wife, Lucy, went through a trial separation. "In the common parlance of the term, we lived in different places," he told me, though it wasn't about infidelity on either his or his wife's part. "It was August 1992 through early January 1993," he added, more sure of those dates than many men are of their anniversaries. "There were times when I said, 'Till death do us part' and I meant it. So did she. Then there were times when the only reason we stayed together was that vow.

"When I got married, I was 26," he added. "I knew I was wholly unprepared to do so. I still wanted to go play basketball, go drinking, hang out with my friends. I was not really ready to live in 'the currency' of marriage. Part of it [the separation] was, I hadn't given it a chance; I felt like I should." He wasn't ready to even consider divorce without taking a long look at his future.

"One of the things about Lucy and I is that we are very, very good friends," Gary said. "That, probably more than anything else, kept us together. I thought I would give it another whirl and see if I could make it work. Part of me is very achievement-oriented. If I did something wrong, I want to identify it and get back on the horse and do it right."

Ten years later, Gary was able to see another side of himself—how much richer his life became after his children were born. "They've really and truly showed me that I have the ability to love," he said. "Because in a marriage, it's a quid pro quo. You're asking, 'What am I putting in; what am I getting?' I didn't feel true love until I had kids. Then I could understand it and appreciate it.

"The whole thing about people turning 40 and being angst-ridden is not something I connect with. My life has only gotten richer."

During his 40th birthday year, however, Gary had a career setback that started with a layoff and turned into a sidestep: He ended up taking a job outside of his field, more to feed his family than to feed his needs of self-esteem. "It was a trying time in my marriage," he said, "because when I gave up, at least temporarily, my career as a journalist,

CHANGING THE MARRIAGE CONTRACT

When you say, "I do," whatever your age, probably the last thing on your mind at that precise moment is that you are entering into a contract. A legally binding agreement. You are becoming, in a sense, an agent of the state—as well as a brand-new husband. But there comes a time in many (or most) marriages when contracts should be revised. Officially or unofficially, experts say. And it has little or nothing to do with divorce.

"I think marriages should be negotiated as often as we negotiate business contracts," says Phyllis Levy, a Chicago-area relationships and marital counselor. "If marriages were treated like businesses, we'd be in much better shape. Every year, you'd have an evaluation of your performance: It would include a performance review and budget reviews, and you'd both ask, 'Is this working for you and for me, and is it profitable for both? Am I getting what I need and want, and are you?'"

It's as much a business plan as it is a love-life road map, and who knows—with the U.S. divorce rate still hovering near 50 percent, Levy's philosophy may propel her to become, before too long, chief executive officer of matrimony.

I gave up what I had been doing since the seventh grade and all through high school and college. It's how I met my wife. But I gave it up for what I thought would be stability of home." Turns out, it was and it wasn't. Yes, the paycheck offered stability. But resentment in the marriage surfaced, bubbling up from how much "giving" Gary felt he was being asked to do. "For some time," Gary said, "I had been one of the most unhappy campers."

A recent job offer back in his original field of journalism gave him the chance to reassess and to make a move that he expects will help make all ends meet, including psychological ones. He got a raise and a bump in title, with only one drawback: His family will have to move. So in a sense, he has decided to move from his roots in Chicago to get back to his roots in newspapers. From the energy in his voice, it's a risk worth taking. During our last interview, he was a very young sounding 40-year-old, indeed.

Divorced and 40

It started in Paris. The beginning of the end of a 10-year marriage in which Dan R., a 40-year-old, faithful-till-then husband, began to have serious doubts about his married life and the rest of his life. He knew that he and his wife were in trouble, even as they took in the sights of the Left Bank, the Louvre, and Luxembourg Gardens—places they had never seen together, which were part of a 10-year anniversary tour for which they had saved for more than a year.

At first glance, it might seem basic, clinical male-midlife-crisis stuff. Yet there was nothing typical about it. No job burnout. No boredom with his wife or lust for a younger woman. Dan, a professor at a Midwestern college and a part-time radio commentator, had a lot going on in his mind and his marriage when he approached his big birthday. Half-over? As in, his life? Maybe. But his marriage, he felt, was dangerously close to being over, finished, despite the baguettes and café au lait of Paris. Truth be told, this marriage had a shaky foundation from the beginning. "I was married at 30, separated at 40, and divorced at 41," he said. Looking back, Dan might say that his was a divorce steeped in psychological immaturity and lack of growth, some lust, a touch of infidelity, and a lot of pain.

"I don't think that, at the age of 30, I realized how emotionally dependent I was," he explained. "It wasn't an unsubtle or spoken thing on my part, it was, 'Boy, if I hadn't met this person, I wouldn't have gotten through school.' At that point, I didn't have a bachelor's degree, and I was a night watchman at a nursing home." Of his ex-wife, he says, "She was the product of the city schools of Cincinnati, an overachiever. She graduated high school and knew she wanted to be a doctor or a medical technician." Dan, on the other hand, didn't have a clue about his eventual profession.

Looking back, he also sees that he was in some ways as dependent upon others as he was on his ex, Nora, who was five years younger. After they met in 1981, they "got serious right away" and started living together. "I turned 30 in '82, then we married in December," he related. They got married despite family histories that were studded with divorce and the fact that they were both "pretty negative" about how long marriages tend to last.

"I was controlling," Dan confessed. "It was clear to both of us that my emotional needs were right there on the surface and would take precedence in the marriage. Everything was a holy war with me." This kind of deal-making doesn't occur in a vacuum, however, as needs of other kinds merge and fit into the partnership. By their 10th anniversary, it had become difficult for Dan to tolerate doubt or, in his words, "to not realize something was wrong in a deep, profound, capital 'W' sense," until it was too late. "My emotional needs were not being met," he said. This time, when he said it, the statement sounded cool, clinical. For he also admitted that he hadn't been "standing on his own two feet," in the marriage or in his career, even as his work in radio documentaries was (finally) picking up. The clincher: He rarely saw his wife, who was in the midst of a 65-hour-plus career as a medical resident, fresh from the med school ranks. (Not surprisingly, they hadn't begun to plan a family.)

A key question that surfaced in Dan and Nora's marriage, but that doesn't surface often enough in others, according to marital therapists, is "Am I meeting my own and my partner's needs as well as I should?" Similarly, it may help to ask, "At what point do I stop looking for others to meet those needs for me?"

Dr. Rosenthal advises many of his clients—from both solid and shaky marriages—to think about needs regularly, both yours and your partner's. "One question a man can ask his lady," he says, is, "are you getting your needs met in this relationship? If not, what would you like me to do differently?" (Of course, that's two questions, unless the guy is perfect.) When I asked him how often I should ask this question, as a dutiful 40-year-old husband, I was thinking, maybe once a year. "A healthy man should ask this question once a month," he says. "Once a year [isn't enough], it becomes a ritual. Once a month, you can get down to specifics."

As for Dan, he admitted he wasn't, well, healthy, at the time: "I don't think I'm being a drama queen when I say that around that time, I'd been 'dry' a couple years. Then I plunged in again and started smoking, drinking, pot smoking—all the old patterns. It convinced me that I was a balls-out pot junkie—and an alcoholic, too."

A lot happened in the next two years. After the divorce went through, Dan began attending therapy sessions; a men's support group recommended by a counselor, with his new girlfriend; and he moved his home a couple of hours away. Fresh start. Four years after the divorce, he was engaged to the woman he'd met when he was 40.

"There's a certain explosive force you feel when, for whatever reason, you realize your life's blowing up," Dan said. "You want to sort out those aftereffects. I was better able to understand my neediness at 44; I had been numb. But my [new] relationship with Laura opened me up to depth of emotion that I felt threatened by. It was important to not get swept away. It became a real fight for clarity.

"One of the reasons I waited to get married again—until I was 44—was because I wanted to be sure I could stand on my own," Dan said. These days, Dan and Laura have a tight bond compared with most newlyweds, largely due to the amount of work they put into the marriage. It's a bond forged on confession, renewal, weekly therapy sessions, and vague notions of kids and a family. Notably, it is not and was not formed in a crisis, according to Dan. Their marriage isn't perfect. They know enough about midlife unions to admit that. But neither are their problems being bottled up and saved for later. They are being managed if not always solved. As so many other couples who have spent time in therapy know, this is a healthy compromise.

"Everybody wants to grow, but growing is a bitch. What makes people change is discomfort and untenability in the situation they are in now," offers Dr. Schnarch. When handled well, the changes that men often notice result in them becoming "softer," Schnarch says, and decidedly more reasonable. For those in the throes of intractable marriages, that's a start.

Single and 40

"I somehow thought I would be married at 36, which was the age Senator John F. Kennedy got married," said Evan B., 42, a corporate lawyer and former prosecutor from western Connecticut. "No one is more surprised than I that I wasn't." Not that he didn't try. He got engaged at 29, but was dumped by his fiancée.

Being single at or after 40 these days means being on the defensive at times—a lot more often than these guys would like to admit. During interviews with more than 20 single types (many of whom were divorced), I felt myself, at times, leaning in a direction that an impartial

FIVE MOMENTOUS MIDLIFE MARRIAGE MOMENTS

No matter how proficient a marital counselor may be, he cannot provide five simple tips to save a marriage in jeopardy. Love and marriage, you certainly know by now, do not work that way. But after interviewing 15 professionals in the field of couples counseling and marital therapy, I can at least offer some of their guidance related to key questions that crop up in marriages at midlife.

So for now, forget "fixing" a marriage. Instead, think about testing it, building it, shoring it up. Think of these, then, as non–Trivial Pursuit questions—with answers that are hardly trivial.

1. How have you faced—and dealt with—divorce among your friends and family? Did you find yourself taking sides? If so, you or your partner may be concealing fears you may have of one day finding yourself in a similar predicament. Fear has a nasty habit of spiraling, at times, into anger directed against your spouse.

2. Do you and your wife look into each others eyes at the moment of orgasm, as David Schnarch, Ph.D., co-founder of the Marriage and Family Health Center in Evergreen, Colorado, and author of *Passionate Marriage*, recommends? If not, is it something that sounds appealing to both of you, or invasive? Among some couples, this kind of sexual move becomes as meaningful as it is sexy. Plus, it can make a longtime relationship feel younger in a hurry.

journalist shouldn't go: I felt as if I needed to shore these men up, somehow, because they didn't seem as confident as I thought they would be. In Evan's recent past, it wasn't unusual for him to date two or three women in the same weekend (condom management, one might say). Yet in the late 1990s–early millennial years, "bachelor" isn't a kind term to men who for one reason or another find themselves unmarried at 40. And Evan serves, perhaps reluctantly, as exhibit A.

"Most of my closest friends are married, with children ranging from toddlers to teens," he said. "They are living in the suburbs and have social lives that basically revolve around kids and their sports." Although his engagement fell through at a relatively early age, Evan

3. Regarding extramarital affairs, can you envision an instance in which you or your partner would have an affair—and your marriage would survive? If not, would it help to learn that nearly half of all married men have sex outside of their marriages? Or that the percentage is becoming similar for women?

4. By the time you've reached midlife, chances are that you realize there's no such thing as a 50-50 marriage. Human beings aren't that perfect in delegating. Or in feeling. The key questions to consider here are: Are you satisfied with a 70-30 split, say, in letting your wife manage the majority of the emotional components of your marriage? How about in raising the children or in so-called household duties? Or, on the flip side, are you satisfied with the amount of time and energy you devote to overseeing the family finances, doing yardwork, and maintaining the car? If you aren't satisfied, can you map out a way to redistribute each of your strengths?

5. Have you prepared for the death or severe illness of a parent, parent-in-law, family member, or friend? How about that of your spouse? Did the writing or sharing of your wills set off anxiety or was your response more muted? How about your spouse's response?

"This is the time you are in danger of losing your parents," says psychotherapist Olga Silverstein, Ph.D., of the Ackerman Institute in New York City. "But you, as men, [typically] think you're free—that you shouldn't need to suffer. The problem is, there's a sense of impending loss, yet nobody has found a whole self by age 40. I'm 75 and I haven't found it yet."

hasn't seen fit to force himself into taking a bride. He's not dating for revenge, either. He's simply reaching the end point of dating "for fun" and finds himself increasingly trawling the waters of dating for a future. Perhaps it's for marriage. Perhaps not. But like so many single men today, he is thought by women to have an incredible advantage, numbers-wise, in the dating pool.

The National Center for Health Statistics tells a different story: The latest data show roughly 2.3 million marriages in the United States each year. Of those, 68 of every 1,000 women ages 35 to 39 get married each year, while 79 of every 1,000 men ages 35 to 39 tie the knot—not a large advantage for men. That's merely 11 more men than women per 1,000 getting married. Likewise, of those ages 40 to 44, 50 women per 1,000 get married each year, while 70 men per 1,000 do the same. Again, not a large margin, especially when you consider the supposedly strong inclinations of middle-aged men to "marry younger."

Perhaps fittingly, within a month of his 40th birthday, and after having dated a woman named Karla more steadily than not for six years, Evan found himself alone once more. Karla broke up with him and moved away. She was more into marriage than he was, in brief. Plus, she was entering her mid-thirties, never having been married herself. She wanted to settle down. Evan wasn't ready.

Wasn't being married by age 40 important to him? I asked.

"The question I asked myself wasn't, 'Will you marry Karla?' he said. "It was, 'Will you ever marry?' I knew the question was larger than one of age. If not her, who? There's never going to be someone better: This woman was the total package—everything a man could look for in a companion. I realized then that if I couldn't put it together with this woman, I wondered if I ever would with anyone else."

Part of the problem Evan (along with millions of other single or divorced men at midlife) faces is that expectations of marriage have shifted profoundly in the past few decades. In some ways, people simply expect too much from the institution. We expect our wives to be passionate lovers at times, and also to be our loyal confidantes. We want them to bond with us intensely at times, but we also want and need them to give us our precious space. Finally, we want romance in the ebullient times of marriage, but we also want a stable partner to nurture the kids, run the household, and share the stresses of the family's career goals, whether it is a one- or two-career family. Did I mention we want them to be our best friends as well?

"I always expected to be a father," Evan continued. "When my dad was my age, he had six children already. Today, my father thinks I'm 'ahead [of the game].' But I think he's ahead."

Two years after the big breakup, Evan finds himself in another relationship, one that involves a bit of a drive—to and from Boston every weekend. That doesn't deter him, though, nor does the fact that his girlfriend is the mother of a four-year-old. She's a never-been-married mom, in fact.

"There's an ugly, obnoxious quote I could tell you about guys in my situation," he said. "It is, 'Single moms don't have baby lust.'" I repeated it to myself silently before I got it. Single moms aren't going to hound the single guys they date to get married quickly and "be a dad" in the ways that singles who are concerned about their biological clocks might. He's right. It is an obnoxious thought. But it may help explain the situation he finds himself in today: mostly alone and not 100 percent proud of it.

On the other hand, when Evan and his friends get together for golf or a motor-home camping weekend, he revels in the role of playboy bachelor, a role that makes him the envy of his buddies. In their eyes, he can be with new women whenever he wants. (In reality, that doesn't happen much anymore. Plus, holidays can be painful reminders of the family life he doesn't have.) He's a good-looking guy who likes sports and has a good job in a top profession. Why shouldn't he, as they say, "get some strange" once in a while? In a way, his buddies are lamenting the sameness of their loves lives and sex lives based on the fact that most of them have been married for 5 to 15 years. Evan laments something else. "Remember," he said. "I was engaged at 29, and I thought I'd be a dad soon after that."

At some time or another, very likely in our forties, most of us indeed will have to deal with questions of sameness, or "dulling of sexual feeling," as I put it to Michael Perelman, Ph.D., co-director of the marital and sex therapy clinic at New York Hospital–Cornell Medical School in New York City. In approaching Dr. Perelman, I wasn't looking for a quick fix as much as a reasoned, seasoned sense of why this so often occurs. "I think the 'dulling' is a reflection of a shifting of priorities in midlife, both in work and in paternity," Dr. Perelman says. "For many men, [work and family] become such a greater source of priority than sexual conquest, which is so frequently a young man's pursuit." This might—I repeat, might—make thousands of men feel a bit better. It's not that we don't want to have sex anymore, it's just that it's no longer number one on the hit parade. At the same time, a solid number three isn't so shabby if it's right on the heels of a worthwhile career and loving family.

In retrospect, then, it wasn't surprising to learn, the last time I spoke with Evan, that he was shopping for real estate with a broker (forget marriage for now—a relationship with a real estate broker may be the real commitment!). And he made certain to tell me that the space would have to be large enough to include play space for a little one. It's the first time in his life that he is looking seriously to buy a home and land. Plus, he's now in a job that he says could last the rest of his life. Finally, his days of squiring women 10 years his junior are behind him. About his current love, the single mom, he says she's "the first person who's a contemporary of mine. She's 38."

Tim L., 39, is an East Coast contemporary of Evan's, though they've only met once. He's a bit younger, but he, too, has never been married. I reached Tim at home one night on a Sunday and realized after we had set the (rather late) interview time that I wouldn't have to worry about waking any small ones or his wife. He had been at the gym earlier that day, so I asked, "Would you work out as much if you were married?"

"I do it about three times a week; twice on the weekend and once during the week," Tim said. "If I were married, I think I might do it less. But I do it much less out of vanity than I used to and more for myself, for health." He also works out to keep active and to stay out of the home/work/home/work routine.

"I don't have a large group of friends that I interact with a lot," Tim said. "But among them, I'm the only one who's not married. My friends say they're jealous. I say mostly they're right, and I don't disagree with them. But I'd like to have more of a constant, dependable intimacy," he added, "with one other person. The kind that sucks out of you a way of being that is more than yourself."

Whether you're single, married, divorced, or separated, if you find yourself entering your forties while feeling distanced from a partner, a new question lingers: Can you ever know yourself too well?

The Body at 40: Midlife Maintenance Time

For a couple of reasons, I spent a good portion of the historic 1998 major league baseball season rooting for the wrong guy. Sure, the country went nuts for Mark McGwire and his 43-inch biceps (or whatever), as he shattered Roger Maris's famed home run record and reset the bar at a mind-boggling 70 home runs. But the fact that I grew up in Chicago as a Cubs fan had me rooting for someone else that summer. An underdog. A humble man. A guy who's not even close to six feet five inches. A guy who doesn't fit the All-American image of a poster boy, at least not universally. No, not Sammy Sosa, who also broke Maris's record by hitting 66 homers. I was rooting for the balding, beak-nosed Cubs third baseman, Gary Gaetti.

Of course, he didn't catch much of the limelight as the Cubs strug-

A MAN'S BODY AT THE 50-YARD-LINE OF LIFE

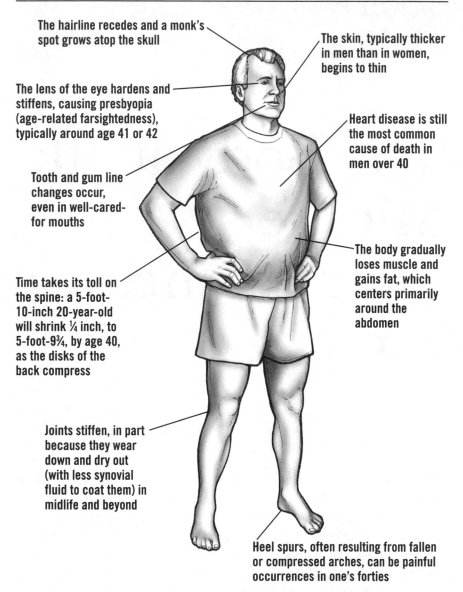

The hairline recedes and a monk's spot grows atop the skull

The skin, typically thicker in men than in women, begins to thin

The lens of the eye hardens and stiffens, causing presbyopia (age-related farsightedness), typically around age 41 or 42

Heart disease is still the most common cause of death in men over 40

Tooth and gum line changes occur, even in well-cared-for mouths

The body gradually loses muscle and gains fat, which centers primarily around the abdomen

Time takes its toll on the spine: a 5-foot-10-inch 20-year-old will shrink ¼ inch, to 5-foot-9¾, by age 40, as the disks of the back compress

Joints stiffen, in part because they wear down and dry out (with less synovial fluid to coat them) in midlife and beyond

Heel spurs, often resulting from fallen or compressed arches, can be painful occurrences in one's forties

gled to make the playoffs, where they were swept three straight by the Atlanta Braves. Slammin' Sammy was the Chicago summer icon. Casual fans thought of Gaetti (if they thought of him at all) as an afterthought, as a one-time World Series champ (with Minnesota in '87) who was signed up in midseason to shore up the infield, hit line drives, and dispense sage advice to younger Cubbies all around him. For Gaetti turned 40 that summer, and I—who had played six years of Little League ball in Illinois, four more of Pony/Colt League, then 15 more of corporate-league softball in New York City—wanted mightily for him to succeed.

My career was over at 38. I wanted his to last all the way to 41—or even 42. It would make me feel younger, I imagined, and I rooted for his body to stay healthy. The newly middle-aged Gaetti wound up hitting a heady .281, with 19 homers and 70 RBIs, while doing his job quite respectably in the field. He was a shining role model for his teammates and for all of us fans and former players who had long since kissed our thirties good-bye. Especially when he doffed his cap.

Hair Today . . .

While Gary Gaetti's main concern in his 40th year wasn't his retreating hairline, we must note that he is one of a distinct minority of Americans who must, absolutely must, wear hats in order to perform their jobs. No hat? He takes a seat on the bench. That's the rule in the major leagues, and one can only wonder whether 20-some years of wearing baseball hats might have inadvertently accelerated Gaetti's hair loss.

BALD TRUTHS

While all men lose hair, they do so at markedly different rates during adulthood. According to *The AMA Book of Skin and Hair Care*, over time, male pattern baldness becomes noticeable in approximately:

- 12 percent of 25-year-old men
- 37 percent of 35-year-old men
- 45 percent of 45-year-old men
- 65 percent of 65-year-old men

We all—men and women, young and old—lose hair as adults, to the tune of about 20 to 60 hairs each day. This may sound like a lot until you consider that an average 30-year-old with a full head of hair has approximately 100,000 hairs—a slightly smaller number for redheads, but a larger number for blondes. At 40, signs of male pattern baldness, or androgenetic alopecia, are common. These can be either early signs (thinning at the crown or temples) or advanced signs (in which the receding hairline has almost met the "monk's spot" atop the skull). If it makes you feel any better, skin and hair experts estimate that up to 80 percent of all men will have some noticeable hair loss during their lifetimes.

Unlike our fathers' or their fathers' generations, however, those of us new to our forties have not one or two weapons to battle baldness, but a veritable arsenal. Today's men may choose from among the topical drug minoxidil (Rogaine); the oral drug finasteride (Propecia); hair transplants; "micrograft" individual hair transplants; scalp-reduction plastic surgery techniques; hair weaves or extensions; or any number of hairpieces. Or they might stylishly shave their heads. Costs range from $350 a year for anti-hair-loss drugs to a few thousand dollars for custom hairpieces to $10,000 or more for surgical solutions.

A few words about treatments for 40-year-olds are in order: First, if you're thinking about drugs to counteract hair loss, your choices involve a clear liquid, Rogaine, or a pill, Propecia. Both work on some heads and don't work on others. And both need to be taken for the rest of your life or else the possibility looms that your hair will revert to the way it was before treatment, perhaps with even less hair because of your advanced age. As for cost, a year's supply of Rogaine bought over the counter will run you about $360 a year, or $1,800 over five years (if prices stay constant). The Propecia pill, by contrast, must be prescribed by a doctor (often a dermatologist) and costs some $600 a year, or $3,000 over five years.

Although some evidence indicates that Propecia is more effective at stimulating hair growth (was it just coincidence that Rogaine's makers introduced an extra-strength version of its product when Propecia hit the scene—more than doubling the strength of the original Rogaine?), Propecia isn't the whole answer, either. Some advisors on the federal Food and Drug Administration (FDA) panel that recommended Propecia be approved for treating baldness believed there wasn't clear evidence for successful hair growth on men over age 41. And for both treatments, as with any drugs, there may be side effects to consider.

For those who are unwilling to go the drug, surgery, or shaved-head route and who want to do something to counteract hair loss, keep in mind that "miracle" lotions and potions that talk about "nourishing" hair won't help. That's because hair cells are dead and baldness is not caused by poor blood flow or undernourished hair. To the contrary, three known factors that cause garden-variety baldness in midlife and older men are: a genetic predisposition to the condition, a man's age, and the action of male sex hormones, primarily (but not exclusively) testosterone.

In the hair arena, there's something else for a man to consider: Baldness can be thought of as the price paid for masculinity. That's because without testosterone, the genetic potential for hair loss wouldn't activate. (That's also why middle-aged women rarely show evidence of hair loss.) Finally, in the words of longtime New York–based writer (and onetime softball teammate of mine in the early 1980s) Guy Martin, who lost much of his hair in his twenties, "There is no cure for baldness because, get this, there is no disease. . . ." Wise words to consider next time you check that hairline in the mirror.

Skin Changes

It may have occurred to you that women seem to spend a lot more time obsessing about their skin than any guy you know does. For good reason. At ages 30 and 40, a man's skin typically will show fewer outward signs of aging than a woman's—as long as the man and woman are from the same part of the country, with the same or similar outdoor habits. That's because when it comes to skin, setting sun damage aside, a man's skin typically is thicker than a woman's. "It's a natural advantage," says Randall E. McNally, M.D., a plastic surgeon at Rush-Presbyterian–St. Luke's Medical Center in Chicago. With age, the skin of a man or a woman does indeed get thinner; but with men, there's more substance to start with—call it a plumpness factor. Thus, the appearance of fine lines and aging effects are muted somewhat, at least in the early stages of midlife.

Compared with the state of medicine even 10 years ago, there's a lot more a man can do to erase early signs of aging from his face without resorting to a facelift. He can use skin care products containing alpha hydroxy acid (AHA) that have proven sloughing, rejuvenating effects. Or he can employ a dermatologist or plastic surgeon who may use lasers or injections to reduce the appearance of fine lines or wrinkles, or even erase them altogether (albeit temporarily—wrinkles will return in a few years).

At 40, the most important numbers that have to do with a healthy

UNDER YOUR SKIN

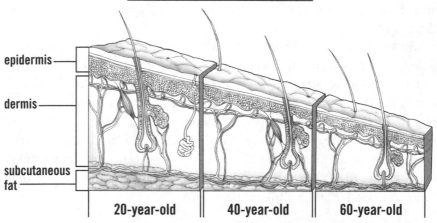

epidermis

dermis

subcutaneous fat

| 20-year-old | 40-year-old | 60-year-old |

With age, the skin's layers become progressively thinner, making them more vulnerable to external assaults.

man's skin have to do with the letters SPF, as in sun protection factor. The more often you use products with an SPF when you work, play, or walk in the sun, the less risk you may face of developing skin cancer. And it turns out that whether you use sunscreens and moisturizing lotions with a SPF of 15, 25, or even 30 (as computed by standards set by the FDA) isn't as important as the fact that you use them regularly when you are outdoors (and that you reapply them after swimming or sweating, as the package directions indicate). Furthermore, in midlife and beyond, it pays to heed the call of skin care experts who advise staying out of the sun—using sunscreen or not—between the hours of 10:00 A.M. and 3:00 P.M., when the sun's rays are the harshest.

Even if you're careful, though, it's difficult to closely monitor potential skin problems. Your skin—not your heart, stomach, or lungs—is the largest organ of your body. Skin cancers and other types of disorders can lurk undetected for months or years on your back, behind your ears, and even on the tops of your toes. And the incidences of basal cell skin cancer (a common, highly treatable type) and melanoma (an aggressive but still treatable type when caught early) have been on the rise in recent years. Years of exposure and overexposure to the sun is thought to be the main culprit in both cases.

Apart from its role in skin cancer, the sun causes elastin fibers in the skin to break down over time, which is why an older person's skin doesn't snap back into place as quickly when you pinch it. There are other causes, too, including such daily activities as smiling, frowning, grimacing, and squinting. These don't seem harmful until you do the math and tote up 25 or 35 years of such musculo-facial scrunching. The other age-related skin changes to note are that you tend to sweat less now and cuts or scrapes take longer to heal than they did in your teens. Eventually, chronology catches up with physiology. Not so much by 30, but certainly by 40.

"With age, there is excess skin around the eyes and a sagging in the jowl area," says James R. Reardon, M.D., a plastic surgeon and director of the Cosmetic Surgery Center of New York in New York City. "One of the dead giveaways [of age] is the neck." Today's top plastic surgeons say that up to 30 percent of their patients are male, up from 5 to 10 percent a generation ago. Not only have plastic surgery procedures become less invasive and more natural looking in recent years but also a better understanding of the biology and musculature of the face and neck have enabled doctors to do less drastic "cutting and lifting" and more targeted "tightening." Of course, it can't be said too often: For those considering an eyelid tightening, laser resurfacing, or full facelift, cosmetic surgery is still surgery.

Seeing the Eyes Anew

Of all the age-related changes that occur within a man's body at midlife, it's odd that the eyes are often, well, overlooked. After all, the eyes are our information processors, drawing in 80 to 90 percent of the input we use each day. Many of us visit a dentist regularly—we were trained to go twice a year as kids, sometimes thrice a year as middle-aged, gum-diseased adults. But who goes to an optometrist twice a year for a checkup when he doesn't wear glasses? And yet when it comes to the short list of what aging experts consider to be true "bio-markers"—the human equivalents of the concentric rings of a tree trunk—changes in vision nearly always come out on top of the list. Around the ages 40 to 42, the eyes invariably begin to show their age. Seeing, or not, is believing.

Inevitably, the eyes' timing slows and attendant muscle flexibility begins to wane. Many optometrists and ophthalmologists describe the midlife changes in brief by saying the lenses of the eye "stiffen" and "thicken" at midlife, which is true enough. But it's not just the makeup of the clear lens that's affected. The muscles that help the lens bend (infinitesimally) in and out, which enable it to focus quickly, begin to weaken, as well. Plus, there are changes to the cornea, which is the first, outside "layer" of the eyeball to take in information. The other major players are the pupil, lens, vitreous humor, and retina.

As with skin, men seem to have a slight aging and vision advantage over women, but it may not be enough to brag about: A major U.S. government National Health Survey once found that when men and women were tested using "usual visual correction" (those who wore glasses or contacts were allowed to wear them during the test), men at each stage of life tended to have somewhat better visual acuity than women did. In brief, some 75 percent of men tested at least 20/20, compared to 70 percent of women. In addition, the proportion of those who had distance-vision problems of 20/50 or worse was 2.9 percent for men, while 3.6 percent of women had defective vision that was at least that poor.

THE AGING EYE

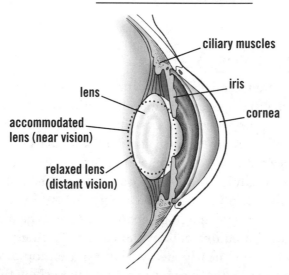

ciliary muscles

iris

lens

cornea

accommodated lens (near vision)

relaxed lens (distant vision)

One of the few true biomarkers of aging, gerontologists report, is the hardening or stiffening of the eye lens that typically occurs in one's early forties. The fibers of the clear lens begin to thicken over time, and within the architecture of the eye, the lens becomes less pliable. That's the leading cause of the need for bifocals in the newly middle-aged.

"Up to ages 40 to 50, little change in acuity has been noted," says Jack Botwinick, Ph.D., director of the aging and development program at Washington University in St. Louis. "But after this time, there is marked decline." By age 70, Botwinick adds, and without correction, poor vision is the rule rather than the exception.

The three major conditions to be aware of in your forties and beyond are presbyopia, myopia, and glaucoma. Of the three, presbyopia—a type of farsightedness—is the most common. It is also the leading vision biomarker in the study of gerontology (the study of the aging process, not just the aged). When presbyopia occurs, the lens of the eye has, over time, become both thicker and less pliable. When the lens can't accommodate for close vision, the images that reach the retina behind it are blurry. Think "dry sponge" at age 50 versus "damp sponge" at age 41 (which one works more quickly?) and you begin to understand why midlife men start to squint more often when checking the mutual fund tables in the newspaper or while pretending to read a menu in a swank, dimly lit restaurant. As a result, the business in bifocals is booming.

It's not just glasses, of course. Along with the now-standard array of disposable and bifocal contact lenses, vision training and laser surgery have become popular means to prevent and correct vision problems. If your vision is good and your eyes are healthy at or about midlife, you might consider signing up for vision training courses, offered across the country at state universities or colleges of optometry and at private optometrists' offices. Unlike lenses, however, there's no guarantee of vision improvement through training and eye exercises. On the other hand, the field of behavioral optometry is growing precisely because many people see results and like the idea of prolonging the youthfulness of their vision. Reading glasses at 41 may be normal, but if they can be postponed until, say, 45, many people will opt for eye workouts as opposed to lasers or lenses.

Leading proponents of these exercises, known as behavioral optometrists, believe that vision declines are inevitable, but they also believe that vision degeneration needn't occur as early in life as many of us have been conditioned to expect. Try these two exercises on for eyes and, if you're lucky, you may not need bifocals or glasses until you're 45 or 50.

Palming. This exercise is anything but high-tech. Simply put, palming is a way to relax the eyes by keeping light out. First, shut your eyes, then cover each eye with one of your palms for a minute or two at a time, with your lower palms resting on your cheekbones. (This way, the eyeballs aren't inadvertently rubbed or pressed.) To further the relaxation, prop your elbows on a table or desk during palming. Repeat a few times during the day. Using the technique not only relieves strain and fatigue, eye doctors say, but also it may improve vision temporarily.

Focusing pursuits. Those who use vision training, including some professional baseball and hockey players, often use focusing pursuits to sharpen not just their eyes but also their whole visual systems, including hand-eye coordination and body-eye movement. In laboratories such as the one at the State University of New York College of Optometry in New York City, performing athletic feats under strobe lights in darkened rooms helps athletes keep their vision stronger for a longer period of time.

An at-home version of focusing pursuits goes as follows: Tape a couple of words from a newspaper onto a small ruler. Hold the ruler out about 16 inches in front of you with the words visible. Now, slowly swing the stick in a small circle, closer to your eyes, then farther away, in constant motion, all the while trying to focus on the words. Reverse direction. Over time, increase the size of your circle and change the words on the ruler. This will give your eyes a more complete, well-rounded workout.

In the area of surgery for vision correction, two laser surgical procedures have garnered most of the attention in the mid- to late 1990s: PRK (photorefractive keratectomy) and LASIK (laser in situ keratomileusis). Both procedures use ultra-sensitive laser beams to reshape the cornea ever so slightly in order to correct nearsightedness, or myopia. Both procedures are highly successful, expensive, and reported to be safe: In FDA studies to approve the PRK procedure, out of 2,500 patients, 100 percent of the subjects improved their natural, or uncorrected, vision. And 67 percent achieved 20/20 vision. For people with extreme nearsightedness, LASIK is usually the better option (more corneal tissue can be removed). Unfortunately, neither of these procedures can correct presbyopia.

As for glaucoma, a disease you don't hear much about in your teens, twenties, or thirties, the operative word is pressure. Briefly, glaucoma, which is a leading cause of blindness in those over 40, is said to occur when eye fluids build up and create dangerously high pressure in one or both eyes. If left untreated over months or years, serious damage and blindness can follow. Treatment usually involves daily use of medicated eye drops or oral medications that work to lower the pressure in the eyes. Lasers are also used in various cases. The key here is early detection, as nearly all blindness due to glaucoma can be prevented, opthalmologists say. It's another reason to consider yearly eye exams after 40.

The Line on Teeth and the Gum Line

At this point in your life, it is time to rethink the phrase "long in the tooth." It no longer just means "old." Because, unlike the years you spent in your teens and twenties (and possibly early thirties), the forties are indeed the decade in which your tooth care invariably changes. It becomes tooth and gum care, on orders of your dentist.

Here's the lowdown on the midlife gum line, starting with a new view of cavities: While the primary cause of tooth loss in those under age 30 is decay, the prime reason for losing teeth in those age 30 and over is gum disease. In other words, over the years, fluoride in our water and toothpaste have done their jobs. Now it's our turn to protect the foundations of our bites, the precise places in which our teeth actually become, through lack of judicious care, "long." So it is not irresponsible to say, "Forget the cavities for now." It's more properly time to plan your plaque attack.

In midlife, if you don't watch it, you could well end up having a team of tooth care experts, from dentist to periodontist to oral surgeon, much like the doctors you visited when we were younger. Used to be, you had a doctor. Suddenly, in your thirties, you added an allergist or internist or, if you developed an ulcer, gastroenterologist to your general practitioner. You'll be doing well if, by 50, you still have but one dentist—no periodontist needed. As David Owen, a toothsome writer and columnist for *Golf Digest*, once wrote in *Harper's Bazaar* magazine, ". . . virtually any dentist will tell you . . . there is enough untreated dental disease already in existence to keep the world's dentists busy until they all drop dead."

Periodontal disease, the condition centered so insidiously along the gum line, is the curse of the baby boomer's mouth. And like it or not, whether we know it or not, some 75 percent of adults suffer from at least a mild form of gum disease, according to the American Academy of Periodontology. There are two main types of gum disease to confront and consider: gingivitis, the less serious type, and periodontitis, the advanced form.

With gingivitis, bacteria that collects around the teeth and gums amasses into a colorless, sticky material called plaque. Left unchecked, plaque can form an even harder material called calculus, which lodges between your teeth and gums. It's the stuff that makes getting your teeth cleaned in your forties so uncomfortable. The good news, if you could call it that, is that gingivitis can be controlled by brushing twice or thrice a day (why not keep a toothbrush at work or at the gym?), flossing at least once a day, and rinsing your mouth really well between times or after meals when you're toothbrushless.

When it comes to dealing with periodontitis, you must shift into attack mode because the bacteria and calculus have themselves shifted into skulking, sticky, gum line-eroding warriors. As you lose millimeters of healthy pink gum line to gum disease, you increase your chances

THE TOOTH AND GUM LINE EXPOSED

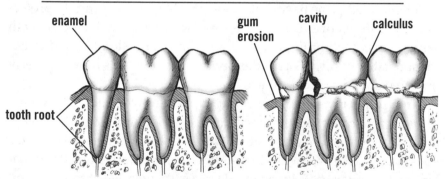

It's inevitable that bacteria will collect along the tooth and gum line, and sometimes this bacteria can form pockets of infection that result in gingivitis. If this mild form of gum disease isn't diagnosed and controlled, more serious erosion of tooth and gum surfaces are sure to follow. The old saws of brushing, flossing, and twice-a-year checkups still apply. The good news is that better brushes (electric and manual) have come onto the market in recent years to much acclaim. Likewise, antibacterial and antiplaque mouth rinses have been shown to benefit midlife mouths, though they'll never replace flossing outright.

of losing teeth and a good-looking smile. (You probably don't even want to know that really advanced cases of periodontitis can result in the loss of shards of jawbone.) The best way to beat periodontitis is, of course, to make sure that your gingivitis never gets that far. So the mantra goes: twice a day, once a day, twice a year . . . smile (key to mantra: brush, floss, dental cleaning . . . smile).

Back to Basics

Blame it on evolution. If we had never evolved from four-legged creatures into two-legged ones, chances are we'd suffer a lot less back pain than we do in modern times. And we do suffer: The most harrowing statistic bandied about by back experts is that 80 percent of the total population will suffer back pain at some point. I prefer a couple of more pointed numbers, however, to get to the here-and-now of the hurt: In the United States, up to 20 percent of the entire population and some 50 percent of all working folks suffer some form of back pain each year. At last count, more than $20 billion a year was spent directly on back care.

But back to evolution: Is it just coincidence that millions of 40-plus men get up out of bed on many mornings looking like the cavemen from which we've descended, all hunched over and hurting, afraid or unable to stand upright, just waiting for the joints of the spine to "lube up" and the stiffness to ease? Or is it a payback of sorts? Truth is, if we spent more time each day on all fours, stretching and crunching and putting in the 15 minutes a day that orthopedics wizards advise, we would all hurt a lot less. And for a lot fewer years. The so-called inevitable decline of the spine that sets in for so many in the late thirties and early forties is indeed somewhat "plastic." In fact, it can be pushed back at least 5 to 10 years, with dedication and a working knowledge of the back's components. Even without the commitment of 15 minutes a day to stretching, much nagging pain can be eased through lifestyle changes and orthopedic accessories.

In the briefest of summaries, the spine consists of 33 vertebrae and some delicate but quite responsive sheathing. As a structure, the spine supports the trunk and houses the spinal cord, spinal canal, and nerves. If you were to take a peek between vertebrae, you would find squishy discs and cartilage—the whole package ringed with layers of muscle.

SHOPPING FOR A MONEY-BACK GUARANTEE

Not long ago, I made an appointment with a chiropractor. My back wasn't hurting. I merely wanted to check out a newfangled store called the Better Back Store, and I thought I could better sort through the merchandise if I had a little professional help.

"In order of importance for doing on-your-own correction," says Doug Kennedy, D.C., a chiropractor in private practice in Boulder, Colorado, who was kind enough to lead me on a professional's tour of the shop, "you need to figure out where you spend most of your day—in a desk chair, driving a delivery truck—and go from there." In the back store, he went straight to the ergonomic office chair department, where all sorts of moveable, bendable, height-adjustable chairs sat at attention. "You'll need to sit in 5 to 10 different chairs before you'll feel the right one," he says. The goal: to prevent poor posture and the "creep" of disk material from the center of the spine outward toward the back of the spine.

"You want lower lumbar support," he adds, "but if the chairs are too pricey or your company won't pay for one, you can retrofit your chair with one of these portable back supports." He was speaking of the plethora of soft but firm foam-and-fabric inserts that are available as portable back braces. Obus is one reputable brand. They often cost less than $50, and they provide ergonomically correct, meaning slightly curved, spinal support.

Dr. Kennedy also mentioned that, ideally, you want your seat pan (the part your buttocks rest on) to be able to move back and forth. By doing so, it enables you to

After all, the vertebrae rely on muscles, ligaments, and tendons to keep the slightly S-shaped spinal column from collapsing. No wonder there's so much pain. There are so many chances for things to slide out of whack, so many chances for the dreaded pain and herniation of disks that we hear about so often in our forties.

Upon entering midlife, and all through their forties and fifties, most men would benefit greatly by performing even five minutes a day of exercises aimed at helping the back. That's because various forms of back pain and early-stage degeneration of the spine tend to be cumulative in nature, often caused by muscular weakness. This weakness may occur in the lower back—the lumbar region of the spine—or it may be shift the angle of your lower back and your hips throughout a long day. "It helps to change a lot of the circulation and the neural input," he explains. During extended computer or desk sessions, your spine craves movement, even if it can't tell you until pain sets in.

At home, one of the best things you can do to keep your spine in line is to rethink your pillows. Most people, Dr. Kennedy says, tend to favor overstuffed pillows in bed, which put a crick in the neck and thus the top group of vertebrae in the spine. A better choice, whether you use an ergonomic pillow or a relatively flat conventional pillow, is to add some sort of neck support. This may be a small pillar of Styrofoam-like material that actually slides into your pillowcase (the foam props up your neck, while the pillow serves your head). Back patients are also increasingly using foam egg-crate pads to buttress the support their normal pillows provide.

Three other products made the chiropractor's hypothetical all-star shopping basket in a back store: a back support "roll"—a tubular foam pillow that's about half the size of a baguette, only thicker—for use by serious commuters or vacationers while driving; a horseshoe-shaped, inflatable neck pillow for use on airplanes; and a large inflatable gym ball or exercise ball, which many health clubs have offered in recent years as props in fitness classes. Often used for rehabilitation of people with back injuries, the huge balls enable patients or exercisers to safely and slowly stretch their spines backward, then forward, in a greater range of motion than a mat on a floor would allow.

hiding in fleshy folds of the stomach, where abdominal muscles reside. It can hardly be overstated that millions of cases of back pain could be prevented had the owners of those backs worked out their abdominals regularly over the past 5 or 10 years. The reasoning is straightforward: The more stress and weight your stomach muscles can handle, the less pressure will be placed on your lumbar, or lower spine. Fitness trainers' standbys include abdominal crunches and oblique crunches.

Abdominal crunches. Lie flat on your back, with your legs extended and your knees unlocked. Cup your hands loosely behind your ears with your elbows out to the side. Keeping your lower back in contact with the floor, raise your upper torso a couple of inches off the ground.

THE SIMPLEST ANTI-AGING WORKOUT

In the East, they talk of yin and yang. And they know their martial arts. As you look ahead to fitness in your second 40 years, you may want to bear in mind an East-meets-West watchword that is particularly apropos at midlife: balance. As Richard Restak, M.D., neuropsychiatrist with Neurology Associates in Washington, D.C., and author of *Older and Wiser*, points out, perhaps surprisingly, "the best single exercise that can be done any time and without any special equipment involves nothing more elaborate or complicated than standing on one foot for as long as possible and then switching to the other foot." Then, one is advised to repeat the drill. No fancy footwork needed.

Though a simple exercise, it is deceptively powerful in that it builds strength, balance, and flexibility. And it is practiced around the world, especially in Asian cultures that favor practicing martial arts moves well into midlife and later life. Closer to home, researchers at the National Institute on Aging have long used measures of standing and balance to gauge what is "normal," neurologically speaking, throughout life. Truth is, in America, we're somewhat late to the game.

Look up as you lift your head, neck, and shoulders off the floor. Hold for a second, then lower to the starting position. Immediately begin your next crunch without relaxing in between. As a general guideline, aim to do crunches for 10 minutes a day, in three to four sets, at your own pace.

Oblique crunches. Lie on your back with your knees bent and your feet on the floor, then slowly lift your head, neck, and right shoulder toward your left knee. Lower yourself, then repeat, this time lifting your left shoulder toward your right knee. Repeat up to 40 to 50 times, each time alternating the shoulder you lift.

It's also important to work the hips and hamstrings, which are the overlooked helpers of the back, serving as anchors of sorts for the lower torso. It makes sense to strengthen them as a means to counteract some of the expected degeneration in the spine that may surface in middle age. While most men at least know about the connection between strong abs and a strong back, less common is the knowledge, gleaned from athletic trainers and physical therapists, that strong hamstrings and hip flexor muscles can also prevent back pain and injury.

To work the hamstrings (backs of the thighs), perform a skier's stretch. While leaning your back against a wall, slowly bend your knees as if you are about to sit down on an invisible chair. When your knees reach a 90-degree angle, hold the position for 20 to 30 seconds, being careful not to bend your knees farther. Slowly rise, and repeat 10 to 12 times.

To work the hip flexors, begin by sitting on the floor with your legs straight and splayed out to form a 60-degree angle. Bend forward, trying to lower your torso slowly as you reach out to touch the ground between your feet. Rise, and repeat 10 to 12 times.

After a few weeks of performing these exercises three or four times a week, your back will feel stronger. And for good reason: Part of it will be stronger.

Instead of doing strengthening exercises, many a man says "Thanks" for the golf clubs he got for his 40th birthday and heads to the course without a second thought—or a stretch. Then one afternoon a week or a month later, he returns home grabbing at his back, which has responded to this surge of interest in golf by serving up repeated, angry stabs of pain.

"I don't consider golf exercise," says Michael Nehring, D.C., a chiropractor at the Boulder Back Pain Clinic in Colorado. "But a lot of people who play simply get up and go out early, before they've had a chance to warm up. Golf involves flexion and rotation, and those are some of the worst things you can do to a spine, especially when it's not warm."

To counteract these golf-related ills and many other sports-related problems in midlife, consider another of Dr. Nehring's offerings: The precious synovial fluid that bathes the joints (not just those of the spine but also the knees and shoulders) and keeps them lubricated and warm is mostly produced during the day. When production of this fluid drops at night, the joints of the spine tend to stiffen. Add to that the fact that production of synovial fluid decreases as you age and the connective tissue in the joints grows less pliant. In the morning, disks take time to once again be properly bathed in synovial fluid. This means that in your forties, not only do you need to warm up carefully and slowly before morning sports but also you can't simply blame the mattress anymore for the lower-back pains that seem to crop up more frequently.

THE BACK'S ANCHORS

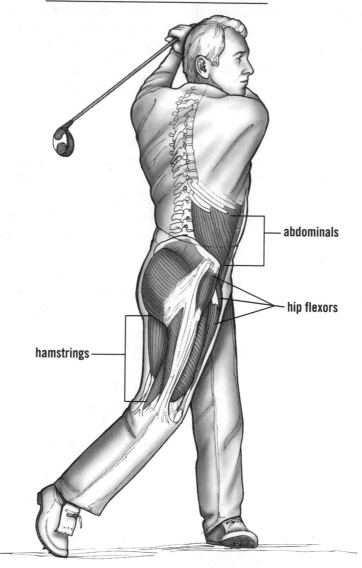

abdominals

hip flexors

hamstrings

Many men could avoid lower-back pain by strengthening their abdominal, hip flexor, and hamstring muscles.

There's something going on back there, and it isn't always pretty. "One-third of adults between the ages of 20 and 40 have at least one level of significant degenerative change in their backs," Dr. Nehring explains. But that doesn't mean treatment or surgery is necessarily needed. What it means is that care should be taken as well as preventive measures. The spine is all about architecture. When you think about it that way, which you're more likely to do at 40 than at 20, you'll begin to appreciate the need for periodic maintenance and shoring up from time to time, instead of waiting for a signal to sound. You can't always beat back pain, it turns out. But you can often outsmart it.

Stronger Bones and Joints

Long before Michael Jordan won his first NBA championship with the Chicago Bulls, he had concerns about bones and his career being shortened. In the spring of 1985, his second pro season, while he was flying impossibly high for the Bulls and his shoe sponsor, Nike, he was repeatedly grounded by stress fractures. The small bones of his feet apparently couldn't take the pounding—even while encased in ultra-cushioned high-top sneakers. How could this happen to such a young Bull? The answer is that bones are living tissue—and people of all ages don't pay attention to this often enough.

Bones may look dead, all right, especially when viewed as part of Halloween costumes or in creepy scenes from slasher horror movies. But those are, for the most part, the bones of dead people. Even into our sixties and seventies, healthy bones and joints remain surprisingly resilient, which makes the midlife years prime time for maintenance of the bones and joints.

Under your skin, there's a lot to account for in terms of your skeleton. For starters, the 200 bones in the body average only about 14 percent of a 175-pound man's total weight. In a young, fit man of 30, approximately one-quarter of his bone weight is water. Another 25 percent or so of bone weight can be attributed to collagen, a connective tissue, while the balance—nearly 50 percent—is mostly calcium phosphate, the hard stuff. And here's what you don't see: Inside the bones, where blood vessels, bone marrow, and nerves converge to keep the skeleton healthy and strong, the color is deep red, not ghostly white.

The good news to report, skeletally speaking, is that we can now say with certainty that exercise builds bones in adult life; it doesn't merely slow their decline. (Like women, men can develop osteoporosis—the thinning of bones—in later life, but not in the same numbers. And

(continued on page 80)

TOTAL-BODY TRAINING AND ANTI-AGING HORMONE HELP

Not long ago, I traveled to Las Vegas to get a whiff of the new era of anti-aging at a medical convention hosted by the American Academy of Anti-Aging Medicine, also known as A4M. In a temporary tent erected beside the Alexis Park Resort, Dr. Robert Goldman, a sports-medicine doctor and co-founder of the Chicago-based A4M, preceded by the emotive trumpets from *Chariots of Fire*, gave a rousing keynote speech: "I'm often asked," he said by way of introduction, "'Who in the world wants to be 102 years old?' I answer: 'Someone who is 101.'"

Dr. Goldman is in his mid-40s and wants to stay that way. "Ours will be the first generation to see the end of aging as we know it—a constellation of diseases," he said. "Instead, as we'll see in today's presentations on human growth hormone, age changes can be thought of as 'unrecognizable disease processes,' and . . . aging is, for the first time, reversible."

With all this new focus on hormones and on reported major declines of midlife sexuality and athletic performance, you can see how a guy can get pretty down about getting older. But I also found out, that weekend in Las Vegas, that hormones are not the whole answer to total-body anti-aging. That would be far too simple an answer to a far more complex process. This much we do know about hormones and hormone supplements as potential anti-aging elements.

• Melatonin is a relatively safe and relatively powerful hormone that has been shown to have multiple health benefits, some of which are related to slowing effects of aging. It can help regulate sleep when used on occasion and under a doctor's care. It can also be used as an antioxidant (a protective substance that helps prevent cell damage caused by harmful oxygen molecules known as free radicals) to fight heart disease, reports Dr. Roman Rozencwaig, M.D., of Reddy Memorial Hospital in Montreal. It's available over-the-counter.

• Testosterone is essential to sexual desire, and testosterone levels fall as a man ages. However, blood levels of testosterone below the lower "normal" limit occur in only 7 percent of men ages 40 to 60, which means an even lower percentage of those ages 40 to 50 have levels that would be considered deficient. Testosterone replacement therapy must be prescribed by a doctor.

• DHEA (dehydroepiandrosterone), an adrenal gland hormone, has been found to increase lean body mass and to prevent "the deposition [collection] of body fat," in the words of Judy Kameoka, M.D., of the Center for Health Restoration in Charleston, South Carolina. Muscle mass and body fat ratio is a biomarker of aging; therefore, this could be a relevant anti-aging hormone. Long-term studies, however, have not yet been completed in terms of safety. DHEA is available over-the counter, but dosages vary widely.

• Human growth hormone (HGH), in certain controlled instances, can be helpful to the whole body in terms of anti-aging effects. L. Cass Terry, M.D., Ph.D., of the Medical College of Wisconsin in Milwaukee, gave the A4M attendees a fair, grounded presentation about the hormone, citing study data of 1,000 subjects. In the study, those who took the hormone showed a decrease in cholesterol of 20 points in six months, a 30 to 40 point decrease in triglycerides (fats that contribute to heart disease risk), and increases in muscle performance, sexual performance, and energy levels. HGH must be prescribed by a doctor, often to the tune of $5,000 a year.

"But you have to exercise [to obtain the full effects]," Dr. Terry said. This is a powerful hormone, and it is legal to use in the United States for certain conditions. However, its safety has not been studied over the long term, and the hormone is mighty expensive. Refreshingly, Dr. Terry also told the crowd, "I have no financial interest in anything related to what I'm going to say today."

The other refreshing thing I found in my reporting from the A4M annual meeting was that we can—and do—make our own human growth hormone in our bodies every day. We can even increase production of the hormone to apparently safe and quite beneficial levels, by exercising rigorously and regularly. When researchers talk about HGH these days, the automatic response is to think of a synthetic hormone that's injected into the body. Well, it's worthwhile to remember that the synthetic version was genetically engineered to match what we already have in our bodies. No, it's not as "quick" or "efficient" to build muscles over months and years with methodical weight work, running, walking, or cycling. But from age 40 on, you can indeed turn up the faucet when it comes to producing your own HGH. That's how "natural" bodybuilders do it. And that's how masters athletes do it, as well. Over the long term. Safely, steadily, and at times, mightily.

midlife men needn't have the same concerns about anti-osteoporosis hormone supplementation that women face at 50 or so, during onset of menopause.) The healthful stresses placed on the bones by weight-bearing workouts such as walking, jogging, and weight lifting result in stronger-knitted surfaces at the ends of the bones and help nourishment to flow inside the bones themselves. In short, bone mass can be increased in midlife, which will offer you protection in late life.

Similarly, nutritional changes that boost your calcium intake will make a difference to your bone health later on. Sources of calcium include milk, cheese, yogurt, canned sardines and salmon, broccoli, leafy green vegetables, and soybeans. Increasing your intake of these foods is important because as you age, your bones lose calcium. A man's bones are thickest and strongest between the ages of 21 and 30. By contrast, the first signs of mineral loss, while barely apparent to the bones' owners, take place soon after age 40.

By 40, there is no major decline inside the bones—it's where they meet that trouble crops up. The result is numerous soft tissue and joint injuries in the forties and fifties, says Frank Jobe, M.D., of the Kerlan-Jobe Orthopedic Clinic in Los Angeles, which counts numerous professional athletes among its clientele.

As joints (particularly those such as knees, hips, elbows, and vertebrae, which bear weight or severe stresses) age, the cartilage that allows them to flex and move freely breaks down. This is called articular cartilage, and it is what so many athletes fritter away, season after season, by subjecting their joints to undue stresses and trauma. Even among the rest of us, garden-variety

A FRIEND IN KNEES

Whether your 40-year-old knees have submitted to the scalpel or not, it pays to be kind to them from here on out. So take a seat and treat those tired-and-true joints with the following exercise. Remember, too, that they may be stiff from having sat too long or too often, at work and at home.

While seated in a chair, extend your legs forward so that only your heels are in contact with the floor. From this position, tighten your quadriceps muscles—the large muscles on the front of your thighs. Hold the flex for a few seconds, then release and fully exhale. Repeat four more times to release a healthy amount of knee-joint lubrication, known in the orthopedics field as synovial fluid.

arthritis begins to work on the joints in midlife, before we tend to worry about it.

Because of this, midlife is a time to be active and, at the same time, prudent. Relatively few men suffer from rheumatoid arthritis, the most serious form of arthritis, in their forties or fifties; but by age 60 or so, there's a good chance that you may have signs of the milder osteoarthritis. Years of flexing and just plain using the joints wear down the cartilage cushions between joints (sometimes chipped or "floating" pieces of cartilage cause joint troubles), and the fluids between joints begin to dissipate as well. Supporting ligaments also stiffen somewhat in later midlife, but remain strong and healthy through the forties when exercised and stretched regularly.

"Virtually everyone who lives beyond early adulthood eventually experiences the effects of osteoarthritis," writes author Kenneth Anderson in his book *Symptoms after 40*. "Signs of joint deterioration usually appear on x-ray films long before the person experiences pain." The pain Anderson speaks of is often apparent by age 60; it rarely afflicts fit 40-year-olds.

In general, you could say that joints age ahead of schedule in comparison to bone tissue. That's why doctors and athletic trainers today advise people in their thirties and forties to consider cross-training when working out, instead of simply telling them to jog 15 miles per week. Cycling, hiking, walking, cross-country skiing, and swimming are wonderful cross-training alternatives, and they are all less stressful to aging knees than jogging is.

Yoga is another of the best midlife defenses—and offenses—against age-related changes of the bones and joints, trainers say. It's an activity in which American women are well ahead of men, and it may be time to play catch-up. Sun salutation, anyone?

In sum, there's more going on inside your bag of bones than you probably imagined. This is a good thing to know in your sixties, but a better thing to have learned in your thirties and forties.

Fitness: Being Strong of Heart

S ome men climb a mountain not because it is there but because their 40th birthdays will soon be here.

In the case of Edward E. McNally, an attorney with the Chicago-based law firm of Altheimer and Gray and an occasional climber who grew up in the flatlands of Illinois and who never worried much about fitness as a young man, the facts of the case belie some of the claims. "I didn't try to summit Mount McKinley because I was going to turn 40," McNally said, not long ago. Let the record show that he was 39 years old at the time of his Alaskan climb.

"Objection!" he might have said (but didn't).

"I also climbed McKinley in 1992, when I was 36," he did, in fact, say.

Though McNally was into his 40th year of life when he set out in Denali, Alaska, to re-climb Mount McKinley—the tallest mountain in North America, at 20,320 feet—the decision to head up the hill again indeed was made in his mid-thirties. And it had as much to do with unfulfilled dreams as it did with age. Perhaps more, if you take his word for it. For he didn't quite reach the top during his first ascent. He and his team of nine other climbers got within about 2,000 feet of the summit before being forced to turn back due to treacherous weather.

The first time he tried to ascend McKinley—or Denali, as the locals call it—he trained harder, aerobically, than he ever had in his life. For four months, he worked his five-foot-nine-inch frame five days each week, combining 30- to 45-minute runs (many of which were performed indoors in winter in an Anchorage health club) with light freeweight work, to build endurance and strength. After a couple of months, he began filling a backpack with gallon jugs of water and wearing it while trekking, to simulate the rigors of climbing with weighty packs. He began climbing at low, then medium, altitudes to prepare his lungs for the high-altitude challenges ahead.

McNally wasn't what most people would call a technical climber; he wasn't even necessarily a jock. In truth, after working in Washington, D.C. at various jobs for most of the 1980s, then again in the early 1990s as a speechwriter for President George Bush, he more properly might have been called a wonk.

McNally suffered from asthma as a child, which hampered his breathing at times. He recovered enough to be able to play ice hockey without an inhaler, as a youth and teenager, and even played informally in college, where one night he had his two front teeth knocked out by an errant puck. (At least then he looked like a jock.)

When he moved to Alaska in 1992 to become a state deputy attorney general, it wasn't long before friends, natives, and local lore teamed up to tempt him into training for a physical challenge that would test his heart and mind in new ways. He wanted to be ready.

Working out became a hobby in his new home, then a routine. He wasn't after bulk; he wasn't after speed: He was after cardiovascular fitness of a medium-to-high order. "You don't have to be in the best shape in the world to climb the route we climbed," McNally told me. "But you should be in the best shape you can get into, given the time constraints we all have to face." It was more about tenacity than strength, more about a marathon than a sprint. And the training drove home a fundamental truth that McNally had never before taken seriously: that what you do in your thirties and early forties very much affects how you will feel—and move—in your late forties and fifties. Indeed, many serious mountain climbers stay with the sport well into their forties and early fifties.

Hearty Advice

By the time he turns 40, a healthy man's heart will have beaten, without incident, more than 1.5 billion times. (By age 80, God willing, it will have recorded some 3.2 billion thuh-thumphs.) Also by age 40, in the absence of prolonged, rigorous exercise, a typical heart—a fist-size bundle of muscle, arteries, veins, and extraordinary electrical activity—will have started to weaken. It tends to become more fatty, less muscular, and more laden with useless connective tissue. This is why doctors have learned to look for early signs of heart disease on or about a man's 40th birthday—because there is often much to be corrected or improved upon during his forties.

The heart in middle age, however, is remarkably resilient. That's worth remembering when you learn that heart failure occurs some 400,000 times each year and that heart disease is still the leading killer of men in America today, responsible for more than 500,000 deaths annually. Barring hereditary heart disease, however, like the kind that killed 52-year-old running legend and author Jim Fixx in 1984, or severe obesity, like the kind that contributed to actor John Candy's fatal heart attack in 1994 at age 43, the heart can withstand years of abuse and still, literally, come up for air. In early middle age, the untrained heart will typically welcome the rigors of a doctor-approved, three-to-four-times-a-week training plan.

PROGRESSIVE CORONARY ARTERY DISEASE

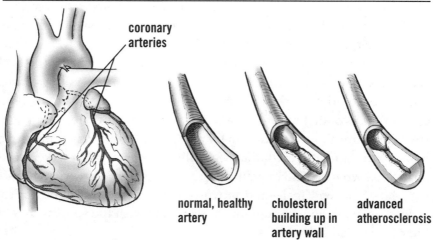

coronary arteries

normal, healthy artery

cholesterol building up in artery wall

advanced atherosclerosis

With age, as the level of cholesterol in the blood increases, the cholesterol accumulates on arteries' walls, which are themselves growing thicker. The net effect of these changes is to force the heart to work harder to pump blood throughout the body and back to itself. Eventually, the pressure of the blood against artery walls may build to a point at which heart attack or stroke becomes likely.

Gradual changes that occur in midlife go unnoticed by millions of men, and rightly so, for the heart can overcome a lot of abuse. But should it have to? In many ways, that is up to you and your doctor.

As the musculature of the heart begins to wane, the heartbeat may weaken a bit. This means less blood is pumped with each heartbeat, and a kind of sluggishness sets in. While this sluggishness may go unnoticed by desk jockeys in their forties, the decline in blood flow will announce itself during hard physical work or exercise. You can bet on it. In general, your pulse will not rise as high as it used to unless you take steps to maintain or build your cardiovascular capacity.

What you're aiming for, at 40 or so, is to reduce your risk factors for heart disease, some of which may have been present—but silent—as far back as your teens or twenties. Smoking and family history of heart disease are two such examples. Cholesterol is a third factor, which is why you want to strive to keep your total count under 200 milligrams per deciliter (mg/dl)—some doctors even say you should shoot for 150—while your total cholesterol divided by HDL (high-density lipoprotein) should equal 4 or less. Make sure that your doctor gives you measures for all forms of cholesterol, including HDL; LDL (low-density lipoprotein); total cholesterol; and triglycerides, a combination of fats in the blood. (Higher triglyceride levels can reduce levels of HDL, the so-called good cholesterol.)

Diabetes and high blood pressure are other major risk factors to watch for, both of which should be parts of your annual 40-plus physical. The tough thing for many men to realize is that if they haven't paid attention to heart-healthful living before hitting 40, they may be battling the effects of up to two decades of degradation. "Being male and 45 are risk factors for the other risk factors," notes Amy Roberts, Ph.D., physiologist at the Boulder Center for Sports Medicine in Colorado and a consultant to the Colorado Avalanche NHL hockey team. "But the most prevalent risk factor is inactivity."

Edward Lakatta, M.D., a heart disease specialist with the National

How Does Your Heart Measure Up?

Even with all those low-fat Snackwell's cookies around, heart disease is still the most common cause of death in men over 40. As cholesterol levels rise, cholesterol accumulates on artery walls (which themselves thicken with age), and the result is higher blood pressure in those arteries. In addition, arteries may clog, which forces the heart to pump harder, raising the risk of heart attack or stroke. Here are the national averages for men—remember, they're just averages. *Note:* Even if your total cholesterol is better than average, any reading over 200 is considered high.

Age	Total Cholesterol (mg.)	Blood Pressure
30	200	125/76
40	220	129/81
50	230	134/83

Institute on Aging, likes to startle people with the fact that atherosclerosis, or narrowed arteries, has been identified in a substantial number of individuals ages 15 to 24. Yet when you think about diseased arteries today, it is time to toss out the notion that it's all about cholesterol clogging up the works. Sure, that's part of the story. But there are a couple of aging changes to note as well, changes that often go unreported. First, even healthy arteries tend to narrow in middle age. The insides of the arteries begin to close in a bit, while the outsides become stiffer with age.

"Consider that the heart, pumping blood, forces it through the vessels," Dr. Lakatta says. "With each heartbeat, the vessels expand somewhat to accommodate the blood. Stiffer vessels are less accommodating, and when the blood is pumped into them, the pressure will be higher than in 'normal' arteries. The heart will then have to do more work to pump out its blood into this higher-pressure system." A blood pressure reading of 120/80 usually means you're in good cardiovascular shape; the borderline high blood pressure (hypertension) level is 140/90. The first number (systolic pressure) refers to the force exerted when the heart contracts; the second number (diastolic pressure) refers to the decreased force between contractions, or when the heart chambers are refilling with blood.

Whether or not you're new to fitness regimens, it helps to realize that not only does aerobic exercise build the heart muscles themselves but also it actually spurs your body to grow new blood vessels—thousands of them, like tiny branches on a tree in spring. That helps to ease some of the pressure Dr. Lakatta is talking about. And, of course, this angiogenesis, or birthing and branching of new vessels, doesn't happen overnight. We're talking about weeks to months.

One way to look at middle age and the heart, then, is to separate what is and isn't age-related change: Before you try to build more branches in your vascular system, you have to know what changes are due to deconditioning (or lack of exercise), and what changes are due to vascular disease (your heart and blood vessels). Then it's time to get a bit more serious about your plan, while not forgetting the fun.

Still Hustling after All These Years

Randy H., 41, has always known how to have fun. In high school and college, he was part of the partying crowd and part of the jock crowd, too. Tall and lanky, with long, frizzy blond curls, he assumed the nickname Struggs in high school. It was short for "Strugglin'," which is what he looked like he was doing when he ran his drills on the football field. "I just had to try harder than the gifted athletes," he said. He wasn't after "smooth," though; he was simply out to make the team. And he did.

Some 25 years later, the six-foot-one-inch Struggs is still struggling—this time to fit a fitness regimen into his crazed life as marketing executive, husband, dad, coach, fisherman, long-distance commuter, and volunteer outdoorsman/chaperone for his daughter's overnight Princess Scout camping trips in summer. He's committed to keeping his body in decent shape, he says, despite the heavy business lunches he finds himself sitting down to three times a week. His solution? To get out of the office two or three times a week at midday to play basketball. Serious adult basketball, YMCA-style, elbows and all. It's a combination of aerobic and anaerobic (sprint-level) exercise, with a little bit of plymometics (jumping, explosive movement) thrown in to complete the mix.

Despite the millions of calls for aerobic exercise that go unheeded, trainers often say that the most important choice you make in planning a workout regimen is to plan workout elements that you'll enjoy doing regularly. If that means playing tennis once or twice a week instead of chaining yourself to the treadmill every day, fine, even if it isn't as aerobic as other sports. If it means mixing a bit of easy mountain biking into a summer running routine that's gotten stale, by all means, make the effort.

"I usually weigh 184 or 187," Randy reported, "depending on whether it's before or after lunch or a workout. I'm skinny but pretty solid, although there's a little more flab on my stomach than there used to be." On the positive side, his resting pulse rate, as measured by a doctor who was checking him out for a midlife insurance-related phys- ical exam, turned out to be admirable. "When the doctor measured it and it came back at 40, he said, 'Wow, that's really low. Are you in re- ally good shape? That's really good. You're either dead—or you work out a lot.'" (A more normal range of pulse rates around age 40 would be 60 to 75.)

Randy's physical exam at age 40 showed that his total cholesterol was 200; his HDL was 55; his LDL was 140; he had a total/HDL ratio of about 4 (4.1, to be more precise); and his triglycerides were 159 mg/dl. "Most of those are pretty normal," Randy said, "except for triglycerides, which are elevated. But my doctor made no recommen- dations about those, and I didn't know what triglycerides were. I called a few people, and nobody knew exactly what they are either—except that it's 'that T-stuff that ultimately leads to clogged arteries.' It never would have hit me, except that my father just had a quadruple bypass at 66. So I'm wondering if it might be genetic."

Might be, experts say, although this instance may be borderline. One rule of thumb in cardiology is that if neither of your parents has shown evidence of heart disease by age 70, it's not likely to be genetic.

Reviewing his lifestyle changes through his thirties, Randy said he wished he could take more credit for them. But, instead, "I owe it all to my wife," he said. "She started cooking in a healthy way; it's one thing I also learned as a wrestler in high school. You've got to 'manage' what you eat—and you have to exercise. That's it.

"So I play basketball—hard, for an hour—three days a week," Randy said. "Some weeks, I play five times, some it's less. But it's full steam where we play, and when I play, I'm not as good a basketball player as the rest of them. So I have to out-hustle everyone." In other

THE GUM DISEASE LINK

It's almost too cruel a finding. In the late 1990s, reports filtered out of dental re-search labs that not only do middle-aged people need to begin thinking about gum disease, but that bacteria from that disease might lead to heart disease or heart attack. Talk about a reason to floss. . . .

Although the research is very preliminary, James Beck, Ph.D., epidemiologist at the University of North Carolina at Chapel Hill, has reviewed stacks of studies and believes that if you have periodontal disease or another oral infection, your in-creased risk of cardiovascular disease ranges from 20 percent to 280 percent. Yes, 280 percent.

No, the research isn't close to being proven. And the National Institute of Dental Research has provided only about $3 million for studies of mouth infections related to heart, kidney, and lung diseases, among others. But that's a start. Especially when you consider that not even 10 years ago, we thought ulcers were caused in large part by stress. Now we know that bacteria cause ulcers and that antibiotics prevent them. It's something worth remembering as you brush and floss tonight.

words, he's still strugglin' and playing, although he's not skying quite so high for rebounds as he did in his long-haired years.

Training like a Super Bowl Champ

On a snowy spring afternoon that looked more like Juneau, Alaska, than sun-splashed Denver, I pulled my car into the visitors' parking lot of the Denver Broncos' practice complex and headed for the training room. I was hoping to find out how a war-beaten body like John Elway's—one that had shoulder problems all year and a torn biceps just before the season opener—was able to get into condition to per-form as if it were 10 years or so younger. (For, at almost 38 years of age, after 19 years of college and professional quarterbacking, Elway had taken thousands of bone-jarring hits and survived.) Walking past team photos that date back to the 1960s and past mini-meeting rooms marked "Offensive Line," "Running Backs," "Linebackers," etcetera, I soon found the office of Steve Antonopulos, head athletic trainer for the

WHAT A CARDIOLOGIST HAS FOR LUNCH

"I always recognized, from early on, that the single largest cause of death in America was heart disease" says Elliot Barnathan, M.D., 43, a researcher and cardiologist at the University of Pennsylvania School of Medicine in Philadelphia, in explaining how he came to be a heart specialist. "Some people in medical school didn't think it was exciting, but I'd say it has always suffered from a lack of [public relations]. People are more frightened of AIDS and cancer, but heart disease kills more people, by far, each year. And when it hits young people in their prime, it is devastating."

As a journalist, I often wondered how doctors actually decided on a specialty. Cynically, I believed they often went where the highest salaries were. But Dr. Barnathan sounded different when I spoke with him. He spoke highly of his years of university lab work, even though it could hardly be called lucrative. He was helping to save lives, in the long run, except he was doing so in a lab, not in a dramatic emergency room.

After working at the University of Pennsylvania for 10 years and attaining tenure, Dr. Barnathan took a leave of absence from the school and joined Centacor, a Pennsylvania-based pharmaceuticals firm. "I used to do 'basic' research—cell biology, test-tube kind of stuff," he says. "Now, I'm doing clinical research with patients, clinical trials. One study we're doing involves 7,800 patients; one we just finished involved 2,399. Another drug we're testing has a total of 15,000 to 20,000 subjects in the trial."

But what about the subject named Dr. Elliot Barnathan? I wondered. What's he doing to pump up the life of his heart? For instance, what does he—the blood lipid ex-

Super Bowl XXXII and XXXIII champion Broncos, who has been with the squad since 1975 and was dressed in athletic wear emblazoned with official team horse-head silhouettes.

I asked him what advice he might give 40-year-old weekend athletes about preserving their bodies—hopefully well into their fifties and beyond. You know, things that Elway did. To toughen up. To last.

"Number one, your metabolism changes," Antonopulos says. "So what you ate at age 20 and got away with won't work in your late thirties." It's also crucial to "maintain the flexibility in your joints—we gauge the players' range of motion on the weight/strength machines," he says. Weight training, he adds, is a very important part of attaining

pert—eat for lunch? "Half the time, I don't even eat lunch," he says. "I'm kind of a busy person, and I often skip it. But when I do eat it, I'll have tuna or chicken salad on wheat bread. I don't like lunchmeats—they're high in salt. Occasionally, I'll have roast beef. Or a salad. But it's not my main meal."

At home, dietetically speaking, things seem to be more strict. "In general, we have virtually no red meat at home," Dr. Barnathan says. "And we've been a skim milk family as far back as I can remember. But it's largely because of my wife. I also eat egg whites (without the yolks) for breakfast, and we never eat butter. We've switched to canola oil (an unsaturated fat), and long ago began using olive oil (a monounsaturated fat). But honestly, I'm a little schizo there: I won't eat egg yolks, but I'll grab a piece of bacon that we've made for the kids."

I was surprised to find that Dr. Barnathan's cholesterol has risen as high as 230, but not so surprised that he's found ways to bring it down to 180. "I haven't started taking cholesterol medication yet," he adds, even though it is at the heart of his research. As for exercise, Dr. Barnathan, who stands five foot nine and weighs 160 pounds, knocks around the basketball court a bit—which is somewhat aerobic—but he says hip and knee problems keep him from running regularly. He considers himself "slightly obese, but not too bad." He also plays golf and tennis, "maybe a couple times a week" to give his heart at least a bit of a workout. A cardiologist's work is never done.

"joint integrity," which means being able to perform at a high level, injury-free and without compensating for chronic pain from overuse or muscular weakness or imbalance.

"With our older players and also with the younger ones, we try to train and stabilize their lower backs and torsos. We give them [abdominal] crunches to do—because in order to explode off the line, you have got to be 'stabilized,'" Antonopulos explains. In other words, treetrunk legs are only the beginning.

The keys to Super Bowl-type explosiveness, then, start in the middle. Football pros and fortyish weekend athletes alike should aim to maintain strength in the following areas.

Abdominal muscles. Try daily abdominal crunches. Correct form matters more than how many you do. Lie flat on your back, with your legs extended and your knees unlocked. Cup your hands behind your ears, with your elbows out to the side. Keeping your lower back in contact with the floor, raise your upper torso a couple of inches off the ground. Look up as you lift your head, neck, and shoulders off the floor. Hold for a second, then lower to the starting position. Immediately begin your next crunch, without relaxing in between. As a general guideline, aim to do crunches for 10 minutes a day, in three to four sets, at your own pace.

Extensor muscles. At the gym, weight-machine work such as crossover pulls are a good bet for strengthening these back muscles. Reverse flies, however, can be done at home. To do them, lie facedown on a bench, grasping a 10-pound dumbbell—or whatever weight you're comfortable using—in each hand. Starting with your arms hanging straight down toward the floor, lift the weights out to the sides until your arms are parallel to the floor. Try to do two sets of 10 to 15 reps, twice a week.

Hip flexors. Do interval training that includes sprints and guided stretching routines. Hip rotator stretches are an excellent way to work the inner-thigh muscles and the lower back. Lie on your back. Bend your right leg at about a 90-degree angle, keeping your right foot planted firmly on the floor. Cross your left ankle over your right knee. Put both hands behind your right thigh and pull your leg toward your body as far as you comfortably can. Keep your left knee pointed to the outside of your body. Hold for 30 seconds, then switch legs. Do three sets of 10 to 15 reps, three times a week.

*Glutes.*Though many workouts target the gluteus maximus, the gluteus medius muscles, which are located along the sides of the buttocks, "are often overlooked," according to Antonopulos. Strengthen them by doing lunges with moderate weights. To begin this exercise, balance a barbell behind your neck, resting it on your shoulders. Grasp it with your hands slightly more than shoulder-width apart. Your feet should be shoulder-width apart, with your knees unlocked and your toes pointed out slightly. Keep your chest out, your shoulders back, your stomach tight, and your back straight. Your head should be in line with your spine. Step to your right with your right toes pointing in that direction, landing heel to toe and pressing your hips down until your right thigh is parallel to the floor. Your left leg should be extended with your left foot planted firmly on the floor. Your right foot will point to the side while your left foot and your torso remain facing forward. Hold for a second, then push back with your right leg and return to the starting position. Continue on the right side for one set of 10 to 15 reps, then switch to the left. Do three sets on each side.

Cardiovascular system. Antonopulos makes sure his players engage in regular aerobic activity such as running, hiking, or bicycling, "even though football is largely anaerobic." You, too, should aim for 30 minutes of aerobic exercise, three or four days a week.

It turns out that Antonopulos got hooked on aerobic training when he ran his first—and only—marathon, just before he turned 40. (He's now pushing 50.) "Before that, I was hell-bent for leather," Antonopulos said of his workout mindset. In molding a marathon-ready body, he actually slowed down and wised up, while building up his heart and lung power at age 39. "Ever since then, I've been more focused on health," he allows. And the key for every aging athlete, he still finds, is to stay with it three to five days each week. There are, in short, no shortcuts.

"I feel better at 49 than I did when I was 20," Antonopulos said. If only John Elway could say the same thing.

Why Fitness Matters

In a sense, you could call the kind of work Antonopulos did while training for his marathon "aerobics," though he calls it just "running." But perhaps "targeted aerobics" would be more apt because his training was targeted toward the fitness goal he wanted to reach. The same goes for the kind of work that lawyer Ed McNally did leading up to his first climb of Mount McKinley. As you'll recall, he worked out carrying a pack filled with jugs of water. Whatever you call it, their goals were to improve their cardiovascular fitness. Each man strove to train his lungs and heart to inhale and process as much oxygen as possible while such things as altitude, age, attitude, and decades of deconditioning worked against him.

Today, people in middle age who want to improve their bodies need to know more than their cholesterol count, blood pressure, and heart rate: They need to know their "max VO_2," as well. Used to be, only athletes paid any mind to this measure of fitness, the maximum

BOX SCORE

PROTECTING YOUR HEART

It's never too early to prevent heart disease from taking hold. Here are time-tested guidelines to start you off toward a cardio-friendly future.

Decrease stress. If you didn't pay much attention to the links between stress and health in your twenties and thirties, the early forties are an apt time to experiment with a few stress relievers and incorporate one or two into your life.

Meditation (minus the religion, if you prefer) is quick, easy, and inexpensive. For sound advice, consult the book *The Relaxation Response* by Herbert Benson, M.D., president of the Mind/Body Medical Institute at New England Deaconess Hospital in Boston.

Increasingly, yoga-based exercise is finding its way into both health clubs and the lives of men who formerly shunned it. Elysabeth Williamson, a Boulder, Colorado, yoga instructor, believes that "partner yoga," a specialty of hers, not only reduces stress and improves cardiovascular performance but also builds intimacy between longtime couples—a true affair of the heart.

Invest in yourself. Let's face it, a 30,000 mile tune-up of your sport-utility vehicle costs about $500, including the trumped up charges for flimsy air and oil filters. Isn't your cardiovascular system at least as important? The same amount of money can buy a decent-quality treadmill or an aerobic cross-trainer, either of which might help you stick with a year-round aerobic training program. Even if the cost is closer to $750, that's still less expensive than many health club memberships.

Think multivitamins. Since most men don't eat their recommended minimum of five servings of fruits and vegetables daily, consider adding a quality multivitamin to your diet. It should include 5,000 international units of vitamin A, 60 milligrams of vitamin

amount of oxygen processed by your heart, lungs, and vascular system during peak exercise. But over the past 10 years or so, it has become a much more telling statistic because it enables you to track incremental progress as you train.

One of the most important measures of VO_2 in regard to midlife men took place in the mid-1980s, when Michael Pollock, Ph.D., a researcher at Mount Sinai Medical Center in Milwaukee, was able to prove that our hearts don't age as fast as we thought they did. Dr. Pollock, past president of the American College of Sports Medicine, followed a group of elite masters (over 40 and) track athletes for more

C, 30 international units of vitamin E, 70 micrograms of selenium, 400 micrograms of folic acid, and 2 milligrams of vitamin B_6. In recent years, folic acid and B_6 have been shown to have exciting promise in cutting heart attacks.

Know your drugs. By the time a man is 45, he should be well-acquainted with the latest anti-cholesterol and heart-protectant drugs, including pravastatin (Pravachol), clopidogrel (Plavix), and lovastatin (Mevacor)—even if he doesn't need them. Of course, the decision to take prescription medication is one that must be made with your doctor. Another option is to consider regular use of aspirin, as advised by your doctor. Now, it's true that exercise and diet are more natural ways of helping to prevent heart trouble. But don't be too proud. Heart attacks and death, are, unfortunately, also natural.

Keep "heart charts" at home. It doesn't matter whether you prefer manila folders or computer files, it's time to keep track of your annual blood pressure and cholesterol counts, in their own personal domain. (Don't rely on your doctor to keep them handy for your use.) Your goal is to track your progress in keeping both counts steady, or decreasing, well into your forties. Women already do this with the mammograms that they begin having at age 40 or so. It's worth requesting copies of all your physical exam files from here on out, just as you do with your mutual fund performance updates. Both are investments in your future.

No smoking—including cigars. You've heard it before, you'll hear it again here: As dangerous as cigarette smoke is to your heart, lungs, and family, do you honestly believe that cigar smoke doesn't find its way down your nose and throat and into your lungs . . . even when you don't inhale? Enough said.

than 10 years to see if cardiovascular aging could be slowed through exercise. He found that it could, impressively.

Prior to Dr. Pollock's work, it was assumed that our heart rates and max VO_2 declined by about 1 percent each year in mid- and later life, or about 10 percent per decade. Most of Dr. Pollock's athletes, however, who continued hard training into their fifties and sixties, were able to show that their heart and max VO_2 functions declined only about 5 percent over a decade—50 percent less than the initial assumptions. Some even showed no decline at all.

This bodes well for many of us who are looking ahead to 50 or 60, if we remain active. In fact, Dr. Pollock, who died in 1998, had pointed out to me that what he found with highly trained athletes should be easier to reproduce among people who are untrained, or weekend, athletes. That's because at 40, they may start off in a lot worse shape than masters runners, and they might be expected to have had bigger declines in cardiovascular power over a decade of relative inactivity. "I am not trying to say there is no aging curve," Dr. Pollock said. "Rather, I think it is much less dramatic than has been assumed."

"Actually, the max VO_2 stays the same [as we age]," says Dr. Roberts, commenting on related but more recent work than Dr. Pollock's, "but stroke volume, a related measure, goes down." Stroke volume, in short, is the amount of blood that is pumped back to the heart with each beat—or the amount of blood that the heart can squeeze out. "And our squeezing power goes down with age," Dr. Roberts says.

Curiously, in the same way that we have peripheral vision, it turns out that we also have "peripheral compensation" in our cardiovascular systems that begins to kick in when we reach 40 or 50, according to Dr. Roberts. This enables our hearts to be used more fully—although it's a physiological trait that is often underused, just as many nonathletes don't use or train their peripheral vision to see more fully. "It is more related to peripheral muscle adaptations," she says, "and it's amazing that we have this adaptation in our bodies. Now researchers have found that when you train someone who is 50, they can have the same results as [those of] younger populations."

The News in Heart-Rate Training

"Bee-Beep. Bee-Beep." Now that the heart-rate monitor has become an almost standard feature of upscale fitness machines and as a wrist-watch-type training accessory, there are a few things worth noting about the use and misuse of such monitors. For one, a trusty workout plan could use an update. You may know the one: Exercise at least 20 minutes per day, three or four times a week, at 70 percent of your heart rate capacity. If you don't have a monitor, you may have used a formula to figure out your target heart rate: 220 minus your age—40, say—multiplied by 0.7 equals 126 beats per minute. It's the so-called training zone, and it served us well for a while. But it isn't as accurate as it could be, experts say, because all bodies and hearts are different.

"People always think that the highest heart rate is the best reading," Dr. Roberts says. "They'll work out and then come in and report to me, 'My heart rate went up to 210.' What they don't understand is that a lot of what determines the heart rate is genetically predetermined based on the size of one's heart as well as its ability to contract. That doesn't change with training. But it does get a little stiffer with age.

"Sometimes, there's a higher heart rate in a man who's in worse shape," Dr. Roberts says. "Sometimes, if you just look at a person—at the thoracic cavity—there are limitations on the heart rate." A bigger heart, for instance, will tend to have a slower heart rate. "I see many people in their forties who are 'off the charts,' either because they can't reach the maximum heart rate prescribed for men at their age or their heart rates reach higher than the charts," Dr. Roberts explains. In short, target heart rates are mere averages. "They think they may have a heart attack—or that something's wrong with them—if they can't match up with the [heart rate] charts that are posted on the fitness machines in the gym," continues Dr. Roberts, a 34-year-old, five-times-a-week runner.

As a way to help personalize heart rate training as well as improve performance of elite and weekend athletes, sports medicine experts like Dr. Roberts have, in recent years, developed a new approach to track performance. It's called lactate-threshold training, and it picks up where the old pulse checks leave off. In brief, it finds the precise level at which your body moves from aerobic (steady breathing) to anaerobic (sprint-type, hard breathing) exercise, then sets about raising that point gradually and safely.

The goal is to enable you to breathe easier at higher workloads (and to be able to train harder). The way to do that with today's technology is to gauge your metabolism, your rate of "perceived exertion" while running on a treadmill, and the level at which your body starts to use lactate (or lactic acid) as fuel for a workout—the lactate threshold. You've heard the phrase "Feel the burn." Now sports docs like Dr. Roberts measure the burn, then build you a training plan that will push that burn farther off into the future of your future workouts. This is how Olympic athletes find their training levels; the principles are now filtering into a few mainstream medical centers across the country. Besides the Boulder Center for Sports Medicine, the Olympic Training Center in Colorado Springs, Colorado, also uses these techniques (and developed many of them).

The Mackie Shillstone Sports Medicine Center in New Orleans is another of the centers that offers a specific cardio-fitness focus. Step one is to start taking any healthful aerobic steps. Step two is to stay with them for three to six months. Step three is to look for some expert counsel, such as Dr. Roberts's or the Shillstone Center's or that of a doctoral candidate/trainer at a local university's physiology, sports medicine, or physical education department.

A Wake-Up Call at 39

Like most slightly out-of-shape, on-the-cusp-of-40-years-old guys, Mark C., a New York City talent agent, had some guilt to consider as he approached the big birthday. He hadn't paid much attention to cardio-fitness in his twenties or thirties. His family time and agency career always seemed to take precedence.

He always had this feeling, he recounted shortly after his 40th birthday, that if he didn't join a health club or start a running or biking program by 40, he probably never would. Mark said that his weight never climbed to 20 pounds over normal for his size, but as he aged, some nagging disaffection set in.

A health scare at 39 gave him the final push to put a fitness plan into action. "I bought a treadmill," he said, "and started running for two reasons: One, it was the last year to face up to my weakness; plus, I was feeling tired and sluggish a lot, which eventually sent me to the doctor. [Fortunately, the scare turned out to be not much more than a temporary immune-system malfunction.]

"I went from being completely inactive to running four or five times a week," Mark said, "which means I'm up to 16 to 20 miles a week. I started on the treadmill. It was like a game to me. Plus, I couldn't run outside at first because I could not do more than 5 minutes at a time without stopping. It was embarrassing. Then I built up over a series of weeks till I could go for 30 minutes—till I was respectable enough to go outside."

What I found curious about Mark's tale of the treadmill was that he rolled out his story in waves. At first, he denied that turning 40 was a major turning point. Why the denial?

"This had nothing to do with age. It's purely a health thing," Mark said. "I started running at the same time I started eating less fat." Like his compatriot Ed McNally, Mark at first said it had nothing to do with age. Then he conceded that, well, all right, maybe age did have something to do with it.

Marathon runner and masters athlete Hal Higdon has heard this kind of talk before. In his book *Fitness after 40*, he summarizes, "Ask any runner why he runs, and the answers that come back are: It is fun, it makes him feel better, he enjoys the easy camaraderie at races. But tucked away in the back of his mind is the fact that running will make him live longer, that he can cheat Father Time."

It's time to stop trying to "cheat" Father Time. It's time to start working with him.

Food: Enjoying the Lean Years

Fat at 40—that's where you don't want to be. But nature plays a cruel trick on us beginning at around age 30, a trick related to what physiologists call body composition. It's a bit more involved than the pat middle-age spread idea, but in short, it's about fat versus muscle. From age 30 through age 50, men's bodies typically and gradually become proportionally less muscular. What may have begun in your mid-thirties may not be apparent until your late thirties or early forties: Lean muscle tissue is giving way to slower-to-burn fat. The amount of each that you have in your body may be predetermined at certain points in your life, but there's a lot a 40-year-old man can do to keep his body looking like it did at, say, 34. That's a worthy goal for the first few years of one's forties. More important, it's an achievable goal.

Hungry? If so, is nutrition the first thing you think about? Probably not. But consider: The Food and Drug Administration food police say that, in the interest of good health, we should be getting 60 percent of our daily calories from carbohydrates, 10 percent from protein, and no more than 30 percent from fat. On average, men in America today consume only about 47 percent from carbohydrates, about 15 percent from protein, and 34 percent from fat (the balance comes from alcohol). In a way, we don't even need to worry about protein to get our nutritional house in order: Merely cut fat by 4 percentage points and notch up the carbs by a modest amount, and we're on our way. That won't make us skinny; then again, that's not the goal. We're trying to make a mid-course correction at age 40, not revolutionize our eating behavior. A year at a time will most likely be fine (unless your doctor has other plans).

You could point to a million studies about weight and health—okay, maybe a few thousand—that tell you it's not wise to be obese. Obesity has been linked to diabetes, heart disease, cancer—hell, even lousy self-esteem. The study that caught my eye, however, surfaced in early 1998 from folks at the University of North Carolina. It looked at the weights of 324,000 people (no small experiment) of various ages and checked on them over a 12-year period. Instead of using just weight, the researchers figured the body mass index (BMI) of each subject, which is a more complete measure of thinness or fatness. (BMI equals body weight in kilograms, divided by height in meters squared. It takes a little math but is telling: 20 to 25 is a good range for guys.) In brief, the study found that just 2 percent of the men from ages 30 to 44 who had BMIs between 19 and 25 died during the 12 follow-up years of the study. During the same time frame, 5 percent of those who were of the same age and had BMIs over 30 died. Of those ages 60 to 75, 38 percent of the thin men died, while 44 percent of those who were obese died. It's enough to make you think twice about, if not lay off, the ice cream.

Attacking Fat at 40

Barry G., 42, an electrician who lives in Los Angeles, has a fondness for Häagen-Dazs and a sizeable belly. He hates his gut, but he's carried it around for at least 10 years. He stands 5 feet 10½ inches, weighs 260 pounds, and is uncomfortable about the fact that he's beginning to get comfortable with being a guy with a gut. He's tried at least six different kinds of diets—from Weight Watchers to nutrient shakes—from his late twenties through his thirties, with varying degrees of success. Make that failure. The bottom line is that, although he lost 30 or 40 pounds on a protein-shake diet, the weight loss never lasted. So when he was 39, he decided to get serious.

During time off between jobs—he works on television and movie sets with gaffers and lighting experts—he dialed a toll-free number he found in a respectable holiday catalog, ordered some information, then made plans to spend $8,000 to travel to and attend the highly touted Duke University diet and fitness program in Durham, North Carolina. Even as this multiweek, medically based program has enjoyed success in treating hundreds of clients' obesity over the years—and very likely has saved lives in the process—it doesn't work miracles. It also carries the unfortunate tag of what some unsympathetic types dub "a fat camp." Yet it works for many people because at its core, it is about changing one's lifestyle and diet—it's not about dieting. For instance, its doctors prescribe diet drugs on occasion and when appropriate, but not across the board. It's no coincidence that the Duke center never fully joined the Fen-Phen (fenfluramine-phentermine) bandwagon of the mid-1990s.

Indeed, if there is any one thing that a man of 40 should know about food and nutrition for the rest of his life, it's that lifestyle can certainly postpone untimely death style. When you look at what kills the most people in the United States each year, the results can be surprising. The three most deadly events are:

Heart disease	734,090
Cancer	536,860
Stroke	154,350

It almost goes without saying that all three are heavily influenced by diet and lifestyle, which includes regular exercise.

Exactly 10 days after he turned 40, Barry's wife, Mary, drove him to the airport to catch the long flight to Duke. "I had had a surprise party," Barry said, "and it was one of the most fun birthdays of my life—it's still my overriding memory of that year. My wife hired a band—two guys, actually—who played Beatles' songs, and I got to get up there and sing with them. A definite highlight. And because it was my party, everyone had to listen.

"But I was in bad shape physically," Barry said. "It turned out to be a kind of milestone year, even though I had wanted to go to Duke earlier, when I was 39. Maybe I wanted to go then because I wanted to hit

40 running." And run he did, although for the first few weeks of his serious weight loss/lifestyle program, he walked. For 45 minutes a pop. It was, he found, less stressful on his creaky knees.

Barry's daily regimen included exercise, seminars, low-fat meals in cafeteria settings, more seminars, and a little bit of free time after dinner so he could call home to his wife and baby girl. As an optional exercise, he signed up for psychotherapy, which cost a little more but got him thinking about his food "issues." He was intense while he was there.

"I was religious about the exercise for 2½ months," Barry told me, "and I continued to lose weight. Then I got on a movie project with a big director. Right away, it was as if God took an eraser and wiped it across the chalkboard of my brain. Within a day of starting on that movie, I stopped trying to eat well; I wasn't religious about Duke any more. The first day I went to work, I worked out. After that, I didn't work out till the movie was over. I was working 16 hours a day on this movie at times. I realized later that had I worked two hours a day less on the film, it would've worked out fine, and I would've stayed on the exercise. I was walking—45 minutes at a time—before we started shooting."

I wondered if Barry realized he was blaming an employment opportunity for putting harmful things in his body day after day for a four-month shooting period on the film. Was he being honest about his behavior? Was his behavior immutable? Exactly how bad were his food choices?

Gluttony on the Set

On a "terrible" eating day, as Barry described it, he would go to work on the set before 7:00 A.M. and order up a bacon-and-cheese quesadilla freshly prepared on the catering truck. Or he might choose a bacon, egg, and cheese burrito. No oatmeal with sliced banana for this guy.

As the morning moved on, he allowed that he might eat a couple of doughnuts in passing, usually chocolate frosted. "I mean, they are just there, stacked up." He grabbed them while walking by a spread on the set that included fruit, bagels, muffins, and cereal. Then eventually, by late morning, the caterers set out candy for the crew: a "huge" jar of chocolate covered raisins, Barry recalled. "It's not too hard to put a big

THE M&M DIET

Okay, it's not actually a diet. And it doesn't require that you eat cute chocolate-covered candies that melt in your mouth (not in your hands). But let's say, for a moment, that you have a habit of eating a handful of M&M's or similar candies every day. If you were to eliminate eating just one measly M&M each day from your allotment, keeping all other diet and exercise habits the same, you'd lose one pound over the course of a year. Here's how: Each round morsel packs about 10 calories or so; multiply that by 365 days, and you get a total of 3,650 fewer calories potentially consumed.

Because it takes roughly 3,500 ingested calories for an adult to put on a pound, consider how simple it may be to lose weight—if your goal is to lose simply $\frac{1}{12}$ of a pound each month. That's not ridiculous when you consider that aging-related metabolism changes cause many people to gain about one pound each year once they enter middle age.

old fist in that thing." On other days, the jar contained M&M's or cashews. All this was washed down, he added, with Diet Coke after Diet Coke.

For lunch, Barry often took a pass on the entrées, choosing to sit with his co-workers and chat. "I don't eat that much lunch," he said. "I just wasn't brought up to have a hot meat entrée for lunch." He would, though, have dessert. Afternoon snacks would include fruit at times, but on his worst days, Barry wouldn't have any of it. He'd opt instead for a peanut butter and jelly sandwich or two, which was also provided to crew members to stave off the postlunch munchies.

"If there's dinner, it's like pizza," he said. "I'll have three or four slices of that. It's never about hunger, though. I don't know a fat person who eats because he's hungry. Why then? Habit, maybe. Or boredom, emotional distress. There's lots of reasons."

So how has he done from ages 40 to 42?

"Two years later, I think about the exercise part [of the program] every day. But the food part I'm doing absolutely nothing about. I almost always think I should get on the stick again and do it. [The Duke educators] believe in exercise six times a week, with weight lifting every other day. So I think about it; I just don't practice it currently."

Because he brought up emotional distress and because it's true that countless men face intense career pressures in midlife, I asked Barry how the Duke doctors tried to help him and the others de-stress. "Obviously, they didn't work for me," he said of the half-dozen or so stress reduction and relaxation techniques. "Not that I doubt that they work. But you have to be motivated and focused to make them work. I remember in relaxation class, while there was a lot of deep breathing and I was supposed to focus on a part of my body, I was thinking, 'Okay, . relax the calves and neck . . . but what's on TV?'"

So was the program a success for this 40-year-old hyperguy? In a way. While at Duke and immediately after, he lost a total of 37 pounds in about 10 weeks. His waist/abdomen size improved by 1½ inches, while his total cholesterol dropped from 205 to 146. Similarly, his blood pressure plummeted from its "normal" range of 136/90 to 88/56. "Let me tell you, baby, that's what exercise will do for you," he halfheartedly bragged.

"I did get my money's worth," Barry added upon reflection. "It's just hard to practice that stuff. I definitely learned about nutrition on the program, although you lose what you've learned when you don't practice it. I came back wanting to stay healthy and natural. It was a forced lifestyle. And whenever I've put myself through that, I've done great." But for Barry and for far too many of his brethren, weight loss is a short-term idea that lasts weeks or months maybe, while true lifestyle changes take effect over years.

Here's one way the Duke experts help obese clients visualize a year-round, sensible eating plan: Imagine a jar filled with 365 pennies. Better yet, don't imagine it: Fill a jar with 365 pennies. Then remove a fistful of 10 or so for the major holidays and a holiday weekend or two. Take another 5 out for birthdays and anniversaries; then grab another 10 for special-event parties and dinners. Place these separated pennies in a pile. These are your "slip up days" from a year-round eating and exercise plan. You now have two groups of pennies before you: a jar of 340 healthful eating/workout days and a pile of 25 slipup pennies. To all those people who believe that once a diet has been broken, it's broken, this suggests that there's another view. Or perhaps 340 other views, that say, in effect, that one day is only a day. If you have a plan, a lifestyle, that is reasonable and effective over the long term, then you can "cheat" for a day or two and not lose your focus.

But back to the present and future: "It's hard for me," Barry related. "The weight doesn't drop like it used to, that's for frickin' sure. One of the things that came out in my shrink interviews at Duke was—if you want to get a little Freudian—that when I go for the stuff like ice cream, cookies, or chips, it's childlike stuff. Maybe, in some ways, I'm looking for my childhood again."

"I'm not worrying about my biological clock, I'm worrying about dying," he said ruefully, relating that both of his parents died before age 60. "I'm past my prime, but I'm not past the point of having the ability to get in great shape." In other words, for all of Barry's diet-and-eating shortcomings, he still holds on to a realistic goal.

Pritikin Program Redux

After talking with Barry, I was reminded of an earlier interview I had with Robert Pritikin, 45, director of the Pritikin Longevity Program in Santa Monica, California, and son of its late founder, Nathan Pritikin. Even though I'd written about the Pritikin diet before and had heard a number of estimable endorsements of its menus, I wasn't thinking about its food. Instead, I recalled Pritikin the Younger once telling me that his family's regimen could not only treat but also actually help reverse heart disease and some cases of the most common form of diabetes. Like the program at Duke and the heart disease reversal regimen developed by Dean Ornish, M.D., president and director of the Preventive Medicine Research Institute in Sausalito, California (which combines low-fat diet, exercise, meditation, and group support), the Pritikin ideas about long-term health stress a combination of methods. Dieting alone won't bring you the maximum benefits, neither will walking 35 or more miles a week on the treadmill or ingesting handfuls of vitamin supplements. In absence of making dietary changes, "you've got to walk 70 miles to lose one pound," says Pritikin in his book *The Pritikin Weight Loss Breakthrough*. But together, the dietary, exercise, and lifestyle changes can delay deaths and save lives.

"We call it the deadly quartet," Pritikin told me, "when a guy with a gut, who is middle-aged, has high blood pressure, high cholesterol, high levels of insulin in the blood, and high triglycerides. And we have found that a simple program of daily walking and a primarily vege-

HEARTBURN HELP

When it hurts, it hurts near the heart. But the pain of heartburn is actually esophagus pain. During an episode, the muscular, expandable part of the digestive tract that links the mouth and stomach temporarily backs up at its southerly opening. A small leak, of sorts, occurs, allowing the contents of the stomach to back up into the esophageal tube. The burning is a product of acidic stomach contents reaching the tissues of the esophagus. Call it esophagus burn, if you want to be precise. And realize that it happens more frequently in middle age for three possible reasons: the musculature, or valve, weakens slightly with age; food sensitivities may develop, including those to caffeine, fried and fatty foods, or foods high in citric acid; and the fact that some medications such as aspirin or ibuprofen can trigger heartburn, and the use of these increases with age.

As for treatment, try not to lie down after eating or at the outset of the attack (let gravity help you keep the food "down"); and don't be shy about taking antacids. Most remedies, including the newer heartburn prevention drugs, contain acid neutralizers. Also, gastroenterologists advise, eat smaller meals and reward yourself with more healthful snacks, rather than wolfing down three large meals a day.

tarian diet can affect people's sensitivity to insulin. Their resistance to insulin goes way down, and their blood sugar levels come down, as well." In other words, these lifestyle changes can help patients reduce or get rid of the medication they formerly needed to control diabetes. Food and exercise could be thought of as medicine—not just to prevent midlife morbidity but also to reverse disease processes that have already begun. That's a powerful way to look at lifestyle change, much more powerful than thinking of a yuppie or hippie lifestyle. And I couldn't help but think of Barry telling me that diabetes contributed to his father's untimely death.

"When we first started, we had severe 'cardiacs' here," Pritikin says of the Pritikin Longevity Program. "We were the 'Last Chance Hotel.' People came here with one foot in the grave and the other on a banana peel. Since then, we've been getting a younger and younger population. We now have guys in their thirties and forties who come here for prevention." Pritikin's latest crusade is to help millions outsmart what he dubs their "fat instinct," the physiological craving we humans all have for the fatty foods that have enabled us to survive and evolve over centuries. (One simple trick is to eat more potatoes and fruit, foods that rate highly on the satiety index, which rates feelings of fullness.)

Strategy Sessions for Midlife Meals

When midlife men appear at the offices of the Dave Winfield Nutrition Center in Hackensack, New Jersey, they often arrive with sorry histories of fast-food eating and sporadic, if any, regular exercise to their credits. (Only the uninitiated look around for Winfield himself, the sinewy ex-major-league all-star whose donation got the center built.) If they then meet with Lorna Pascal, R.D., nutrition coordinator for the center, they probably won't get off easy. Pascal, though, acts more like a guidance counselor than a coach. "Some guys, I ask, 'How much do you not want to be here?' But I don't get obsessed with the scale. I also ask them, 'What are you doing with your eating behaviors?' These are questions they are not used to answering."

After requesting that a client keep a detailed food diary for a few days, Pascal moves him on to plan primary, then long-term, goals. The primary goals may include such things as reducing cholesterol or losing weight; the longer-term part of the plan—significant weight loss—may take an entire year to achieve. That's fine with Pascal, who usually can make a dent or two in a guy's poor behavior right away. "You know," she says, "even when low-fat chicken or fish is called for, a 6-ounce portion is sufficient. I often see clients who are up to 8 or 10 ounces; and people don't always think about quantity when they're making changes."

As for smaller goals, Pascal advises that men around age 40 can begin to make significant lifestyle changes by writing down the steps they plan to take; by choosing relatively low-fat meat and fish options, such as turkey breast or haddock, and decreasing portion sizes; and by making sure that other sources of protein are the lowest in fat (per ounce) available, such as legumes or beans. Pascal has no problem with people who consider themselves "part-time" or "weekend" vegetarians. It's a start.

"Some people still think a person's going to die if he doesn't eat a 10-ounce steak once in a while," says Pascal, whose center charges roughly $45 to $75 per session. "I tell them that grains plus starchy vegetables can also give them protein. The problem I've seen with carbo-hydrates is that people were eating almost a pound of pasta because they considered it healthier than meat." In other words, carbs have calories, too. "That's wonderful if you're a marathoner," she points out about loading up on carbohydrates, "but believe me, most of the people I see are not marathoners."

What Works for Men

In summing up strategies for hundreds of men in their forties, Pascal says, "I think they like it simple; they don't want to hear a lot of theo-ries. They want to know: 'What should I eat?'" She jokes, "Much as I want to smack them over the heads when they say, 'I don't cook' . . . I say, 'Do you read? You can buy a really simple cookbook.' I give them instructions for shopping, even guiding them to supermarkets that have 'home meal replacements' or prepared take-out, such as broiled chicken or vegetarian lasagna. Even if you're using just three ingredi-ents, I tell them, as simple as that, it's worth it to try to cook something from scratch.

"I never say never," Pascal says of her nutrition-deficient clients. "I don't say, 'Never have a doughnut or a hamburger.' Because if they're coming to me for help, I have to lay it on the line for them. I'll tell them to make a small change that could become a big thing. 'If you could change what you're doing for lunch, it would be a big change,' I'll say. I might tell them to alternate going out and staying in at the office for lunch: I'll ask, 'Can you bring in lunch occasionally; can you do soup and salad occasionally?' Hopefully, men are getting comfortable ordering this way or not eating the entire portion of chicken and fish that's served to them. 'Can you restrict yourself to not eating the whole portion?' I'll ask."

Another way that Pascal and her staff connect with male clients who need dietary overhauls is to sing the praises of certain snacks. "I think snacks are helpful," she says, "especially because of the ways people live today—and especially for the man around 40, who is a busy person." Those who are often making extra efforts at work are also skipping meals and grabbing fast food on the fly. "They tell me there's no time," Pascal says. "I tell them it's worth doing, not only for nutri-tion but also for tasting the food, lessening the stress.

10 ALL-STAR SNACKS

Experts advise people in their forties to eat six times a day. Since you'll need to stock up on supplies for your six mini-meals or your three small meals and three healthy snacks, it's time to go shopping. Consider these foods and ideas as stops along the somewhat-noble nutritional path.

- Have half a bagel (save half from breakfast if possible) with 1 tablespoon of low-fat cream cheese. It contains only 200 calories and is quite filling.
- Try a scoop of low-fat or nonfat cottage cheese on one slice of whole-wheat toast and preserves. You'll get high satiety, high calcium, and low fat and calories.
- Quaker Fat-Free Mini Rice Cakes are not the most filling critters, but taste-wise, calorie-wise, and nutrient-wise, they make this list rather easily. Five cakes provides 50 calories.
- Honey Maid Honey Grahams are available in a low-fat variety. Eight crackers give you good taste, satiety, "mouth feel," and not too many calories—110. Sure they're smallish, but where can you get eight cookies that'll deliver the same goods?
- Orville Redenbacher's Butter Light Popping Corn is not as good as the gooey, illegal movie kind, but it's the best of the microwave bunch when you're at home with a steamy movie. Five-and-a-half-cups contains 110 calories.
- Update the old classic celery sticks and cream cheese, using low-fat cream cheese to fill the half-pipes, with a smidge of sun-dried-tomato spread. The spice makes all the difference (though it is sodium dense).
- Health Valley Fat-Free Healthy Tarts are a filling snack alternative that are not only low-calorie but also relatively fiber-rich: They contain 3 grams of fiber and 150 calories per bar, and the red raspberry packs a lot of flavor.
- Newtons Cobblers, Fig Newtons' fat-free upstart cousins, are quite moist and tasty. Peach-apricot rates raves. One cobbler contains 70 calories.
- Tofutti Cuties are not a bad little dessert if you're tired of the frozen yogurt route. They contain soy protein (from tofu) and are relatively filling despite their "kiddie" size. With 5 grams of fat each, they have 150 calories and great taste, too—especially the chocolate.
- Substitute two tasty Hershey's Sweet Escapes crunchy peanut butter bars for Reese's Peanut Butter Cups; have one in the afternoon and one at night. The total calories will be only 180, versus 250 in Reese's.

"I truly, truly believe that people will feel good when they have good habits—exercise and nutrition," Pascal says. "What can we work on this week, these two weeks, to make a strategy? Usually, there's no strategy at all." Interestingly, Pascal counts "grazing" as a decent style of living with food. Six small meals a day might be a better approach to feeding hunger and then feeling close-to-full for hours at a time.

A Concise Cholesterol Game Plan

The goal at the Winfield Center is similar to those at other medically based places of weight loss: cholesterol improvement. Dietitians look for improvement after 6 to 8 weeks. After a prospective client takes a blood lipid (fat/cholesterol) profile test for weight loss, he will be guided to lose no more than one to two pounds a week over 12 to 25 weeks. "Patience is a very good virtue," says Pascal, "even though Americans like a quick fix."

Fortunately, there are a couple of areas in midlife nutrition planning that are amenable to the so-called quick fix; cholesterol is one such area. With planning and professional dietary help, you can see measurable gains—losses actually—within eight weeks. In the not-so-old days, doctors and midlife men used to use the benchmark of 200 as a key: If the level of blood cholesterol was above 200 milligrams per deciliter, it was high; if it was under 200, they could still have steak for lunch and dinner.

Then HDL and LDL came into the picture, rather prominently, in the 1980s. In brief, HDL (high-density lipoprotein), the "good" cholesterol, is said to help keep the bloodstream clear of blockages by acting as a sort of arterial garbage truck. With all the warnings about cholesterol, many people never learned that small amounts of this fat-soluble substance are actually essential to good health. Exercising regularly and eating fruits and vegetables packed with vitamin C, such as oranges and broccoli, will help boost your HDL level. LDL (low-density lipoprotein), on the other hand, has been described as a delivery truck intent on dropping off cholesterol in cells throughout the body before the HDL and liver can team up to flush and excrete it.

Today, your doctor should be giving you readings of HDL and LDL along with your overall cholesterol. So the midlife scorecard should read under 200 overall, with HDL above 45 or so, and LDL below 130 or so. (Of course, these numbers are just a gauge.) Your diet will affect your cholesterol—with fatty foods and oils doing the most damage— yet exercise or lack thereof can contribute mightily. The prescription of less saturated fat (choosing olive oil versus butter or margarine, for instance) and 30 minutes of aerobic exercise three or four times a week will bring noticeable results in weeks, as opposed to the months it would take if diet or exercise alone were used.

The standard food-based cholesterol-fighters are all forms of soluble fiber, which is most abundant in vegetables, fruits, beans, and whole grains. During digestion, these foods bind with cholesterol and help usher it out of the digestive tract before your body can absorb it and before arterial plaque builds up. The latest cholesterol-fighters to make the news are such foods and nutrients as soy, garlic, onions, and flaxseed. What fiber was to the 1980s, these may turn out to be in the opening years of the new millennium. In fact, the chemical properties in soy appear not only to help control cholesterol but also to help prevent some kinds of cancer.

Without getting too technical, here are some midlife anti-cholesterol strategies for you to consider.

- Do aerobic exercise for 30 minutes three or four times a week.
- Eat garlic of some kind every day.
- Add fiber to your diet by eating oatmeal, oranges, and raw carrots to your diet regularly.
- Use olive oil and canola oil (sparingly) instead of butter and margarine—and stay away from the artery-clogging trans fatty acids found in commercial bakery products.
- If you aren't ready to go vegetarian, start thinking of meat as a side dish instead of as a main course.

The Beverly Hills 902"40" Diet

By most any account, Michael Barnathan is not Arnold Schwarzenegger. Sure, the two of them both live near Hollywood. And yes, they've both spent countless hours on movie sets, killing time while waiting for

God-knows-what special effects to be set up. Yes, they've even worked together, on the 1996 comedy *Jingle All the Way*, which Michael helped produce in his late thirties. (He works as an executive with 1492 Pictures.) And, if you want to know the truth, their paychecks have excess zeros, at least by the standards of lunchbucket workers across the United States. But no, Michael Barnathan and Arnold Schwarzenegger don't have similar bodies.

Barnathan, in fact, now 40, spent most of his thirties not exercising at all. He'd never really been fat, first of all. And unlike Arnold, when he traveled for work, Barnathan never shipped an 18-wheeler full of free weights and aerobic and strength-training machinery on location. For most of the 1990s, while Schwarzenegger was eating carefully pre-pared meals and downing buckets of supplements to help sculpt his body up or down as screen demands dictated, Barnathan was well-satisfied eating whatever was dished up by the catering truck. And when he dined with agents at hot Hollywood eateries, as he frequently did, he didn't count fat grams or calories when it came time to order.

After he turned 39, things changed for Michael in the food and diet areas of his life. "I've always had this thing in the back of my head, that if I didn't start doing something by age 40, I may never do it," he said. "I'd never been to a gym, never ran. I didn't like running, particularly, and I even took the chance to make fun of a couple guys I work with who always run. I was never terribly concerned," he added, "because my weight was always within 10 to 15 pounds of my lowest-ever weight. I just wasn't happy with it."

After telling his wife about his plans to trim down, Michael real-ized that his brother, a researcher and cardiologist, may have subtly influenced him, too. "I started eating less fat, although it was a health thing, not an age thing," he said. "Now, I eat a lot of salads. I don't eat butter. I've cut out dairy that has fat in it; I actually like sorbet. And it turned out that what I like to eat works for a low-fat diet. In my case, I'd much rather have a great peach or plum than a piece of chocolate cake."

When most of us think of comfort foods, things like ice cream and pudding and grilled cheese come to mind. But in Barnathan's case, he recalled, "My mother used to go shopping on a Thursday—and by Sunday there'd be none of the fruit left. I actually have a problem in that area, because in the summer, if there's a lot of fruit sitting there, I

(continued on page 116)

Small Change Adds Up to Big Results

Here are 10 simple, surefire things you can do in your forties to alter nature's course, including the nature of your belt line.

1. Think of healthful eating habits as a marathon, not a sprint. According to the experts at the Duke University Diet and Fitness Center in Durham, North Carolina, even if you slip up twice each month on birthdays or holidays, a healthful lifestyle practiced on 340 out of 365 days each year is not bad. And it's still quite effective in managing weight.

2. Eat more tomatoes, especially cooked tomatoes or those found in tomato sauce and paste, which are especially good not just for taste but also for their lycopene. Lycopene, a nutrient and carotenoid found in tomatoes (and in lesser amounts in watermelon and pink grapefruit) appears to protect against prostate cancer and cancers of the digestive tract. This is based on research reviewed by experts at the Harvard School of Public Health and is intriguing for yet another finding: When lycopene is consumed with a little bit of fat, such as with the cheese on pizza or with the oil in tomato sauce, its effect is most protective.

3. Get more folic acid, either by taking a multivitamin containing 400 micrograms per tablet or by eating more pinto and kidney beans, asparagus, or brussels sprouts. (Even orange juice has some folic acid.) You may be able to cut your risk of heart disease by a full 10 percent, depending on your age and health status.

4. Eat at least four fruit or vegetable servings a day. Yes, it's true, the federal guidelines call for five servings a day. But that may not be realistic for everybody. Most people in the United States eat only three or fewer per day. So eat four, be proud of your fiber intake, and consider a supplement with a variety of antioxidants, like vitamins A, C, and E, as well as selenium.

5. Outsmart your 'fat instinct.' Robert Pritikin, director of the Pritikin Longevity Center in Santa Monica, California, and son of its late founder, Nathan Pritikin, suggests that most people crave fatty foods in part due to evolution: Fat storage is what enabled our ancestors to survive when food was scarce. These days, we don't need such protection. To work around that fat instinct, try adding exercise to your lifestyle (it creates a craving for carbohydrates instead of fat); then consider upping your intake of

potatoes, sweet potatoes, fruits, and beans, all of which rate highly on the satiety index, which rates feelings of fullness.

6. Eating six smaller meals per day is another way to outsmart your instinct for fat-laden foods. Most people try to eat three meals a day and a few snacks. But if you are able to divide your eating into six smaller meals a day—or three small meals with snacks like fruit and low-fat yogurt in between—you'll have a much better chance of controlling tendencies to overeat. Even if you practice this just on weekends and one day during the week, you'll find benefits. Low-fat cottage cheese on toast with fruit is another popular meal/snack substitute.

7. Think zinc. Not only is zinc getting high marks from dietitians and doctors for its possible immune-boosting benefits, but numerous urologists have given the nod to zinc (and the herb saw palmetto) as a way to help prolong prostate health. Beginning in middle age, zinc supplements may help reduce irritation from the conditions of prostatitis or benign prostatic hyperplasia, a nettlesome swelling of the male sex gland. The research isn't all in yet, but it's a safe supplement when you stay within the label guidelines.

8. When you travel, pack for your stomach. Because so many of the nation's frequent flyers are men ages 38 to 43, it makes sense to heed the advice of seasoned, altitude-weary warriors. Bananas, oranges, apples, low-fat energy bars, and yogurt cups (when well-padded to prevent them from spilling all over your carry-on), are worthy weapons against inedible airline food and the hunger pangs that hit just when the pilot announces, "The good news is, we landed ahead of schedule. But we'll have to sit here on the runway a while, as there's still another plane in our arrival gate."

9. Try 15 to 20 slow-motion chews per forkful. It truly helps you feel more full while eating the same amount of food that you used to scarf down in 7 or 8 bites. You see, Mom did know best. Even 30 years ago, when you didn't need to worry about your . . . you know . . . fatgramscholesterolcaloriestriglycerides.

10. Drink more water. "Eat" it as a snack. Even if you can't handle the eight, eight-ounce glasses per day shtick, shoot for at least six. (Coffee doesn't count. It's a diuretic, which means it actually causes you to lose valuable fluids.) And start keeping a water bottle in your desk at work, plus an extra in your car's glove compartment. It's not just lucent lubrication. It's an inveterate appetite suppressant.

will eat one after another, all night long. I could easily consume seven or eight peaches or plums. I'd much rather do that than eat 10 Oreos." Some problem, most guys with a gut would say.

"I know most of my numbers," Barnathan continued, speaking from a cell phone in his car on a Los Angeles freeway. He said that his blood pressure was a normal 120/60, his cholesterol level was 192 (although six months earlier it had been 238), he wasn't sure about his body fat ratio, and his height and weight are 5 feet 9 inches and 168 pounds (although "180 was my top weight").

There may have been one other motivator for the major change in Barnathan's eating habits at age 40: "I remember that one of my father's friends had a heart attack at 43 and died not that long after. So [as I approached 40], I was thinking a little more about mortality and about my father and his friends—and the early forties was the time you'd [begin to have] heart attacks." So, he thought at 39, "I've got a year to take this seriously. My cholesterol was kind of high, and I'd slipped from being careful about what I ate. My doctor said, 'If this keeps up, in another year, I'll probably suggest that you start taking cholesterol medication.' That was it for me." For Barnathan, that was the time to lay off the fettucine alfredo at the Hollywood hot spots and head back to the salads made of cilantro and baby greens.

For other men, he represents one clear case study of someone who has exercised and eaten his way backward, finding himself with a better body at 40 than he had at 35.

Sex: The Best Is Yet to Come

Pick a number between 1 and 10. But before you do, consider your last erection. Was it last night? Last week? Last month? No matter. If 1 is as limp as a wet sock and 10 is as hard as a brick, go ahead and award your most recent erection the score that most suitably applies. This, you'll soon see, is no idle exercise.

In fact, Ken Goldberg, M.D., a urologist and director of the Male Health Institute near Dallas, swears by this scale. He admits that it's simplistic, but it's also deceptively powerful in resolving problems of midlife male sexuality. And men, he finds, respond to it rather well. They don't actually get excited about the prospect of slapping numbers on their penises. It's more that the firmness gauge gives them a scale for something that they're not used to putting into words—the fact that their erections have been changing or not performing or both. It is Dr. Goldberg's job to help set things right. When I asked him, after rating myself a stalwart 7, why he developed this tool for his patients, he didn't chuckle. Men, he says, are numbers-oriented creatures.

"The reason I went to a number system with guys is that I found they couldn't really communicate about themselves sexually. Beauty,"

From Wet Dreams to Dry Dreams

Sure, it may have been a while since you experienced a wet dream. But you may be surprised at how active your genitals are at midlife, even while you slumber. A study of nearly 150 men at the sleep labs of Baylor College of Medicine in Houston and Eastern Virginia Medical School of the Medical College of Hampton Roads in Norfolk produced the following data.

Age	Avg. Number of Erections per Night	Avg. Total Time Erect (min.)
under 40	4.2	141
40–49	3.9	134
50–59	3.65	127.5
60–69	3.6	109.5

Goldberg says, "is in the eye of the beholder. And some men who consider themselves 8s, who are older, well, we'd probably consider them 4s or 5s. The scale is more of a mechanism to get them talking. I've found that it's worked quite well, and the interviewers at our clinic like it. We have lots of guys who come in with erectile problems and get prescriptions to treat impotence. Then, after they use it, they rate themselves again and say they're 12s. They want to buy a gallon of the stuff."

If men are, as Dr. Goldberg says, numbers-oriented creatures, they are also more than that. As Norm R., a 40-year-old, never-married contractor from Atlanta, told me, in reviewing his sex life, "Quantity is less of an issue now than quality." After years—make that decades—of dating, Norm's notion of numbers, of how many women he's slept with each month or each year, has, well, softened.

"I'm ambivalent about conquest," he said. "It's not so much about conquest for me now. It's more about the experience of being with a woman." While he fancies himself a solid weekend athlete and enjoys a good cigar, he said he's been told by numerous women that he rates very high on the scale of having a feminine side. It doesn't bother him at all, though it might have at 32 or 33. Yes, he still considers one-night stands occasionally. But he's more proud, it seems, of having a true ability to empathize, to understand the way women think. To Norm and untold others who find themselves questioning their sex lives at 40, there's an obvious conflict to ponder: the decades-old drive to score versus a psychological softening of sorts, and, finally, a physiological softening.

"It doesn't surprise me that I'm ambivalent about conquest," Norm said. "I won't say that I don't get something out of a new thing these days. But it's more about the quality of what I get than about the process of getting it." Think of it: By age 40, he's come to consider the chase a "process." Maybe it's a relief to have it filed away just so.

"I love sex; it's a great thing," Norm related. "But I've become jaded about casual sex. Good sex now requires intimacy. A friend of mine said something the other day; he's 30—out of the mouths of babes. He said, 'I don't want to sleep with anybody unless I like her now.' I'd change that to say, 'I want to like her a lot.' I don't want to sleep with her and have this awkward moment the next morning when I really want her to leave. I want it to be a case where I want her to stay, lounge around, and I'll fix breakfast. There'd be no reason to leave. We could grab a paper and hang out; maybe go sit on a blanket in the park."

Penises That Think?

While many of us would agree that men are numbers-oriented creatures, Dudley Seth Danoff, M.D., suggests in his book *Superpotency* that we are also "penis-oriented creatures." Aiming his user-friendly guide squarely at the male midlife sex-help market, Dr. Danoff went on to state, "I want to demystify the penis and empower men to enjoy every ounce of pleasure that their wonderful organ was intended to give." He added, certainly not as an afterthought, "Penis power is the power of positive thinking as applied to your penis." Heady stuff, if not quite overstating his case.

Does this thus mean that penises can think? Obviously not. But the way that we think about them clearly does change as our bodies age and, in some cases, become less responsive. And it's worth knowing that for men, sex changes occur slightly more often in their forties than they did in their thirties. We may be single, married, or divorced, in love or in lust, and yet we can't help but wonder: How will sex change over the next few years? How will it feel? Will our erections get no-ticeably softer even if we're healthy and eat our bran? What is consid-ered normal for a man of 40 who's moderately healthy? And how can we improve on that?

The first thing to do is acknowledge age 18, then swiftly move on. The teenage penis (which by all accounts doesn't think), "seemingly wants to explode to orgasm every few minutes," says Bernie Zilbergeld, Ph.D., a sex therapist and psychologist based in Oakland, California, in his book *The New Male Sexuality*. "And what orgasms they are. The force is explosive and the pressure is immense; large amounts of semen fly across the room." The decline in a man's virility, Dr. Zilbergeld goes on to say, proceeds gradually but often imperceptibly.

This is good news, actually. It has become popular in sex education circles to talk about how the most powerful sex organ is the brain. What, then, would be the second most powerful male sex organ? The skin, of course. At least that's what the experts say. Fortunately, for most men at midlife, the brain and the skin are stable, healthy, eager partners when put to the test of libidinous arousal. They're team

The Erection Decades

After being bombarded with references to female biological clocks, men are finally starting to hear about their own. When researchers at the National Institute on Aging began tracking men's sex lives for a long-range study on what might be considered normal through the years, they found that age 18 may not be the peak for every guy. Typically, there are more sexual escapades at 30 than at 20. There are not quite so many, however, at 40. Here's how the self-reported orgasm scores stack up.

Age	Avg. Orgasms per Week	Avg. Orgasms per Year
20	2	104
30	2.3	121
40	1.6	84
50	1	52
60	0.7	35

NOTE: Numbers are assumed to include masturbation.

players, if you will. Setting penis power aside, then, or even the power of positive thinking as applied to erections, one can easily see that the capacity for good, even great, sex should remain within most every guy's grasp around the age of 40. It all depends on how you view sex or how you might view it a bit differently while pondering changes you may soon make.

"Four is the max," said Craig G., 42, of Los Angeles, when I asked him how many times he thought he was capable of having intercourse in one night. "Maybe five, but I'd have to be incredibly motivated. Now, it's usually once." For the record, Craig is married, pretty happily, to a woman four years his junior. He recalled that when he was in his mid-thirties, during their courtship phase, there was a time when he and his wife "went at it seven or eight times from Friday night till Sunday morning—all over the hotel suite, on every chair and couch, in the bathroom." As for their recent sex life, he related, "I don't think it's an age thing or a stamina thing. It's more a matter of being with a woman you've been with 5 or 10 years. The relationship isn't sex- or passion-driven anymore, which is too bad, in a way." (Even as he was talking about the changes in his sex life, his three-year-old daughter showed up, tugging on his sleeve for attention.)

Some experts in men's psychology would go further. They believe that the sex-driven relationships of your youth don't serve you well for the times you face in midlife. "Fundamentally, to understand men," said Tom Fiester, Ph.D., a Boulder, Colorado, psychologist who helped found the Boulder Men's Center in the mid-1980s and who for the past 15 years has run a number of men's groups, "you have to understand that men are drug addicts with their feelings and emotions. Because we don't know how to have our own, we become dependent on women." He believes that it's not healthy for women to control the goodies when it comes to sex in a young man's life. ("If you want to be with me, then you'll have to do X," Dr. Fiester says.) That's how patterns of give and take develop, instead of a deeper sharing that leads to acts of love and intense sex, which don't show up in middle age as frequently as they should.

When it comes to the work that it takes to develop layers of emotions, which seem to surface more easily among females, Dr. Fiester sounds almost cynical. "It's not developmental," he says. "It's a job skill. I used it in my thirties when I was trying to get laid. But it was still not okay to be sensitive or feeling in our daily lives. Guys would try for a while, then say, 'Screw this. It doesn't get me anywhere anymore.'" It's not that guys are inherently greedy in their youths when it comes to sex; nor are they inherently burned out or bored by sex in their late thirties and early forties. Rather, role playing may have been more powerful than we ever admitted. Until, that is, we started to question it.

The midlife men who go to see Dr. Fiester and sign up for group and individual therapy don't typically attend for a simple tune-up. "They're in pain," Dr. Fiester allows. "But at 40, it's not usually too bad. You've been in La-La Land up to that point. Or you've been on cocaine and alcohol and pussy. But now you are going to have a chance to be alive."

Forget, for a moment, all about the firmness of your erection. "Preparing men for this if they haven't experienced it is worthless," Dr. Fiester says, "because the wonderfulness of a soft penis does not occur to a man till he's got one."

End Zones versus Erogenous Zones

There are erogenous zones and there are erroneous zones, and then there are erroneous erogenous zones. When looking for ways to develop layers of intimacy and layers of a sex life that go beyond the genitals, it helps to know which zones are which. At this point in your life, since you're reading this book, you probably aren't just looking to score. So toss out the sports analogies, forget about getting to the end zone, and entertain some options.

Think back to the sexperts who talk about the skin as being the body's largest sex organ. Erogenous zones are "parts of the body directly wired for sexual stimulation," says Erica M. Goodstone, Ph.D., a New York City sex therapist. These areas tend to be patches of skin that are richly bundled with nerve endings and often are paired with a rich supply of blood vessels. One way to update your lovemaking in your forties, then, is to reconsider erogenous zones as erogenous "areas." It's a broader, less push-button philosophy of foreplay or afterplay. For instance, in both men and women, the often-overlooked face and neck are rife with erogenous areas: lips, cheekbones, eyes, ears, wherever skin and hair meet. Further down, the shoulders offer up some sexy epidermis, especially in the clavicle, which longs to be a cradle for the tongue.

Moving beyond the breasts (for now), depending upon how comfortable your partner is with her body, you may find that her armpits are every bit as erogenous as her nipples. So, too, may be the abdomen, especially the lower part of the belly, beneath the navel and above the pubic hairline. (This is not an area of the body often lingered over by an excitable 19-year-old, which is his loss.) Don't waste the waist, either, experts advise. Massaging and cupping her hips and curves are ways to accentuate her femininity and acknowledge the power it has over you, even if that's uncomfortable for you to say aloud.

As for the breasts, the nipples are not the only hot-wired areas. As one 38-year-old woman complained to me in an interview, she wished men would go easier on her aureoles: "Men think nipples are turn-on buttons." That's about all they concentrate on, but the sides and undersides of the breasts, it turns out, are notably thin-skinned. Likewise, the cleavage, an upside down "V," can become a destination for sexy friction. Use your imagination. And leave the bra on once in a while.

BED CHECK: FIVE THINGS MEN DO RIGHT AT 40

1. Last longer
2. Become scouts for new positions
3. Know how to use our tongues
4. Don't worry about simultaneous orgasms
5. Last longer

You already know about the inner thighs, but untold numbers of men ignore the rest of their partners' thighs for no good reason. The skin around the hamstrings, at the back of the thighs, is quite appreciative of light fingertips and lips and, well, you can take it from there. The backs of the knees are also too-often ignored. On the whole, a man who's been with a partner for a long time would be surprised at how little of her lower body he has have been attending to. Of course, it goes both ways.

One married, female, 40-year-old lawyer from Long Island, New York, told me, "A man who says, 'I love your thighs' is great, even though you know you have fat friggin' thighs. Or if he says, 'I love your ass—the way your cheeks stick up in the air' you know he's focusing on you. If the lights are on and he's looking at my big butt, I think, 'He must really like me.'"

The point to keep in mind about erogenous areas is that, as with the genitals, there's as much psychology as there is physiology in making things great. Speaking to that point, the Long Island lawyer related, "A woman is a whole body, not just a vagina and breasts. I can't tell you how much pleasure I get from the right touches to the back of my neck, the small of my back or when my toes are sucked, my fingers, too or my back rubbed. The thing is, it takes the fun out if I have to tell my husband that this is what I want. The best lovers don't need to be told. If you see that a man is operating 'intellectually,' it can be a real turn-on."

Hot Lips

With all the talk of turn-on buttons and sex the way it ought to be, some men may be surprised to learn that women find their kissing skills sorely lacking. Maybe it's not the skills that are the problem, but the notion that kissing isn't as important as it used to be. So many other things have entered the picture of a sex life at midlife. Who spends time going back to the basics? That's exactly the point, many a woman may say.

One night, while my wife was away on a too-long business trip, I discovered a piece of writing on the Internet by an author whose name I recognized—a woman I'll call Lynne, with whom I used to work when I lived in New York City. I'd always thought she was smart, flirty, and sarcastically witty; she often wrote about sexy things for men's and women's magazines as well as for audiences online. I don't believe I'd ever kissed her socially.

This particular example of Lynne's writing was about what many men do wrong when they kiss women and what fewer men do correctly. For starters, she bemoaned that guys have never gotten over the first-base, second-base concepts we learned in junior high. "A bad kisser, whether he likes to secrete a gallon of drool or waggle his head like a dog menacing a bone, seems to be simultaneously thinking: 'When can we get to step two? And three and four? Is she aroused yet?

Can I put my hand on her breast now?' He sees kissing as the next step on a carnal quest."

A man in midlife ought to know how to kiss better, or be open to a little re-education. A great kisser, Lynne and other women say, is a guy who kisses as if he will never touch another part of that particular woman's body, as if he will never desire to touch another part of that body. He sees, feels, and tastes the kiss as the goal, for however long the kiss may last. If performed warmly and honestly, this kiss will undoubtedly lead to more horizontal pursuits. I downloaded some of Lynne's words that night, wondering, for only the briefest moment, about those horizontal pursuits.

Advanced Intercourse

Historically and intellectually, the *Kama Sutra* has been teaching couples how to expand their sexual boundaries for millennia. About two millennia, you could say, give or take a few hundred years. Long before *Penthouse* put its spread-eagle views of women on glossy pages and on the Internet, noblemen of India were learning from a book about how to get more pleasure from sex and how to provide their partners with more pleasure. Besides featuring scores of illustrated intercourse positions, the *Kama Sutra* told men (and it was written for men, women being subservient), in florid but clear prose, that they weren't quite finished when they were "finished."

The *Kama Sutra* instructs readers that a man's job is to include such niceties as kissing and stroking, according to Anne Hooper, a former editor of *Penthouse Forum* and author of *The Ultimate Sex Book*. And if a woman is somehow left unsatisfied by an act of intercourse, the man should "rub the yoni (vulva)" of his partner with his hand. Think of it: What may have been groundbreaking, sexually speaking, shortly after the birth of Christ has become coin of the realm in sex-help literature of the current millennial era. Even so, even with pay-per-view cable TV and countless Internet Web sites, many of the featured sexual positions haven't gotten their fair share of publicity these days.

To correct these oversights and expand men's midlife mission to move beyond the missionary position, a handful of carnal highlights are offered here, to be used however you choose. Remember, though, that the *Kama Sutra* advocates love as well as acrobatic, high-level intercourse.

The widely opened position. In this position, the woman is on the bottom with the man on top. During penetration, she arches her back slightly, lifting her bottom just off the bed (or floor), with her feet planted soles downward. While supporting herself with her shoulders and her arms, which are joined behind her head, she spreads her legs generously, enabling her clitoris to benefit from increased friction. Her partner takes care to support himself with his arms. It is not so much about thrusting, when performed correctly, as it is about gliding. The friction sought here is light and pleasing—caressing, as opposed to chafing.

The rising position. This move employs the woman's calves. As the man kneels facing his partner, who is on her back, he raises her legs up toward his head, allowing her ankles to straddle his neck and rest upon his shoulders. He enters her carefully and clutches her calves as she begins to press her thighs together. This squeezing brings more profound sexual feeling than usual, as the pressure of the vagina bears down intensely.

The mare's position. Rating quite high on the erotic scale, this position enables the woman to control much of the lovemaking. It starts with the man on the bottom, sitting upright, legs barely spread, and leaning back on his arms for support. His back is at about a 45-degree angle to the bed. His partner is in front of him, facing away, until she backs herself toward him and slowly squats down onto his erection. Her bent knees are astride his thighs, which means there's a bit of flexibility required. The bonus for the man is that she can use her vaginal muscles to bear down on the penis, fairly milking it. The woman's bonus is two-fold: She can receive breast or clitoral fondling from one of her partner's hands during intercourse; plus, the vaginal muscles she contracts during intercourse are the same ones that quiver at orgasm.

The Joy of Toys

If ever there were a modern business enterprise that could be said to be devoted to a certain quiver at orgasm, it would likely be a San Francisco–based store and catalog outfit called Good Vibrations.

Located in a newly trendy, but formerly dowdy part of town (Valencia and 23rd Streets), Good Vibrations is aptly named—it sells more vibrators and sex toys than fishermen sell baskets of shrimp uptown at Fisherman's Wharf. Well, perhaps not quite. Even so, the proprietors have been gleefully marketing sex toys while publishing erotic books and erotica catalogs for some 15 years. From standard faux-penis rubberized dildos to $75 imported vibrators that are designed to be powerful and discreet, the goods at Good Vibrations are marketed with a certain joie de vivre, not to mention irreverence. I first learned of the Good Vibrations gang when I attended a sex education conference in the early 1990s. I had never before perused a catalog that featured whole theme sections of vaginal toys, vibrating gizmos, and unashamedly, butt plugs—or anal plugs, as they are called in sex therapy circles.

The educate-with-pleasure spirit is apparent at the flagship store, and for couples looking to spice up their sex lives, $50 to $75 can go a long way. "Our best-selling sex toy of all time isn't really a sex toy—it's the Hitachi Magic Wand, a handheld massager," reports Anne Semans, co-owner of the shop and a sex-book author.

Kent A., 40, an accountant from Oregon, has never visited Good Vibrations. But he's the kind of guy they would love to have on their mailing list. "I have no doubt that the reason our sex life is so good is our ability to discuss what we want and push our boundaries," Kent said when interviewed for the *Men's Health* Life Improvement Guides book *Sex Secrets*. "For example, we enjoy watching erotic movies and discussing our thoughts about the situations. And we love our sex toys. My advice to my fellow man: Don't be intimidated by using toys. We've found that they greatly enhance our sexuality, and believe me, we've tried most of them—vibrators, dildos, butt plugs, nipple clamps, cock rings, you name it. It's ridiculous to think there's something wrong with these. I see them as fun and useful tools to help make sex better and more satisfying.

"Now I'll admit," Kent added, "that it has taken us a while to get to this point." He allowed that he and his wife discussed beforehand what they wanted to try. When I later asked his wife about his revelations to his fellow men, she said she had no problem whatsoever with his notions of sharing some of their more private preferences in public. That is, as long as he runs them by her first for approval. Her husband believes that most men are afraid to "go out on a limb, to talk about the things we want to do or want to have done to us." Cruising through your thirties toward forty has a way of either opening you up or shifting you into an uncomfortable kind of cruise control.

Forbidden Sex

There aren't too many things that can make comfortable partners uncomfortable with each other, but one of them is anal sex. Despite our culture's increasing openness toward sexual experimentation and freedom, strong moral and religious grounds continue to place anal sex in a taboo category for many adults. Millions of other people, however, have had a brush or two with anal sex and don't mind sharing that fact with others. When University of Chicago researchers asked more than 3,400 Americans about their sex habits for a scientific survey in the mid-1990s, they found that more than 25 percent of the men and 20 percent of the women respondents had tried it.

That's a lot of apparent comfort with a tricky kind of sex. The fact is, if you are considering anal sex, you need to know that unprotected anal intercourse is still the most risky sexual behavior in regard to possible transmission of the HIV/AIDS virus. So no matter how well or how long you've known your partner, use a condom and a lot of lubrication with water-based products such as K-Y Jelly or Astroglide. Besides guarding against sexually transmitted disease transmission, a condom will also protect against bacterial infections from microscopic fecal matter. Some couples feel safer using two condoms.

Too many men decide to introduce anal sex into their relationships without explaining why it's so potentially fascinating to them. Once the fun begins, a confident guy should offer himself up as a willing participant, in case his partner wants assurance that a finger or two, or a small sex toy, doesn't hurt and indeed provides pleasure. In fact, it's long been known that the prostate gland contains highly charged sexual tissues. Both male and female rectal tissues are highly sensitive, and partners who have been shy about touching those areas may find themselves a bit more brave as they approach midlife. For some men and women, it is a highly charged event that boosts their self-images of being not just randy but sexually aggressive and thrill-seeking in bed.

"I slept with a woman I hardly knew, in college," Neil T., 40, a commercial artist in New York City, told me, "and things got hot pretty fast. She was visiting from out of town and had no inhibitions," including about anal sex. Though the event happened some 20 years ago, Neil sounded quite proud as he relayed the memory. The woman's being a near stranger and a visitor, their risk-taking behavior, and his penile pleasure combined to form a vivid, lasting memory in the sex bank of his brain. Now married and the father of two children, he has trouble finding time for quick acts of sex, let alone the time or the impetus to introduce into his bed at home a romp replete with anal sex. His wife, it also appears, hasn't been hankering to try it anytime soon.

Of course, any kind of anal sex may always be scary to some. Could there be a compromise? Certainly. Couples who aren't ready or willing to try anal sex can certainly use light finger caresses, a feather, or even mouths and tongues to explore the sensitive skin of the perineum, which runs from the anus to the scrotum or vagina. To millions of adult couples, these types of activities are not nearly so taboo, though they may have been ignored for years because of unvoiced concerns about cleanliness. That's nothing that a sexy shower or bath wouldn't fix. Consider this anal sex "light."

An Unlikely Vaginal Performance

You could call it erotic art. Yet the "V-Day" performance of Eve Ensler's award-winning play *The Vagina Monologues* that took place on Valentine's Day 1998 in the heart of New York City wasn't meant to be a turn-on. It was meant to get people thinking about vagina power and how society, including those of us who are males, might tap that power more constructively in the future.

So instead of being hot, the special performance included funny and serious monologues by an all-star lineup including Glenn Close, Susan Sarandon, Whoopi Goldberg, Lily Tomlin, Marisa Tomei, Rosie Perez, Calista Flockhart, Margaret Cho, Gloria Steinem, Winona Ryder, and others. It was an unlikely fund-raiser intended to foster media attention and to help fight violence against women. "If your vagina got dressed, what would it wear?" the play asks. "A pink boa," is one response. "What would it say?" is another question. "Oh, yeah," comes the answer. Women were urged to celebrate their vaginas this night.

Y MARKS THE SPOT: A MIDLIFE SEXUAL SECRET

When a man has a plastic lifelike model of a penis on his desk, you can assume he won't be shy when it's time to talk about sex. Such was the case when I visited Jed C. Kaminetsky, M.D., a urologist at New York University in Manhattan, for an interview. Of course, he knew the physiology of the phallus, but I found the lesson he taught me about the clitoris more intriguing.

"It's a lot like a penis, anatomically," he said. He went on to explain that the clitoris that we see during sex, located within the elusive areas of the labia, is only half the story. There's a lot more underneath the surface of the skin, in terms of nerves and sexually charged tissues. And yes, you can even call it erectile tissue.

When Dr. Kaminetsky told me this, I thought back to a lecture I once heard while on a business trip to Atlanta. I was on assignment for a woman's magazine at the time; so I had good reason to attend the surprising seminar entitled "The Clitoris, Redefined." It was surprising on two counts: First, the speakers accused the medical community of a cover-up in terms of female sexual pleasure; and second, they forever changed my view of women's most sensitive sexual organ. Even today, most medical illustrations that purport to show women's anatomy depict the clitoris as a pea-sized bud of nerve-rich tissue set above the urethra and beneath a hood of skin. But a subset of sexologists and researchers, including Dr. Kaminetsky, now believe that the clitoris is much more than a buzz-worthy nub: It includes long bundles of nerves, or "legs," and blood-rich tissues, or "bulbs," that are located beneath the skin.

If you consider the old view of the clitoris as a pearl, the new view of the clitoris would include the pearl and the entire shell of the oyster, as well. To get a sense of scale, instead of thinking of clitoris as the period at the end of this sentence, think of

Playwright Ensler has been trying to get that message across for a few years now, starting from a perch on an off-Broadway stage. Hollywood finally heard her call, at least for "V-Day."

The word "vagina" doesn't sound sexy to some folks, all by itself. (Does "penis"?) But that's the point. It shouldn't be considered all by itself, in language or in bed. We sort of knew that, didn't we?

There were a surprising number of men in the audience that night. One 27-year-old woman told me she took a male date to the show, but

THE NEW VIEW OF THE CLITORIS

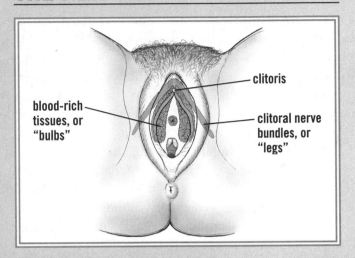

the capital letter "Y," suggests Helen O'Connell, M.D., a urologist at the Royal Melbourne Hospital in Australia.

When you reconsider the clitoris and then read accounts of how many women say their sex lives are more fulfilling in their thirties and forties than they were in their twenties, things begin to make more sense. This has a lot to do with them gaining experience and confidence without losing sensitivity. If only this were made clearer years ago. Nothing about the mere aging of a woman's body should affect a bundle of active, nerve-rich tissues that reach from the visible clitoris down along the perineum and all the way to the inner thighs. Gentlemen, start her engines.

that it may have been "too soon." It was only their fourth date, and it made her uncomfortable to be sharing this forced intimacy with him so early on. Still, the show helped broadcast a view that midlife men would do well to entertain: There's a host of hidden feeling—and often shame—that blocks the potential for millions of women to have uninhibited, gleeful sex. With abandon. That starts down there. Without thinking of any part of their anatomy as dirty or unclean. Or, most assuredly, unsexy.

Part feminist manifesto, part comedy, part "Our Private Parts, Ourselves," and part political treatise, *The Vagina Monologues* has brought talk about the vagina nearly into the mainstream, or at least onto the culture pages of the *New York Times*. Feminist author Gloria Steinem, as may have been expected, didn't honor the vagina just that one night. She wrote an introduction to the published book of the play and re-named the formerly private parts. She declared them the "power bundle," giving credit to a group of young girls who used that term to describe the entirety of the vagina, labia, and clitoris. It turns out that that's not a bad moniker. If men can talk freely about their "tools" or their "Johnsons," ascribing Bunyanesque traits to six or so inches of mannish organ, maybe a celebration of female genitalia—of flesh, lips, nerves, and lubrication—was long overdue.

"In Great Neck, they call it a pussycat," the play relates. "In Westchester, they call it a pooki. . . . There's 'powderbox,' 'poonani,' 'nishi,' 'dignity,' 'monkey box,' 'mongo,' 'split knish' in Philadelphia, and 'schmende' in the Bronx." Whatever you might call it, in most long-term relationships, the vagina is decidedly unheralded, either from familiarity, unfamiliarity, or a combination of the two.

But in the 1950s, long before they were celebrated onstage, vaginas were studied in the labs of pioneer sex researcher Alfred Kinsey, M.D., of Indiana University in Bloomington. Besides finding that the clitoris was extraordinarily sensitive, Dr. Kinsey's research uncovered the fact that the inner lips of the vagina, the labia minora, were equally sensitive. This was a rather startling finding back then. Even today, millions of men have no idea how much pleasure that part of the vagina can provide to their partners. Just think: The G-spot and the clitoris have some company. When it comes to sex research, men are never too old or young to do a little homework.

Sex, Lives, and Videotape

While conducting interviews for this chapter about how men feel about their sex lives at 40, I decided not to start by asking them how things were going in bed. I did what a sportscaster might do: I went to the videotape. I made a point to ask guys what they would include on highlight reels of their sexual histories. It was a backward focus at first, which then lead us closer to the here and now. It was also a way to get them talking, taking things from the top, when sex could hardly have been much better.

While I heard a sense of disillusionment in some of their voices, I also heard a decided sense of earnestness about the future. They were not going to settle for mediocre sex, as perhaps their parents' generation did in their forties and fifties. Here, then, are clips from the highlight reels, blended with some actual and memorable sex stories of today.

The Realist

"I once had sex—and almost but not quite went all the way—in an outdoor fountain at night, in downtown New Orleans with a woman I met that same day," boasted Paul M., 41, of Cleveland. "And it wasn't even Mardi Gras." He was 27, she was maybe 22, and she was wearing a polo shirt and skirt, he recalled. They had their shoes and socks off and were wading in the water of the Piazza di Italia when the urge hit.

"She was drunker than I was," Paul said. "And she's the one who pulled down her underwear while we were going at it. I don't remember if I got freaked or just wanted more privacy, but I couldn't go through with it. There was a guy sitting on a bench, I could see, when I looked over her shoulder. We did just about everything else that night . . . in a bed, with the door closed. But we both passed out.

"Yeah, it's changed since then," Paul added, speaking of his sex life. He's now married, and has been for five years. He's the father of one child, a two-year-old girl. And he hasn't had a true week-or-longer vacation since the birth of his daughter. "Since I turned 40, sex has changed, but not in remarkable ways. It's been subtle, even a little bit sad. It's gotten less dramatic in bed; maybe it's been that way for a couple of years. It's only since I turned 40 that I've been thinking about it, though. Questioning it more and wondering if it's part of a pattern that's going to lock up.

"On the other hand," he continued, "I've started thinking about ways to put some life back into it. Because, to be honest, I've gotten lazy when it comes to sex. I know how to get off and how to get Amy off in a couple of minutes. It feels like cheating, sometimes; it's so efficient. I'd say she's gotten a little lazy, too, though it's easier to tell you that than tell her. I'm not sure how we might change things, and maybe it's got to get worse before it gets better. Know what I mean? Sex at 40 for guys gets a little scary, I think. At least it has for me. And yet I've heard and read that women in their forties get pretty confident about sex. They come into their own when we start to fall apart. Figures. But maybe that'll mean we open up in ways we haven't before."

One of the things Paul has done is to begin reading women's erotic writing. He's not the kind of guy who goes for X-rated videos or Web sites, and he said his wife is kind of prudish about it, too. "Though she's not a prude in bed," he quickly added. This is one of the ways he's trying to keep an open mind, keep fresh, and get aroused without resorting to what he thinks is sleazy or what his wife would, without a doubt, scoff at.

"Used to be," he recalled, "when we were first going out, we made out for hours. Nowadays, you'd call it foreplay. Back then it was just plain lust and smash-mouth kissing. I mean, I used to pick her up and carry her around the room naked. We were testing each other out, sort of, and I wanted to show off a little, be a powerful guy. Not a stud, but a guy who liked to have fun and who wasn't ashamed of his body.

"In those days, sex was hot, and we were both working way too hard during the day, then staying up with each other way too long during the night. We lost a lot of sleep but had a lot of sex. I call them my 'condom years' because, being single in the early '90s, I made sure I always had one or two when I went out or when I brought somebody home.

"These days, I don't use condoms. I wouldn't mind one bit if we got pregnant again. In fact, it'd be great. The fact that I'm a new father at 40 means that every time I come during sex now, I'm thinking, somewhere in the back of my mind, 'This could be the one; this could be the one that turns into a baby.' In fact, now that I think about it, that's the biggest change in the past few years." (The first pregnancy wasn't quite so planned, Paul said. It came quickly.)

"One of the reasons sex is slowing down some between us is probably because we do want to have another kid. And after five years of marriage, who cares about our 'big-time' jobs? (His as a health care consultant; hers as advertising brand manager.) It's time to get that family going. In a way, I think that's meant not as much oral sex, for me at least, and more of a reliance on just plain intercourse.

"Don't get me wrong. I enjoy it, and I'm not having any troubles getting it up or anything," Paul said. "I'm just thinking that maybe there's a pressure taking away from our pleasure. It's almost like blow jobs are a waste for now. We can't afford the sperm, even though that sounds weird.

"Another thing I've noticed, and this is a good thing, is that my wife seems more comfortable grabbing me than maybe she did a few years ago. It probably doesn't have as much to do with age as it does with our comfort level of being with each other. But I get off on her going down my pants with her hands, even if it's just a quick grab in the bedroom when we're getting dressed in the morning. It's like she's saying, 'When we get home . . .' Or maybe she's just doing it because it's fun. It doesn't have to mean anything. It's part of what happens between couples who really like each other, even though we may not be the most open couple in the world when it comes to talking about sex and what we'd like each other to do. I make sure to tell her it feels good, though."

When Paul thought a bit more about his so-called old days, he mentioned that he missed the times that he and Amy used to "fool around more" with intercourse, trying different positions. In particular, he said he still fantasizes about her straddling him in bed while they were sitting up and facing each other. "Three things were going on," he relates. "One, we were facing each other eye to eye, which is a lot different from lying down in bed. Two, she was riding me, and I was helping lift her up and let her down on me. We were both setting the pace and it seemed a little dangerous. I remember wondering if a penis could break if someone fell on and off it at the same time. The other thing was, before we did any kind of rocking or really went at it, we sat there for a long time kissing, just locked together, and it felt as close as it ever has to the two of us being one.

"You hear all that BS during weddings, about 'two souls joining as one in wedded bliss,' and I guess it happens to some people some of the time. But that image of us naked, sitting up, me in her and her on me, legs all splayed, is an image I keep on file. And I don't think there's anything wrong with that. The only thing wrong is that we don't do it more often. That's what I mean about maybe slowing down around 40 and doing things that are more comfortable, more predictable. We tend to fall back on convenience in bed, which isn't the end of the world, I know. But I'm not sure when I'm going to say something to her about it."

The Settler

"I was about 25, she was 21," said Craig G., the married architect from Los Angeles, remembering his single days. "I went over to Paris on vacation to visit a girlfriend who was studying overseas, and she wanted to give me a blow job outside in the street. It was late at night when we were coming home from a bar; I couldn't believe it. She tried to; I said 'No, no, no.' I was drunk, walking her back to her school. What happened was, we walked into this mews, making out. She started tugging at my pants, I was a wimp.

"Then she tried to do it with me on the living room floor of the lounge, where she lived. I said, 'No,' because I was an idiot, first of all. I said something like, 'If we get caught, it's going to wreck your year at school.' It just seemed weird, but I probably wasn't that into her then. I didn't have sex with her till she came back to the States.

"She liked to get a little nastier than most of the other women I dated did. That's probably why I'm remembering all this. Stuff like her sticking her finger up my ass and licking my ass, and wanting me to do the same to her. If my wife did stuff like that, I'd probably still be doing it, too. Although after having a prostate exam, I can see why women don't want to do it so often."

For Craig, the biggest difference between sex at 25 and sex at 40 is simply a decrease in desire. "Sex is not so passion-driven anymore," he told me, "which is too bad, in a way. But maybe it's good, for sanity's sake. I mean, for me, whenever I've been all hot for a woman, it turns out that I've gotten almost manic-depressive. Every time I was desperately in love with a woman, there was also misery. It would make me crazy." So he's settled for a little less as he's aged.

The Stylist

"I've gone out with 42-year-olds, and I've been out with 19-year-olds," said Brian P., 40, a divorced Englishman and hairstylist who works in an upscale salon in San Francisco. "My state of mind might be different because of the work I do, but if I hit it off with a girl, I don't think of her age. I'm just usually attracted to younger girls." His current girlfriend, it turns out, is 26.

"It's not just looks, but an attitude," he told me, of his fondness for women in their twenties (though he still calls them "girls"). "They're usually looser about commitment and kids. I mean, my girlfriend is 26. She would never pressure me about marriage. Kids have come up, but only occasionally." When he flew to England to visit with a dozen friends for a combined 40th birthday party, Brian said, his "mates" didn't give him a hard time about having a young girlfriend.

"In Europe, it's different," he said. "It's no big deal. She's going to be 27 soon; I'm thinking of trading her in. None of my London friends have said, 'She's only 26.' In America, they have. Over there, I could be 50, she could be 20, and it wouldn't be a big deal. If anyone said anything in London, it was the girls—the wives."

The girls wouldn't have said much two years ago, however. That's when Brian dated a 42-year-old, when he was a mere 38. "She was amazing," he said. "A girl from Trinidad. She was in amazing shape. She's a grandmother, at 42, who happened to have the hottest body. It was really great." Ironically, one of the reasons they broke up had to do with children, but not in the way you might think. "Whenever we went out, we had the grandchild with us," Brian said. "It was driving me crazy. We never really split up, though. We started out being friends. Then we started sleeping together. Then it sort of fizzled, but it wasn't about how old she was. If she's 42, and she looks good, and the skin fits, I don't care," he added, half in jest.

"I honestly think it's an individual thing. Some young girls just know what they're doing," said Brian. "I'm not talking about virgins. By 22, they've had some experience. I know some who don't want the lights on. But then I know some who take off their clothes and walk around freely. Some of the girls I've been with do that for a living; they're models. I haven't been with a lot of older women, but sexually, the ones I've been with tended to want to make sure that they're not just going to have sex and that's it. Not just, "Spread your legs and see you in the morning." They're more sensible, because most of the ones I've been with who are single have been burned a few times.

"The younger ones look up to you," Brian continued. "But I never believed in that regaining-your-youth thing with young girls." The fact that they've looked up to him has made him feel older, not younger, he said. He also mentioned a bonus: Younger women, these days, seem to be more adept at or more eager to perform oral sex than those who have been closer to his age. Maybe it's not the sexual revolution, just evolution. And while he acknowledged that he enjoys the "excitement of something new" at the outset of a relationship, he added, "Most of the time that's overrated. One of my friends says, 'Show me a beautiful woman; I'll show you a guy who's tired of doing her.' I don't care if the woman is Cindy Crawford (though it might take longer to tire of her). I know lots of models who get dumped."

The Creative Type

"I went 'around the world' in my twenties—with two women," said Mark H., 39, describing his most memorable ménage à trois. Now a married graphic artist and Internet consultant from Virginia, he recalled the sexual highlight clearly. "One was a Frenchwoman from Paris, the other was her friend from Tokyo (who didn't speak much English), and me, from Ohio. I was living in New York, as an artist, and they were just visiting. They needed a place to stay, and of course, I made the token offer to sleep on the couch. They didn't want me to sleep there. So I slept between them.

"They liked watching, too," Mark said. "There was a language barrier, but it was purely universal language that night. After the Japanese woman, I did the Frenchwoman, then I had anal sex with the Japanese woman. She thanked me. I remember, the next morning, walking the two of them down the street, arm in arm. I never felt so 'from Ohio,' if you know what I mean. I don't know why that was.

"I've also done it on an airplane," Mark said, "with my wife. She wasn't my wife at the time. It was the mile-high club on our way to Europe.

"For years, my responsibility was to nobody but my penis." These days he's kept his sex life decidedly more grounded and closer to home. Having been married for 10 years, and now the father of two kids, Mark said he's learned how precious those pockets of time for sex can be; especially in the morning.

Mark and his wife seemed the perfect candidates for being supporters of quickie sex, so I asked him how he felt about it. "Yes, those quickies are valid," he said, "and the old dry hump is better than nothing." Or is it?

BOX SCORE

SEX LIVES AT 40

Three Things to Ponder
1. Has the firmness of your erections changed recently?
2. Has your partner expressed new interests or desires to you lately? Have you to her?
3. How many erogenous areas of your partner's body have you visited in the last week? In the last month?

Three Things to Remember
1. The brain and skin are the two most important sex organs.
2. Many women's sex lives peak in their early forties.
3. A bout of impotence once in a while is normal in one's forties. Chronic impotence is a different story.

Three Things to Do This Year
1. Introduce one or two fantasies or sex toys into conversation with your partner, or, better yet, into the bedroom.
2. Take partner massage more seriously than perhaps you have in the past. Invest in oil(s). This will pay dividends.
3. Celebrate the quickie, carnally or manually.

"I think that, as we get older, a woman's sex drive slows down. My sex drive certainly outpaces Katrina's. But I'm not going to allow that sort of quickie to become a regular substitute," he stated, "because the more you allow it to become one, the more dependent you become on it. As I get older, I become fixated on that. The whole notion that men can father children daily and women only yearly tells me our drives are way different. As a man, you have to maintain your standards. I mean it. I'm not saying that she's my wife, so I have every right to make love with her whenever I want. It's that I don't want to get used to the drive-up window kind of sex. I'd rather go on a diet and wait for the filet. Because, you know, you do it too much, and where are you?

"Clearly, we're heading into a new phase. If we did slow down, take the time, and caress our wives more," he said of men in their forties, "we would be having more participatory sex. Somehow though, it's hard to be so slow. I don't know why we don't do the sweep of gestures, the massage, that we know that women desire."

Mark wasn't going to take the easy way out and blame the kids. "You have to defend those tiny little pockets of time because the kids are like clockwork. We know one of them will come bounding in at 7:05 in the morning. So if we both happen to be up at 6:40, we both know we're weighing the possibilities.

"Actually, one of the things I'm doing is buying a house with the master bedroom on a separate floor. That way, we'll get an early warning if the children are on the way up. There will be more significant noise; it'll be harder to be surprised. That's a big deal, too," he said. "It's not that it'd be horrible if the kids walked in on us. I'm okay with the 'giving Mommy a back rub' story. But my wife would be a lot more comfortable if there was less chance of being caught.

"I'm convinced we're at a crossroads now," Mark concluded, sounding like a man in his 40th year who's properly concerned. "I think it's normal to slip into this pattern of behavior where it's more women tolerating men's needs for quick gratification instead of fuller commitment. I'm convinced that needs to be confronted."

The Postscript

All this reflection doesn't mean sex is over, not by a long shot. Nor does it mean sex in one's forties is destined to be fraught with questions about ability and desire and staying power. But it does mean sex at 40 is unlike sex at so many other important ages. And it most certainly can get better, the sex gurus remind us. Especially in the age frame of 40 to 45, when a man shouldn't even try to get where he was at 25. It may prove a lot more helpful for him and his partner to simply aim for getting back to where he was at, say, 35. Forty can be a time of renewal, of making love in ways you just never got around to before or didn't quite appreciate the first time around.

Sexual Health: A Midlife Tune-Up

S ex marks the spot.

Of all the age-related markers in a man's life, those related to acts of sex and how he feels about them are, consciously or not, the ones that often mark him as middle-aged. The forties, unlike the thirties, become a kind of sexual proving ground. "How much do I still have?" goes the oft-unstated refrain. "How much can I still do?"

This is the decade, in fact, when sex becomes intrinsically linked with sexual health. To be sure, such links have been forged at other times, as with sexually transmitted diseases (STDs) in the teens and twenties, or with sperm counts in the thirties if fertility was in question. But these were typically more temporary. At 40, annual physicals become the norm—or should. Blood pressure readings, digital-rectal exams, and prostate-specific antigen (PSA) test results don't sound quite so foreign anymore. Blood flow—to the heart, of course, but also to other organs—begins to become a concern.

When you consider hormones, sex drive, erections, or the prostate gland, you find—if you press a man to be honest—that actual experiences feel quite different than they did at age 18, 25, or 35. For starters, libido may languish . . . a little bit. Similarly, when standing, an aroused 40-year-old guy notices from time to time that his erection is pointing straight ahead, not up and angled sharply toward his abdomen, the way it did just a few years earlier. Even a slow, luscious, teasing-and-tenacious act of fellatio may surprise him at its end: He doesn't seem to come as hard as he did before. His manly orgasms have, it seems, lost a little power. (Gerontologists dub this a "decline of the orgasmic reflex.") Similarly, he may notice in his late thirties or early forties that he is getting up in the middle of the night once or twice to urinate. It's annoying and confounding. It's the prostate talking.

As one ex-cop, played by James Garner, asked another ex-cop, played by Paul Newman, in the 1998 film *Twilight*, "Your prostate started acting up?"

"Not yet," answered Newman.

"Well, you're in for a whole lotta fun."

Actually, the fun that Newman's character found in the film came in the form of a love scene between him and a salacious character played by Susan Sarandon. Think of it: a love scene in a late-1990s movie in which the average age of the actors was over 60. Something, perhaps, to look forward to, at least in part.

The Soft Sell of Softer Sex

Your sexual future, for the record, starts with the past. "When I'm taking a sexual history," offers Michael Perelman, Ph.D., co-director of the marital and sex therapy clinic at New York Hospital–Cornell Medical School in New York City, "I always say, 'Tell me about your last sexual experience.' Often patients say, 'Nothing happened.' They'll say they didn't have erections, so they didn't proceed." In these midlife patients' minds, the case is seemingly open and shut. "So I ask them what they asked their partners to do," Dr. Perelman goes on. "They'll say something like, 'Well, I wasn't hard, how can I ask her to [perform fellatio]?' I tell them that even a softer penis can enjoy sensual caresses with various parts of a woman's body." That may strike you as just plain weird. After all, who ever heard of "soft sex?" Or at least, what guy in his twenties ever heard of it?

"I just discovered something," said David R., 41, a Chicago father of two who's been married 10 years and is a consultant in the fashion trade. "It's great, and a woman told me about it—somebody I work with. If I want sex and my wife doesn't, or if I can't get hard, I'll just say, "Screw it," and have her hold my hand while I beat off. At least she's involved in some way. And I'm not going to bed frustrated." Whether David would have ever floated this proposition were it not for his enlightened colleague, we'll never know. The point is, he and his wife joined the soft sex club. Perhaps without knowing it.

This is not about impotence. This is about aging and what is or isn't thought to be normal in the new millennium. "There is some age change in regard to sexuality, beginning at about age 25, although it is imperceptible," Dr. Perelman explains. "There is some degree of neu-rological decline, as well. It usually isn't noticed, though, until the late thirties and forties, when sex becomes less automatic. As opposed to before, you may need some combination of sexual thought and sexual friction in order to evoke a sexual response.

"There are two ways to look at this," Dr. Perelman adds. "One, you may be with a person who excites you greatly but who isn't a great lover, and yet that may be enough to get you aroused. Or you could be with someone whom you may have less lust for but who is sexually prolific. And that may be enough to excite you." Or else, once in a while, you just may need to take matters into your own hand while your partner holds the other.

"The way to feel as good as you did in your thirties about sex, when you are in your forties, is to not try as hard as you did in your twenties," Dr. Perelman continues—not as an afterthought. He advises men to slow down a bit, enjoy the ride, and begin to acknowledge their bodies' responses.

So This Is Normal

Aside from the strictly physiological changes, men in their forties typ-ically become more sensitive to distraction—an answering machine that clicks on, a child's cry. As men between the ages of 35 and 50 tend to function under the most stressful conditions of their lives, it should come as no surprise that by their late thirties or early forties, many of them may require massage or other stimulation to become fully erect. Yet it does come as a surprise to many, sending them perhaps prematurely into the offices of internists and urologists. They may be thinking impotence, when it is actually aging at work.

By one's mid-forties or fifties, the average scrotum, having heard gravity's call, hangs visibly lower than it used to. Around the same time in a man's life, occasionally sooner, the period of ejaculatory inevitability (consider it the point of no return in the countdown to ecstasy) and emission becomes shorter. Eventually, but rarely in one's early forties, this two-stage aspect of a young man's orgasm becomes a single shorter orgasmic reflex. By age 50 or 60, as male hormone levels dip and the vascular system shows signs of sluggish behavior, ejaculations are less forceful, though still potent. In addition, some researchers say, beginning in the fourth decade of life, the penis (and a woman's clitoris) actually shrinks due to falling sex hormone levels.

Fortunately, not all of the news in this area slopes downward. For women in their thirties and forties, estrogen levels decrease gently, which enables their testosterone (the so-called male hormone) to exert more of its hormonal influence upon them. As a result, women now become more easily orgasmic, says Theresa L. Crenshaw, M.D., a sex therapist in private practice in San Diego, in her book *The Alchemy of Love and Lust*. At the same time, men's lowered levels of testosterone may explain why we become more interested in touch as midlife progresses. We desire more kinds of stimulation to achieve similar levels of sexual satisfaction.

If you do the math—softer erection, shorter orgasmic reflex, less forceful climax—things don't appear bright at first. But these normal aspects of aging become a problem only because men make them a problem. And the way to avoid doing that is to do what many active, arousable, and healthy midlife men do: Move from a performance-based sex life to one based on pleasure. This is a subtle but crucial shift.

One example of how to make that shift comes from Bernie Zilbergeld, Ph.D., a sex therapist and psychologist based in Oakland, California, and author of *The New Male Sexuality*, who has heard it all from clients over the years. When I spoke with him in an interview, I felt immediately at ease, as if we were connected in some way. He seemed to enjoy tackling the at-times-intractable sex lives of men. "A lot of men say to me, 'I don't want more sex because I'm not enjoying the sex I'm having,'" he says. "It's easier for men to talk about a lack of pleasure than of pleasure-experiencing."

Here's a quick way to broaden your notion of pleasure at midlife: Start by rethinking your orgasms, Dr. Zilbergeld offers. Make the distinction between partner-induced orgasms and partner-involved orgasms. Partner-induced orgasms occur when a woman physically brings you to orgasm, using her hands, mouth, or vagina. Partner-involved orgasms occur when a woman is merely in the room, on the phone, performing a striptease, or clicking away on a keyboard that's connected to your modem, while you ejaculate as a result of your own manipulation—as our friend David did. He just didn't have a name for it. Don't automatically judge one type as superior to the other. Either way, it works.

As for responding to those who say this isn't "real" sex, there isn't much to dispute. It's real to those who are doing it.

The Hormone Hard Sell of Youthful Sex

So now you know. There are ways to come to terms with the "new" ways of coming. Most of them involve behavior and mindful changes, but there are other options. Since the mid- to late 1990s, the use of anti-aging hormones and nutrients, including melatonin, dehydroepiandrosterone (DHEA), testosterone, human growth hormone (HGH) and pregnenolone, has become a solid growth industry among the not-so-stolidly middle-aged. Sales of melatonin and DHEA, in particular, have moved from the back bins of health food stores and pharmacies to front and center. Testosterone and HGH must be prescribed by doctors and are far more expensive.

Still, countless curious men are popping so-called natural hormones in search of lost vigor and revved-up sexual energy. "Tens of thousands of doctors are prescribing DHEA to their patients to treat a wide variety of ailments," claims William Regelson, M.D., professor of medicine at Virginia Commonwealth University Medical College of Virginia School of Medicine in Richmond, in his book *The Superhormone Promise*. This may be overstating the case, but the fact that hundreds of men have reported better sex lives after taking DHEA has at least hundreds of doctors taking notes—and waiting for scientific proof to filter in.

The well-regarded Massachusetts Male Aging Study, for one, has found that of 17 hormones measured in its subjects, only DHEA showed a direct correlation with impotence. As DHEA levels declined, incidences of impotence rose. But what about DHEA's effects on normal sexual function? Those kinds of studies—absent a disease—are more difficult to fund and conduct.

It's preliminary findings like this, though, that spur hype and hope about maintaining the feelings of a 25-year-old in your 45-year-old genitals. Hold on, our government has said. The National Institute on Aging (NIA) issued a warning about using anti-aging therapeutics in general. "The NIA does not recommend taking supplements of DHEA, growth hormone, or melatonin, because not enough is known about them," the Institute cautions. Specifically, as of late 1998 the NIA had only approved studying HGH, for one, in experiments that involve people over age 65.

One doctor involved in the government's study made a point at an anti-aging convention I attended in Las Vegas that I'll not soon forget: "It doesn't matter what the blood levels of these hormones are; what matters is the target tissue response," said Marc R. Blackman, M.D., director of the division of endocrinology at Johns Hopkins Bayview Medical Center near Baltimore. Be careful, he told doctors in attendance. Blood levels of hormones may seem fine, but how do we know that certain hormones aren't spurring the growth of sex gland tumors, for example, in the prostate? That may turn out to be the target tissue, and who's measuring that? In women, for example, estrogen has been shown to foster the growth of some gynecological cancers.

For more input, I visited the offices of one Colorado doctor who prescribes testosterone and DHEA, among other anti-aging hormones. I scheduled an interview, then asked him if he was, in effect, jumping the gun. Robert Rountree, M.D., a physician at the Helios Health Center in Boulder, told me he was satisfied with the safety record of the substances as reported in the medical journals so far. But he tracks his patients' hormone levels carefully, just in case. Plus, he said he prefers to keep the dosages to a minimum. He seemed to be a cautious yet enthusiastic supporter of the hormones when they are prescribed to active, athletic patients in their fifties, sixties, and up.

For men of 40, then, it may simply be too soon to expect too much from the supplements and hormones found in health food stores. They may be harmless and could prove helpful, but truth be told, men's natural hormone levels usually haven't dropped precipitously yet.

"I think there's some merit in maintaining a longitudinal knowledge of your own body," says Dr. Perelman, "and knowing your testosterone can be helpful." He adds, however, that the likelihood of low testosterone levels at 40 interfering with erectile function would be possible but remote. He continues, "But I think there's merit in something women have been proposing for years: Whether you have a full tank of gas or half a tank of gas, you have enough to run the car."

So we have to avoid being overly concerned about normal age-related changes that in no way diminish our capacity, even if they slightly alter our response.

Impotence Problems and Opportunities

Used to be, a diagnosis of impotence meant a turning point in a man's life—an inevitable decline. It still may turn out that way, but the conclusion is certainly not forgone. With all the talk and focus on impotence drugs—from alprostadil (Caverject injections and MUSE suppositories) to sildenafil citrate (Viagra)—men now have an array of nonsurgical options from which to choose. Implants and pumps used to get all the publicity in this field. No longer.

The Food and Drug Administration (FDA) testing and approval of Viagra had thousands of urologists and millions of men eagerly awaiting its mass distribution. By April 1998, prescriptions were flying out of pharmacies at a rate of 40,000 a day. "Half the men in America will be lined up to get that drug," Dr. Zilbergeld told me when Viagra first made the news. Millions of men have, by now, tried it.

The pill, diamond-shaped and blue in hue, is special because it is the first oral medication for impotence. It doesn't promise to magically produce erections on demand, merely to stimulate those that are on the way and help keep them harder, longer. It takes up to an hour to kick in. (Many men have taken to taking it at dessert, after a fine meal.) It was largely responsible for the heady rise in the price of Pfizer pharmaceutical stock from just over 105 to 113⅜—a jump of over 8 points—in one day, shortly after the FDA said, "Yes, yes, yes."

By early 1999, after the initial euphoria wore off, it was safe to say the drug had made its way into the mainstream of midlife sexuality. It also made its way into the bloodstreams and erections of many men who didn't even suffer from any medical or sexual problem. They just wanted firmer erections. Numerous doctors were happy to oblige them with a loose diagnosis of impotence. Numerous partners were happy, too. The most common side effects are reported to be few, if a bit ironic: nausea, blurred and bluish-tinged vision problems, and headaches (as in, "Tonight, dear, I want a headache."). More seriously, up to 130 deaths have been reported to the FDA among Viagra users, although the drug itself hasn't been implicated directly.

In terms of opportunities for the younger midlife men, Viagra, surprisingly, may not help all that much. After all, it doesn't produce spontaneous erections. And men at 40, for the most part, haven't lost much in the departments of feeling, skin sensitivity, arousal and, fortunately, erectile blood flow. Still, health insurance companies will be grappling with one issue for at least a few years: How much of the cost of medication should be reimbursed for patients who do have impotence and erectile dysfunction? Are two $10 pills per week sufficient? Four per month? What is a "normal" amount of sex for a middle-aged man? Doesn't it depend on his and his partner's ages, health, and libidos? And why should a man's erection pills be covered, when a woman's birth control pills aren't? The difference in cost between four pills per month and seven per week can run more than $2,000 a year.

The question needs to be raised: Could there be too much focus, perhaps, on erections at 40? After all, the sexual health of most 40-year-olds revolves a lot more around issues of aging than it does around those of impotence. Once again, a focus away from erections and onto mindfulness during sex can go a long way. It's how sexual health improves. And it starts not by revisiting or improving upon what you used to do, but starting, in a way, anew. How, exactly, some might ask? One answer would be to work on your powers of touching and receiving touch. Millions of sexual partners don't give this skill much thought; they should.

Elysabeth Williamson, a Boulder, Colorado, yoga instructor, spends hours each week working on this very notion. Williamson notes that improving sex lives certainly isn't her main goal. That has, however, arisen as a notable side effect of her classes and workshops, which teach varying forms of nonsexual yet intimate touch through partner yoga, among other forms. In particular, a program called Phoenix Rising Therapy, in which she has worked with numerous midlife men as clients, has opened her eyes to what some men sorely lack: connection.

"In relationship with another body, the work is more in your psyche," Williamson says. "We work on active listening skills, the quality of touch, opening up out of your core, and co-breathing." She goes on to relate, speaking of some of her male clients, "They want to be touched, and we work on the surrender aspect of that." Again, it's not about sex, but it is inherently sensual. Some men have even gone into a kind of dream state that started with breathing and touch. "There's probably an intimacy factor," she says, "of being with a woman in such a close way. Fear, grief, and sadness all come up." For decades, it appears, men have been the ones "in charge of" intimate touching in their lives. In many cases, it could use some further development. And Williamson's and others' work is chipping away at that rather large task.

The Prostate: A Midlife Primer

For the first half of a man's life, his prostate is mostly about sex and reproduction. It works. For the second half, it's more about aging, annoyance, and sometimes well-grounded fear. It works, but not nearly as well. Each year, some 210,000 American men over age 40 are diagnosed with prostate cancer. Then again, each year, more than 48 million American men over 40 don't receive that diagnosis.

As a reproductive gland, the prostate has a lot to do with sex hormones. Testosterone from the testicles stimulates the growth of the prostate over time; meanwhile, the prostate manufactures milky prostatic fluid, which helps to make up semen. (Semen also includes sperm from the testicles.) With so much recent interest in prostate disease, people sometimes overlook the fact that a healthy prostate contributes mightily to quite pleasurable orgasms, beginning at about puberty.

Benign prostatic hyperplasia (BPH). During a male's preteen years, the prostate, which rests right below the bladder, behind the rectum, and hard by where the penis begins, is smaller than a grape. It reaches the size of a walnut in early adulthood, then after age 40, it begins to grow again. On occasion, it can reach the size of a grapefruit in one's sixties or seventies, even when cancer isn't present. This steady swelling is why so many middle-aged men get up in the middle of the night to urinate repeatedly. In these cases, known as benign prostatic hyperplasia (BPH), the prostate swells enough to crimp the thin, pliable tube of the urethra. The painful burning feelings that accompany BPH and urination are sometimes mistaken for early signs of prostate cancer and vice versa.

MAN IN HIS TWENTIES   MAN IN HIS FIFTIES

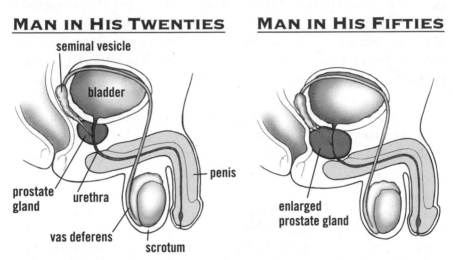

As you age, your enlarging prostate can cause problems with urinary flow by putting the squeeze on your urethra.

On the positive side, drugs or surgery can control most cases. Many men have reported success in preventing and treating BPH using the prescription drug Proscar (finasteride) or extracts of saw palmetto berries, found at many health food stores. In serious cases of BPH, a Roto-Rooter-like procedure called transurethral resection of the prostate (TURP) carves away prostate tissue that impedes the flow of urine. A variation called transurethral needle ablation (TUNA) uses heated needles to kill excess tissue.

Prostatitis. This is the other nagging noncancerous condition that afflicts most men in middle age or after. Basically an irregular inflammation of the prostate, it causes stabs of pain and difficulty urinating. It can be acute or chronic, but surgery is rarely necessary. Antibiotics often cure prostatitis, but not always. Treatments are sorely lacking; sometimes doctors actually prescribe frequent sex or masturbation as a way to tame it.

Before any man is told he has prostate cancer, BPH and prostatitis must be carefully ruled out. That's one reason why there seems to be so much waiting time before a definitive diagnosis of prostate cancer is made.

There are two low-tech ways to make a preliminary diagnosis of prostate cancer: the standard-but-embarrassing digital-rectal exam (DRE) and the relatively new PSA blood test. (The high-tech methods are ultrasound and biopsy.) While nearly every man over 40 submits to a DRE every year or two as part of a physical exam, PSA tests—which measure the amount of prostate-specific antigen (a protein) in the blood—are not yet universally performed. Perhaps they should be,

How Prostate Surgery Can Help Your Golf Game

It may have started as an inside joke, but it ended up as scientific fact: Prostate surgery helps improve golf scores. In a study of 55 golfers with prostate cancer who had radical prostatecomy surgery at Columbia-Presbyterian Hospital in New York City, 36 (or 60 percent) of them reported that their golf game had improved postoperatively.

"The most common long-term side effects of surgery are urinary incontinence and impotence," reported 16-handicap golfer Mitchell C. Benson, M.D., vice-chairman of the department of urology at Columbia-Presbyterian Medical Center in New York City, who conducted the study. "Patients were asked, 'What was your handicap before surgery?'; 'Has your game improved/worsened?'; and 'What do you think is responsible for the improvement/worsening of your golf game?'"

Dr. Benson shared his findings at an annual meeting of urologists in Lisbon, Portugal. It turns out that those 36 prostate patients who became better golfers (dropping their handicaps, on average, by 3) did so by swinging more slowly and rhythmically, mostly due to fear of incontinence should they swing the club too hard. A lesser number, only 8 out of 55 (about 15 percent), said their games got worse because they swing too slowly—also due to fears of leaking urine while they played.

Dr. Benson's conclusion, which gave the doctors in attendance a rare chance to smile, is that "radical prostatectomy appears to offer a golf advantage that has not been reported with radiation therapy."

even though the test isn't perfect and the costs would be enormous. Research shows that the key reason for the rise of the PSA test in higher-risk individuals is that less than 20 percent of prostate cancer cases can be detected using the digital exam.

On balance, when a well-trained urologist combines the information from a DRE (how the gland feels and whether there are lumps) with the level of PSA density in the blood (typically ranging from 1.0 to 10 and higher), he has a rather good idea of what is going on in the prostate. Although the PSA test is just one diagnostic tool, there are good reasons for you to request a PSA at your next checkup. For one thing, a PSA test can detect up to 25 percent of all prostate cancers an average of four years before diagnosis would be made without the test, according to the National Institute on Aging.

The trend line of PSA is more important than the mere number. By keeping a chart of your PSA, beginning in middle age, you will have valuable information that men would never have had 15 years ago. Most men should have the test every two years beginning at age 50 and every year after 60. However, African-Americans and men who have family members with prostate cancer are at highest risk. They should get baseline PSAs in their early thirties and then annual exams starting at age 40. As with tracking cholesterol to prevent a heart attack, by tracking your PSA, you may be able to ward off a major medical event. The reference levels are:

- Less than 4.0 nanograms per milliliter (ng/ml) = safe
- 4.1 through 10.0 ng/ml = cause for concern
- 10.1 through 20 ng/ml = cause for serious concern (but not necessarily cancer)
- 20 through 100+ ng/ml = likely cancer cells

If you are diagnosed with cancer, you'll want to know both your PSA level and your Gleason grade, which measures, on a scale from 1 to 10, the aggressiveness of the tumor cells.

In many cases, urinary problems will be the tip-off to prostate cancer. But, as with BPH, you may notice absolutely nothing out of the ordinary in the early stages. On occasion, you may see blood or pus in your urine or experience burning pain from blocked urine flow. Later-stage prostate cancer brings intense pain to the bones, suggesting that malignant cells have spread.

THE VIEW FROM BOTH SIDES OF THE SCALPEL

"I do not think that radical prostatectomy is a particularly painful operation," declares Patrick C. Walsh, M.D., director of the urology department at Johns Hopkins Medical Institutions in Baltimore and arguably the top prostate cancer surgeon in the United States.

"The last person who can comment appropriately on pain is a surgeon," says Michael Korda, a patient of Dr. Walsh's, who is editor-in-chief of Simon and Schuster publishers and author of *Man to Man: Surviving Prostate Cancer.* Korda, however, takes pains to explain he is "a great admirer of Pat Walsh," and under-scores it by saying, "The bottom line is that Dr. Walsh promised I would be all right—in terms of cancer—and I am. I send friends to him."

Dr. Walsh is best known for having developed, in the early 1980s, a surgical technique that has enabled thousands of men to regain their potency after prostate surgery—something that was unheard of before. The technique, often called nerve-sparing surgery, salvages the nerve bundles that attach to the prostate and send sexual impulses to and from the penis.

The surgery, through its relative precision, also enables a much higher percentage of prostate surgery patients to regain urinary continence—in many cases, months ahead of typical predictions. By patients' accounts, getting out of diapers in a matter of days or weeks is perhaps a greater achievement than regaining firm erections.

In 1994, Michael Korda received a prostate cancer diagnosis at Memorial Sloan-Kettering Cancer Center in New York City, the top cancer hospital in the United States. A few weeks later, however, he ended up choosing Dr. Walsh as his surgeon, despite the fact that he'd have to travel to the doctor's practice in Baltimore, some 200 miles from Korda's home. By way of explanation, Korda detailed Dr. Walsh's ac-complishments and said that he wanted the best possible care.

He didn't leave his recovery solely in the doctor's hands however. Korda penned *Man to Man,* an account of his own prostate cancer diagnosis and surgery, to help men make it through their own harrowing diagnoses with a focus on good treatment outcomes. During his free time these days, Korda sits on a panel of experts for the Harvard School of Public Health's Cancer Prevention Committee. The operative word is prevention. Setting treatment aside, he is now helping to figure out how men may avoid prostate cancer altogether.

Preventive Health: What to Eat and What Not to Drink

Like the PSA test, the concept of prostate cancer prevention is new to urology. But that doesn't mean that you should wait for a tradition-minded doctor to catch up with the latest literature. There are at least four well-founded beliefs about promoting prostate health and minimizing inevitable declines.

- Research at the Harvard School of Public Health and elsewhere points to a low-fat diet as being protective. Over 20 or more years, the benefits could be major.
- The National Cancer Institute recently reported that lycopene—a substance found in tomato sauces—is incredibly prostate-friendly. So much so that men who had just two servings of some form of cooked tomatoes per week had 34 percent lower risks of developing prostate cancer.
- Increasing your intake of zinc, either by eating pumpkin seeds or taking a daily supplement containing up to 20 milligrams of the mineral, can forestall a number of prostate problems. Doses above this amount must be taken under medical supervision.
- Drink less alcohol (it stresses the prostate) and a lot more water. Dehydration, it turns out, also places undue pressure on the prostate.

Treating Prostate Cancer Today

It was after office hours, and the doctor was stumped. "I'm not sure what I would tell him, if he had prostate cancer," said Catherine Klein, M.D., a medical oncologist at the University of Colorado Health Sciences Center in Denver, answering my question as to how, hypothetically, she would counsel her own husband.

Dr. Klein fervently believes that there is no "right" answer for men in America today when confronted with the increasingly common question of how to treat cancer of the prostate gland. The choices, more plentiful than ever, each have their proponents and detractors. See "Know Your Options" on page 156 for a brief summary of the five major methods of prostate cancer treatment. Yet as Dr. Klein explained

By the Numbers

Type of Cancer Cases	Diagnoses per Year	Deaths per Year
Prostate	210,000	41,800
Breast (in women)	180,200	43,900
Lung	98,300	94,400
Colon	66,400	27,000
Skin melanoma (in men)	22,900	17,400

SOURCE: American Cancer Society

to nearly 30 members of the prostate cancer support group Man-to-Man who had gathered not long ago at Columbia Swedish Medical Center in Denver, even the best answers are often best guesses. There simply aren't enough meaningful data to properly compare the prospects of, say, surgery versus radiation in treating the disease. Or, for that matter, "smart bomb" therapy versus "watchful waiting." Each case needs to be weighed on its own.

In Dr. Klein's case, her husband happened to be perfectly healthy and 49 years old—exactly the age at which men begin to take a much greater interest in the workings of their prostate glands than they did at 40 or 45 (though 80 percent of diagnoses are made after age 65). "I guess I'd guide him toward surgery," Dr. Klein said at last, with a quick qualifier: "But that's largely because he is young, and my bias is that getting it out is better than doing nothing."

In 1998, having reached arguably epidemic proportions, prostate cancer was expected to strike some 210,000 American men and kill an estimated 42,000. It is the second leading cancer killer (after lung cancer) among American men, while, for unknown reasons, African-American men have the highest rate of prostate cancer incidence in the world. With the aging of the baby boom population and the rise of early detection methods such as the PSA blood test, these numbers aren't expected to decline soon. As millions more men move into and through middle age, urologists now are able to spot cancer in the reproductive gland years before they used to notice it. (And over half of all prostate cancers are discovered when still localized.)

(continued on page 158)

KNOW YOUR OPTIONS

Here are the five most common types of prostate cancer treatment available. While surgery, or radical prostatectomy, is the most common type of treatment today for relatively young, otherwise-healthy men with prostate cancer, other forms of treatment have gained favor in recent years. Still, urologists and oncologists say it may take 5 to 10 more years to collect solid, scientifically sound data to make comparisons of the various procedures more equitable. Until then, patients are advised to seek second and third opinions before making their treatment decisions.

Cryosurgery

What it does: Freezes the prostate gland using supercooled liquid nitrogen, killing all tissues within the gland—healthy and cancerous

Risks: Because the urethra runs through the prostate, it must be warmed during the procedure to protect it; as a result, some cancer cells may be missed near the warmed sites; less incontinence and impotence are reported than with surgery or external beam radiation

Recovery time: Can be done as an outpatient procedure; takes two to three hours to perform; limited or no blood loss

Outlook: Limited data exist on long-term survival rates; few doctors have years of experience performing it; as imaging techniques improve, so may prospects for cryosurgery as primary and secondary treatment; it is one of the few treatments that can be repeated

Anatomical Radical Prostatectomy

What it does: Removes entire prostate gland and cancer within through surgery; also removes part of urethra that runs through prostate

Risks: Short-term immobility (due to incision); 10 to 20 percent of patients suffer long-term impotence; less than 5 percent of patients suffer long-term incontinence, though more than 50 percent experience short-term incontinence

Recovery time: Generally 2 to 3 months for full mobility; up to 18 months for recovery from all side effects

Outlook: Surgery considered the gold standard for early-stage cancer in men ages 40 to 65; "nerve-sparing" surgery (to protect potency) relatively new—not all surgeons are adept at it

External Beam Therapy

What it does: Uses x-rays and radioactive elements to bombard the prostate and kill or shrink cancerous tissues; patients submit to six to eight weeks of painless daily five-minute radiation sessions

Risks: Urinary flow may be obstructed due to scar tissue buildup in prostate; up to 50 percent probability of impotence following treatment; small probability of damage to rectum and associated fecal incontinence

Recovery time: Minimal, though fatigue often reported near end of treatment period; many patients continue to work during treatment

Outlook: Ten-year survival rates are improving and approaching those of surgery; however, unlike surgery, some prostate cancer cells (however few) often persist within first year of treatment

Radiation Seed Implant Therapy

Employs small metal tubes (seeds) containing radioactive material to deliver high doses of radiation precisely to tumor sites

Risks: Swelling of prostate following implants impedes urination; fewer side effects than surgery or external beam therapy, however; high doses of radioactivity may affect bladder or bowel function if improperly applied

Recovery time: Minimal, as procedure is designed to affect smallest area of tissue possible while remaining effective; patients can return to work or home within one or two days

Outlook: Future appears bright for seed implants, also called brachytherapy, as doctors gain experience with new imaging tools; only seven years of data currently exist, however

Hormone Therapy

What it does: Shrinks tumors and cancer cells by starving them of androgen hormone (testosterone) that normally fuels malignant cell growth; mimics action of castration, using drugs such as goserelin acetate (Zoladex), flutamide (Eulexin), or bicalutamide (Casodex)

Risks: Severe hot flashes, weight gain, swollen breasts, limited amount of time in which treatment is effective

(continued)

KNOW YOUR OPTIONS—CONTINUED

Recovery time: No time lost from work or home life, however, treatment value lessens after two years as body adapts to hormones, reducing their efficacy

Outlook: Bright, but not perhaps as sole treatment; one of the few areas of prostate cancer treatment on which surgeons, oncologists, and radiologists all agree: Hormones shrink prostate tumors, which boosts success of most other treatments

Watchful Waiting

What it does: Uses a set schedule of blood tests and doctor visits to monitor level and rate of change of prostate-specific antigen (PSA) in blood; also uses information from digital-rectal exam (DRE)

Risks: While doctor is waiting or monitoring PSA levels over months and years, some cancer cases may grow so fast as to escape the prostate gland, making surgery or radiation treatments of little use

Recovery time: Not applicable

Outlook: For men ages 80 and over or those in otherwise poor health who may not fare well after surgery and radiation, may (surprisingly) be best option; for younger men, jury is still out—even though many cases of prostate cancer are slow-growing

That should be welcome news, but as urologic surgeon Norm Peterson, M.D., of the Denver Health Medical Center, asks, "Does screening lead to surgery that needn't be done?" Personally, he thinks not. In 1997, he operated successfully on Denver mayor Wellington Webb, 54, in a case that was caught early—and in time—with the aid of PSA screening.

Even so, you may be able to take your time just after a diagnosis. "The very first step I tell men [to take] who have just been diagnosed with prostate cancer is, 'Don't panic—you're going to live for a while,'" says Ken Goldberg, M.D., 50, a urologist and director of the Male Health Institute near Dallas. "For the most part, they are ready to jump and reach for a cure. And that's where a lot of men get mad, get frustrated." They don't always hear—or aren't clearly told—about the risks of urinary incontinence or impotence that occur after various treatments. "They hear 'cancer' and want it out of there," Dr. Goldberg says. "They want an operation." Who can blame them? But if there is any trait of prostate cancer that can be considered close to good news, it is that prostate cancer cells, compared with other cancers, are often described as slow-growing. The not-as-good news is that millions of men who avoid digital-rectal exams and potentially early diagnoses may do so because they focus on the "slow" aspect and dismiss the "growing." Slow-growing tumors, however, can still be lethal.

In recent years, debates about hormone and cryosurgical (freezing and thawing) treatments have swept through prostate cancer support groups and medical circles and onto the Internet. Doctors who perform surgery proclaim their method as the best. So do supporters of newer forms of radiation therapy. So how does a man go about fighting (or not fighting) the so-called male cancer that may (or may not) result in his early death? "The way to summarize it is controversy," offers Dr. Goldberg, who has treated up to 300 prostate cancer patients in his private practice and authored a book titled *How Men Can Live as Long as Women*. "Maybe uncertainty is a better word."

While each of the major treatments has shown at least slight improvements in incontinence and impotence rates over the past decade, the more critical numbers will remain the 10-year recurrence and survival rates. So even as the prospects of less-invasive procedures such as radiation seed implants and cryosurgery appear brighter, the medical proof of their efficacy has been slower to appear.

"There isn't any 'right' answer," Dr. Klein reminds men. "As a doctor, you struggle with this a lot." At the same time, Dr. Klein points out that in terms of funding, breast cancer and AIDS research are decades ahead of prostate cancer research. Between 1991 and 1996, the Department of Defense—the nation's second largest source of cancer research support—earmarked $485 million for breast cancer research, compared with less than $20 million for prostate cancer. Both diseases are expected to cause between 40,000 and 45,000 deaths each year. Dr. Klein and her colleagues hope that prostate cancer patients can learn from women's health groups and AIDS activists in lobbying for more funds as well as by volunteering for research studies when they have the chance. But men, and especially older men, don't join clinical trials with the same fervor that women do, Dr. Klein adds.

STDs: A Guide for Grown-Ups

"Aren't we done worrying about sexually transmitted diseases (STDs) now that we're middle-aged?" Good question. Here's the tough answer: "The thing I see in this area, among men most often in the 40-plus group," says Dr. Goldberg, "is the guy who does something on the side. He may not have anything, but he sure thinks he does. Guilt and anxiety drive him in here. Some tend to be repeat visitors, and they certainly have reason to be concerned. One guy in his late thirties recently came in—very successful, has a wife and family. He came in because of bumps he felt on his penis. He said he had gone back to someone he'd been with before and she'd given him herpes. He couldn't believe that would happen at this point in time. He couldn't believe he could do that to his wife. Some of these guys feel bulletproof." Stories like this are the reason you should read on.

HIV and AIDS. As we move into the third decade of the HIV/AIDS watch in America, we can begin to feel better, if only slightly, about the prospects of beating this most deadly sexually transmitted disease. From its murky origins as GRID (Gay-Related Immune Disorder) in the early 1980s, HIV/AIDS has taken a brutal, selective toll on the nation and the world. Disproportionate numbers of poor people, intravenous drug users, and gay men have died from the disease.

At last count the grim numbers were 612,000 AIDS cases reported in the United States since the disease's first appearance, with 380,000 deaths recorded. (The incidence of HIV is much higher—about 1.7 million cases since 1981.) Now the good news. For the years 1994 to 1997, the introduction of new drug regimens (including combining AZT and other drugs with protease inhibitors) has slowed the march of AIDS cases in the United States. Both AIDS cases and AIDS deaths showed drops, while an increasing number of people with HIV, the virus that causes AIDS, were living longer.

For men entering middle age, whether married or single, the chances of contracting HIV are not much different than they were 10 years ago. The bottom line is behavior, not age. It's about knowing your HIV status (home test kits are now available) and knowing the status of your partner (or all of your partners). If you're unsure of a partner's status, use condoms and dental dams, when appropriate, to block the exchange of bodily fluids. And don't let your guard down just because

A GUIDE TO MALE SEXUAL HEALTH SOURCES

American Foundation for Urologic Disease
1126 North Charles
Baltimore, MD 21201
This is a good organization to contact for fact sheets about and comparisons of various prostate conditions, including but not limited to cancer.

The Prostatitis Foundation
Parkway Business Center
2029 Ireland Grove Road
Bloomington, IL 61704

American Social Health Association
P.O. Box 13827
Research Triangle Park, NC 27709
This organization is an excellent source of information about sexually transmitted diseases.

doctors have gotten better at keeping people with AIDS alive longer. As of this writing, there is still no cure.

Herpes. The numbers are startling: Up to 40 million Americans have genital herpes, although perhaps 25 million don't even know they have it. It is spread when virus particles are shed during sexual contact. The hallmarks of this viral STD include blisters or lesions on the genitals, buttocks, and thighs, which appear four to eight days after infection. They then recur a few times each year, for varying lengths of time, bringing pain, swollen glands, headache, and malaise.

The important point to note about herpes today is that, unlike what doctors believed 10 years ago, the disease can be spread even when there are no apparent sores or visible outbreaks. The "shedding" of the herpes virus has been tracked more closely and it is every bit as contagious as it was in the early to mid-1990s. So now the rules are: if you're looking for near 100 percent safety, no unprotected sex during an outbreak or between outbreaks. Fortunately, if you already have herpes, the use of valacyclovir (Valtrex) or another antiviral drug may reduce the risk of transmission to less than 5 percent in many cases. If you don't have the disease, make certain you know your partner's status.

Chlamydia. Your teenagers probably know more about this STD than you do, yet it strikes, often silently, four million times each year in the United States. That makes chlamydia the most prevalent sexually transmitted disease, by far. It is spread by contact with mucous membranes, and it sometimes announces its arrival with burning and itching in the penis or pain accompanying urination. Abdominal pain and fever are other notable symptoms, but again, they are not universal. Antibiotics are effective against chlamydia, but if left untreated, it can cause infertility and sterility. The only good news to report here is that incidence seems to drop with age.

Gonorrhea and syphilis. Both of these STDs, known as the premier venereal diseases a few generations ago, are caused by bacterial infections, and both date back centuries. Gonorrhea is much more common, striking at least one million times each year in the United States, while syphilis afflicts roughly 150,000 persons annually. Gonorrhea may not have visible symptoms, but many sufferers report pain with urination that occurs from 2 to 10 days after infection. This STD is spread by contact with infected mucous membranes in the mouth, throat, and genitals.

Syphilis is passed by sexual contact from genitals to genitals, or from mouth to genitals. Its hallmark is a canker sore that may first appear up to three months after infection, primarily on the mouth, penis, or around the rectum (in women, sores may appear on the vulva and be barely noticeable). If untreated, severe fevers may follow. Both diseases respond well to antibiotics—the sooner the better.

Genital warts or human papillomavirus (HPV). You hardly want to think about warts on your genitalia, but it probably wouldn't hurt to know that genital warts are highly contagious and that they are spread by a sneaky virus. There are approximately one million new cases of HPV in the United States each year. It's tricky in part because there are so many variations of the virus and because they can go undetected for weeks or months. They often appear on the penis, in the urethra, or in rectal areas. Sometimes, the small, painless, fleshy warts disappear without medication; at other times, doctors must remove them by freezing (cryosurgery) or laser surgery. There are no appropriate antibiotics, as the disease is viral, not bacterial, in nature.

Urinary tract infections (UTIs) and cystitis. Technically speaking, urinary tract infections and the bladder infections known as cystitis are not STDs, because they have numerous causes. They commonly occur when tissues around the urethra are irritated, making them more vulnerable to infection by normally occurring bacteria. "You can get bladder infections from having sex too much," one 41-year-old married woman told me, speaking of the (painful) first few months after her marriage.

But while that may be true, it's not the whole story. Men and women may also get bladder infections when lower urinary tract infections aren't properly treated and spread upward into the body. A lower urinary tract infection typically hurts while you urinate, whereas cystitis causes pain during and after urination. Antibiotics and a quick diagnosis are your best bets to control UTIs. In the research for this book, I was surprised to find out how many men, especially single men, mentioned their midlife battles with UTIs. Sexual health experts offered two possible causes of the uptick, though this has not been well-studied: one, a relationship between age-related inflammation of the prostate and resultant infections; and two; a higher incidence of "silent" STDs, including chlamydia, among many midlife men than perhaps were evident a generation ago.

Condoms Come of Age

As a never-married man of 40, Norm R., an Atlanta contractor, has dated half a dozen women over the past few years. He considers himself a sensitive lover and a rather selective partner. I asked him, one night, how the AIDS era has affected his love life.

"It's affected me marginally," he said. "I say marginally because venereal diseases have always been around, and I've always been careful. I also say naively, because I have always been a little less alarmed about AIDS than you'd think I would be considering the hype that goes on in the press: I imagined it was mostly a homosexual problem. Safe sex involves condoms, and I've had a level of trust, along with basic safe sex practices.

"However," Norm added, "I've noticed in the last 6, 8, 10 years, that no one takes this frivolously any more. Ten years ago, the discussions were about birth control and a little bit about whether you were healthy—meaning herpes. It was situational before: Are you healthy? Now it's, 'What's your sex life been like? Who have you been with?' If you want to get rid of that condom, then you have that big conversation."

"The question I had," said Joe S., 41, a married East Coast music critic, "was: Is there such a thing as a condom that doesn't subtract from the experience? I'd always heard about lambskin ones, but they don't really protect you from STDs or other infections. And my wife kept getting infections for some reason. So we needed to use some protection for a while."

I considered Joe an aficionado when it came to condoms, because, like anything he does, he researches the heck out of it first. In this case, he and his wife took this as an opportunity, not a challenge. They put libido and latex together for a few weeks' time. "I'd occasionally used one of the standard brands, in my youth, but I found them so distasteful that I could never imagine using them as a form of birth control," Joe said. These days, however, he was pleased to find LifeStyles Xtra Pleasure condoms, made by Ansell, an Australian firm. They are wider than the old skintight condoms, with an oversized, but quite effective, bulbous tip. The extra latex surface area is put to good use during intercourse—all sorts of new friction, providing a frisson.

Also rating highly in Joe's highly unscientific survey was the Crown Skinless condom, a Japanese import that is incredibly thin and allows more than a modicum of heat transfer. Finally, the silky domestic standby, the trusty lambskin condoms that have been sold for years, passed muster in our 41-year-old judge's and wife's opinions. Of course, any aficionado knows that these rubbers aren't exactly rubber— and they aren't made of lambs' skin. The truth is, it's lamb intestines that you slide around your erection. Also, the truth is, you don't much think about materials and composition in the moments that follow.

Family Matters: Now More Than Ever

The first thing to remember about midlife family life is that, for the most part, you're not screwing it up. This bears repeating: You're not screwing it up. As family responsibilities mount between the ages of 40 and 45, whether you are married, otherwise partnered, separated, or divorced, you'll likely feel pressed. You'll also likely feel stressed, perhaps by children, perhaps by parents. Meanwhile, at the office, these are supposed to be the peak, go-go-go years for millions of career-oriented men and, increasingly, women.

"In 1950, 12.6 percent of married mothers with children under age 17 worked for pay," reports Arlie Russell Hochschild, sociologist and author of *The Time Bind*. "By 1994, 69 percent did so." That's a 500 percent increase in working moms, in less than half a century. No wonder dads are feeling it, too. In addition, the hours both men and women put in at work have increased steadily over the past few decades.

One reason you're not screwing up is that, at 40, chances are that you've just arrived at this sometimes intractable crossroads. You would do well to remind yourself and your family that there's time to work things through, even when it feels as if you're cursed with a lack of time. Welcome to the club, wizened 42-year-olds say. Pick your spots of time with your family. Don't promise what you can't provide. Be consistent.

And even though you're talking about emotions and activities instead of money and individual retirement accounts, go ahead and make an annual budget. Then, if you're feeling optimistic, make a two- or three-year budget of family time. Tough as it may seem, it will enable you to figuratively breathe a bit. You'll be able to "air out" your family time, much the same way that you have long-term financial

A Father's Way with "Family Planning"

This is not your father's family planning. But during an interview I had with Boyd P., a 42-year-old church-going Mormon father of four from Arizona, I was struck by the concerted effort he had made to budget his family time into his yearly office calendar. He offered it as a template of sorts, proof that dads do more than make deals at work.

Date	Event	Family Members Involved
Apr. 29–May 2	Women's Conference (Utah)	Tammy
May 16	Utah Dance Recital	Cathy, Boyd
June 10–15	Stake Youth Conference (Utah)	Boyd, Tammy, Jeff, Susan
June 10–15	Trip to Grandmother's in Tucson	Cathy, Chandra
June 21–23	Nevada Bankers Speech (Lake Tahoe)	Boyd, Tammy
July 12–20	Midwest and Hill Cummorah Pageant	Whole family
July 14–17	Girls' Camp	Susan, Boyd
July 18–25	BYU Gymnastics Camp (Provo)	Cathy
July 19–25	Shakespeare Workshop (Cedar City)	Susan
July 23–26	Shakespeare Festival/Pick up Susan	Whole family
Aug. 14–15	Rafting Weekend (Arkansas River)	Whole family
Aug. 28–29	Church Campout with Chief Hosa	Whole family
Nov. 25–28 (Thanksgiving)	Family Reunion (YMCA; Colorado)	Whole family

investment goals as well as short-term, liquid cash for your immediate future.

The second thing to know about the new world of family, which debuted during the 1980s, is that the new math is frightening. It is why you might feel you are botching things at home even when you aren't. Consider this: Now that more than half the women in America are working, for millions, day care has become a necessity, not a luxury. And if you and your wife or ex-wife work, there's a good chance that your children will be in day care or school up to nine hours a day, often five days a week, followed by maybe one good hour of family time. So do the math: $9 + 9 + 9 + 9 + 9 = 1 + 1 + 1 + 1 + 1$. In other words (or other numbers), $45 = 5$. Does it? How can this be?

As sociologists would say, this means that 45 hours of nonparental care each week must be balanced, from a typical dad's perspective, by one hour a night—or five hours per workweek—of quality time. (We'll just assume, for now, that all is perfect, warm, and wonderful on the weekends.) Of course, this doesn't work out mathematically. For the men who have children (and this chapter is mostly aimed at those who do), serious questions about commitment to career versus family will arise, as may issues about caring for parents. Those in the middle of the baby boom generation (that is, those born between 1955 and 1960) find themselves squeezed from both ends, often without a clear sense of how to allocate time, money, and emotions in the way that's most beneficial to all, including to themselves.

The key question is what do you, as a midlife man, do to maximize the midweek quality time? And what do you do to assuage dad guilt? That's what this chapter will tackle. You'll find, at a minimum, a handful of real-life ways to improve family time. While well shy of perfection, this may be enough to right your course. Because just as nobody's perfect, nobody's family is, either.

Gone Fishin'; Not Taking the Corporate Bait

"Here's what I think of as quality time," said Ronnie S., 42, a Dallas advertising account executive, husband to Katrina, 41, and father of Laura, 9, and Sam, 7. "For Katrina, it's taking the kids to school or even walking them to the bus stop. Quality time for me is coaching Laura's soccer team, which is one hour of soccer a week, or going to Sam's game once a week. Maybe because Katrina is no longer working, it takes an enormous burden off me." Ronnie can work harder at working during the week, then work harder at playing on weekends.

When I asked him what he thought about the formula in which 45 hours of day care butt up against 5 to 10 hours of so-called quality time, he didn't have to pause and think. "It doesn't make any sense," he said. "What we decided, after Sam was born, was that we had tried it for a while, but the pressures were so big. Plus, my income was bigger. It just made it a no-brainer; Katrina would leave her business. Not only were the kids better off, our marriage was better off, too.

"The focus was never, 'Ron, can you quit your job?'" he added. "The question was, for her, 'If you are dividing your life as mother, wife, and businesswoman and you're putting 50 percent into each, that doesn't make sense.'" Nor does the math work out. "So we threw it out of the window. Her quitting meant that, because she was home, I could come home at night not feeling guilty. I leave at 6:15 in the morning and get home at 7:00 P.M. But I shut out my job completely on weekends." His last comment was said with a touch of machismo. He wanted me to know that he absolutely leaves the ad agency stuff downtown on Friday night. It'll cook till Monday. That's the deal, or so he thought.

Later in our interview, Ronnie contradicted his comment about "not feeling guilty" when he gets home at night, enabling me to see the conflict that so many men feel but do not express. At one point, he told me that kids deserve close-up, personal time with their parents, and "you can't make it up on the weekend." It's not that easy. So he counts doing homework with Laura and Sam as quality time, as unsatisfying as it may seem to seven- and nine-year-olds. One night, for instance, it was long division with Sam. Ronnie harked back to the days before calculators, when you had to draw the division boxes, move the decimal points over a bit, and proceed to make sense of a bigger number being divided by a smaller one. "I had to go back and learn it again," he said. But to see Sam's face when he connected, Ronnie added, was worth the time spent, 10 times over.

"Any face-to-face time with my kids is quality time," he added. "I think people make too big a thing of the weekends. For us, it's just that

HOW TO TAME SIBLING RIVALRY IN QUALITY TIME

Sometimes, just when you think you've set aside the right amount of time to spend with your kids on what you hoped would be a perfect Saturday or Sunday, all hell breaks loose. They won't stop fighting with each other, no matter what you say, no matter what you do. This is no way to wind down the week, you think, especially when this was supposed to be your catch-up quality time. But when you stop to analyze the chaos a bit, you may find that it's not so strange or unpredictable. Sibling rivalry has a rhyme and a reason.

Don't think quality time, think solo time. Experts at the Erikson Institute for Advanced Study in Child Development in Chicago believe that the best solution to sibling rivalry is for each parent to take each child for solo time as often as possible. But downplay all the expensive sporting events and ice shows that are so often centerpieces of family time. Instead, put one child in the car when you go for a car wash. Put the other in the minivan when you head off to do the weekly shopping. Take one to the library with you, the other to the garden center. Just make sure that they each have personal attentive time with you, the experts advise. Quite often, that's really all there is to the whole deal. Their rivalry is as much about getting your attention as it is about getting their own way with brother or sis.

Sam and I will go fishing. Or all of us will go out and play golf together—although that can be as stressful as anything." All things considered, he'll take the rowboat versus the golf cart when it comes to family time. But chores may be pushed aside without guilt. Priorities, you know.

However, "in the new job I've taken, technology is starting to horn in on what I consider my private time," Ronnie griped. "Because I have the ability to take a laptop home, the expectation is that I will do that, so I'll always be connected. But I don't want to be connected. I want to shut down. The technology that's supposed to make your life easier also makes it tougher because the expectation is that you'll always be available." Sure, the money is better than at his last job, but is it enough to make him sit down and answer e-mail on Saturday or voice mail on Sunday? Hardly.

The formal agreement he's made with Katrina holds that weekends are totally family time. "So when she and I took a 45-minute walk around the lake a couple months ago, I shared a lot of the pressures of the job with her—specifics, like having to bring the cell phone home on Friday night. The truth of the matter is, now they're asking for more at the office, even though I've always worked a lot of hours. I said, 'Honey, for the first six months or year, I'm counting on you to know that I'm going to be gone a little more than you're used to. Can you help me deal with the guilt?'" (Likewise, in describing the upper echelon employees in the firm she studied for *The Time Bind*, Arlie Hochschild reported, "The 12 top managers I interviewed all worked between 50 and 70-hour weeks.") He continued, "My kids know that Daddy has a new job. They actually help me deal with it. Laura even said, 'Dad, are you okay? Is something wrong? Are you mad?' I had to tell her that I wasn't mad; my mind was just somewhere else."

Ronnie is adamant that either he or Katrina or both be at every one of the kids' soccer and baseball games. "It kind of sets up a schedule for us," he said. "Then it's just dividing up who goes to each game. We try to balance that so that we're spreading ourselves equally. As far as other times, like spring break and Christmas vacation, my time off is dictated by my kids' school's Christmas break."

Most of us have gotten used to Take Your Daughter to Work Day. But Ronnie takes that idea one step further. The entire family makes occasional trips downtown to see Dad's office, the place that they so often call to talk with him. On the days when he's going to be working late or heading straight to the airport after work, it helps, he said, for them to have an image of his office and the people with whom he works. It's no wonder that Hochschild's full book title is *The Time Bind: When Work Becomes Home and Home Becomes Work*.

Some boundaries still remain, however. In Ronnie and Katrina's case, the subjects of moving and job promotions have arisen repeatedly. Over the past seven years, Ronnie has turned down two promotions that would have required him to move. "Each potential move has become more of a family issue than a work issue," he said. "It's not that I lost ambition, but becoming a vice president at the agency wasn't as important as coaching Friday night soccer. I would tell my boss, 'You know, my wife doesn't want to move and my kid has special health needs.' He seemed to understand. But in the old days, if you did that, you were gone. Guess what—I wasn't gone. I came back whole."

To underscore the difference a generation makes, I asked Ronnie if his dad would've made the same decision. "No, he would have said, 'This is my job.' We moved around; his focus was 100 percent on the job. My focus is: Do I have an opportunity to make twice as much money if we move? If not, will it give me a better quality of life?"

We move, as family men around 40, from quality time to quality of life. When Ronnie and I spoke on a day in midsummer, he talked a lot about fishing with his son and a bit about his involvement with Indian Princesses with his daughter. The father/daughter wilderness weekends, where there's a one-on-one ratio between dads and daughters, is the main reason Ronnie commits time to the Princesses. "It's a lot more personal than Girl Scout campouts," he said. "Plus, Laura doesn't like fishing so much."

Evidently, this topic triggered bittersweet memories of his own childhood. After he criticized his father for not being around much during his grammar school years, he also said, "I didn't grow up with resentment, but you're 'me-centric' when you're little. I remember that fishing with my father was the only time I could relate to him when I was young. When I got to high school, he bought a boat that we could barely afford. We went to a bunch of lakes around Madison, Wisconsin, and he taught me responsibilities on that boat. My dad gave me a love for fishing, and I knew it was time we could spend together. Today, it's time that I can completely relax. I am totally there. Maybe that's what he gave me—a legacy. It's a great memory."

Do Dads Matter?

I was surprised to find a cover story in, of all places, the *New Yorker* that asked the question "Do Parents Matter?" "Of course," I thought. I figured it must be a case of headline bait-and-switch to scare some parents into buying that issue. Then I read the 5,000-word article, which mostly featured the work of Judith Rich Harris, an author who unearthed findings that showed that, when it comes to how kids develop their personalities, children's peer groups seem to matter every bit as much as, and perhaps more than, parental influence. She summarized her findings in a controversial book entitled *The Nurture Assumption*, which kicked up a fuss among family therapists. Two weeks after the *New Yorker* story, *Newsweek* published a similar cover story.

Harris's findings, which were hailed at a national conference of American psychologists in the summer of 1998, added another aspect to the ongoing debate about nature versus nurture in child development. They implied that parents may be trying too hard to shape their kids' development by reading them bedtime stories religiously, engaging in carefully controlled bouts of quality time, controlling their school and play environments, and so on. What it really comes down to, Harris and her followers argue, is the children's interactions with their peers. It's a "new" form of nurture that counts, not so much parenting or genetics.

Consider: As a dad, when you're trying to get your young child to eat something new, do you nibble it first and then say "Mmmm-mmmm," hoping little Tiffany will take a taste? Or have you noticed that it works a lot better to have a few of Tiffany's toddler friends take a few bites to show her all is okay with the tasty new treat? The implications of the second tactic are that parents would do well to evaluate their children's peer groups a bit more carefully and perhaps expend a bit less effort at shaping the behavior of their kids. (The midlife fathers I spoke with weren't ready to do that, though.) Looking at it another way, the 45 = 5 math once again doesn't work out. Whatever the kids are doing in those 45 hours away from working parents may well have the greater effect.

The "parents matter less" theory has some experts questioning anew all the effort that parents put into trying to raise the best kids around. Parents, however, think, that they are doing the right thing. I talked to a half-dozen fathers and mothers before concluding (albeit unscientifically) that indeed they are doing the right thing. Theory, schmeory, you shape what you can shape. You create positive, loving environments when and where you can. It's not about math. It's about caring, about doing your part, especially if you're pressed for time as a family. Then, too, you don't change generations of parenting behavior because of one new, supposedly groundbreaking theory, no matter how many plaudits or awards a researcher might win.

Divorced but Still Their Dad

The case of Dan T., lends support to the belief that parents do matter. This 42-year-old engineer and salesman from Minneapolis, is a divorced father of three. He didn't plan it like this, not by a long shot. His 10-year marriage broke up 6 years ago, after his wife had an affair. "I'll tell you what," he explained, "I've seen a lot of marriages come and go, with that midlife crisis stuff. But Pam's and my breakup wasn't about that. It was just a 'drifting.'" Remarkable, I thought. A guy gets shafted, and seven or eight years later he calls it 'just a drifting.' Too kind, I thought. Too kind. . . .

Once the pain subsided, he decided to remain close to his ex-wife, mostly for the kids' sake. Then, two years ago, he started dating Shereen, a ticket agent for Northwest Airlines, who is also divorced and has two kids of her own. It's not quite the Brady Bunch, but it's close. In both cases, Dan and Shereen's spouses strayed from their marriages, which means Dan and Shereen can relate to some of the same emotional pain and readjustments.

Dan has also made sacrifices in his career, much the same way that Ronnie did. Dan states flat-out that he would be a vice president of his engineering firm had he taken an offer and moved to the head office in California five years ago. He got the same offer, for the same position, a second time, a few months before our series of interviews. "I pretty much had an open door," he told me. "Someone came and went in the job; now number two is there, an empty-nester with a crappy marriage. She's going to be my boss. That's okay. I wanted to stay here and be close to the kids."

To keep his closeness to his two boys, ages 12 and 15, and to make sure he matters, Dan has long coached both of them on soccer and baseball teams. "This is the ninth year I've coached with my youngest guy," he said. "Want to know where I got it? My dad missed only one high school game of mine. He and Mr. Rushing, my friend's dad, would go to the games together, even the road games. I remember them huddled up in a blanket in the spring. One of my coaches found some old photos and sent them to me. There was my dad, in the background, with no one else in the stands. I tell you, if I have missed stuff with my kids, it's only because of work. And it's not very often."

Preplanned time with the kids is largely dictated by sports and school schedules. Dan works out of his home, so even when his ex-wife is at work, the kids have a parent to come home to after school and during summer vacation. Both parents like that now that the boys are old enough to get in trouble. "If I'm in town," Dan said, "I see them every day after school. It's the exception to the rule if I don't see them during the week."

In terms of formalities, the divorce decree states that Dan has the kids every other weekend and once during the week. He and his ex have reached an amicable settlement. I still wondered how. (I never believed the Bradys were perfect, either.) "It's worked out remarkably well," Dan said, "I think because we said to each other, 'Just because it didn't work out with us, let's not be silly here.' Fortunately, I don't have any problems with her as a parent. And she doesn't have any problems with me going to all the games with the boys."

But that's not quite the whole story. "Most divorced parents play the lawyer game," Dan pointed out. "We didn't. In fact, although we get along really well, I had my attorney put a special clause in the divorce agreement, just in case. It says that when I'm coaching the kids, it doesn't count as a formal visit. I thought of it as we were going through the visitation clauses. I said to the lawyer, 'You know, I coach Jackson in soccer and baseball, and Miles in soccer, baseball, and basketball.' I just wanted to protect myself so that this didn't 'count.' My ex-wife was cool with it. It may have seemed silly to put it in writing, but both attorneys said, 'Why not put it in to be safe?'" And possibly to protect his interests, in case of another kind of "drifting."

As a bonus of sorts, the boys happen to be great athletes. This gives Dan a lot of one-on-one time before and during the games and traveling to and fro. It makes up for the fact that they don't always plan a formal vacation during summer or winter holidays. (They did, though, make it to London last year, even meeting up with Shereen and her kids, who cashed in some airline freebie miles thanks to her job with the airline.)

The part of the story that Dan wishes he could change has to do with the quality time that he missed out on with his stepdaughter, who was seven when he and his ex-wife married. He was only 25, and perhaps not ready to settle into the family routine that he had married into. As she hit her teens, Dan was focusing on the young boys, and thus missed a lot of her "games" in high school (which apparently were not of the sports variety). That still rubs at him a little, although his stepdaughter is now 23 years old and married herself. As she has a two-year-old daughter, Dan is a grandpa at 42, at least through marriage.

"You always kind of wonder," he told me, "Do I have the same passion toward a baby that's . . . well, she's my granddaughter, but not my blood. She was over here last Saturday night; we were babysitting. At one point, I just looked at that little thing and said, 'Shereen, you're only 40; let's have a kid.' She said, 'What? Are you kidding?'" It was the kind of scenario that happens only on television. Or was it?

Sharing Responsibilities, Sharing Lives

There's no denying that fishing, camping, and team sports are solid ways in which fathers can bond both with their children and their wives. Yet sometimes, geography comes into play, as in making the big move across state borders. Other times, it's in a less drastic fashion, as in taking more responsibility for what goes on in the geography of your family's kitchen. Just ask Karl T., 42, a maker of fine jewelry and former Californian who not long ago moved to Santa Fe, New Mexico, largely for the sake of his family. He works out of his home but also subcontracts, or "outsources," as he likes to say, a lot of the rote work that he used to do himself.

A father of two girls, ages 4 and 8, Karl has been married to Julie, a physical therapist, for 13 years. At midlife, he seems proud not only of his family but also of the work that he has put into his marriage and the skills he has honed in the kitchen. He reigns over meals the way most dads reign over lawn-care duties, and he feels closer to his kids because of it. "It started when I was 12," he said. "I was home with my two younger brothers, and my mother would leave me with money to buy groceries and cook, while she was working.

"I used to do a lot of stews that I learned from the Galloping Gourmet on TV. Once, my mom had a fit because I bought fresh mushrooms instead of canned for something called hunter's stew. They were expensive, but I didn't know the difference." Karl kept on cooking his way through high school, until he left for the Navy in his late teens. By the time he married Julie, they realized that he would probably play the Doting Gourmet in their newlywed kitchen. "It just kind of happened," he said. "I'd say I do five dinners a week and she does two. But whoever cooks, the other person cleans up." Often, while he's doing prep in the kitchen of their two-story home and while his wife is at work, the kids play or watch videos within eyesight or earshot him.

As Karl's jewelry business in southern California grew from a one-man shop into a retail store, he and Julie began spending less and less time together. Later, after their first child was born, the stresses hit home. "I'd work all day in the store, maybe she would bring me lunch, then I'd go back to work until we closed at 8:00," he said. "And holidays . . . forget it." For anyone in the jewelry business, Christmas starts in the summer with manufacturing and doesn't let up until after the New Year, when special orders are finished.

"I realized that if I wanted to see my kids grow up, if I wanted to enjoy the wonders of Christmas, I couldn't really have a store," he added. "So I eventually sold my business, and we moved here. Actually, I sold my home and my business in two weeks, and didn't have to list either one. We took that as a sign." Karl, a bearded, rugged-looking fellow, and Julie, a fitness buff who works non-nine-to-five hours as a physical therapist, took at least a half-dozen road trip vacations over the years before they found the right spot. They wanted a spot where he could design jewelry and she could help mend misaligned joints and where the kids could go to public school and thrive.

These days, they take hikes and mountain bike rides together as husband and wife. More than occasionally, they do rides over the red rock landscape with their kids in tow, the youngest one literally strapped into a rugged-wheeled kiddie trailer. Perhaps without realizing it, they were reaffirming the "primary relationship" that brought them together, in the words of marriage and family therapists.

"A certain amount of dependence has shifted in recent years," says Roslyn Schwartz, psychotherapist and director of the Marin Family Therapy Center in northern California, "in which women no longer say to their husbands, 'You're helping out.' It's become, 'You're sharing responsibility,' instead." While that may seem as if it innately means more work and more stress for the average guy and father of two, wives increasingly have become co-wage-earners. This means that, yes, husbands have to pitch in more at home; but they may in fact have more free time if their wives are pitching in big time on the salary front. This wasn't the case just a generation or two ago.

These days, in fact, Julie also acts as a part-time sales representative for Karl's line by making sales calls across the country. With so many multiple roles in the family, there's more juggling than most dads are probably used to seeing on a daily basis. It got a lot more complicated when their second child was born, Karl allowed, joking, "Things were simpler before Erin was a Fig Newton of my hallucination." When I asked him how he and his wife have crafted what seems to be a pretty equitable marriage-and-family unit, he added, more seriously, "I've got to tell you, Julie and I have had a lot of therapy in our 13 years of marriage. The problem is, you get comfortable in a relationship. You get locked into what you're doing." Where there's stress, it helps to have stress relief somehow built in.

So what did they do about the increased complexity and potential for complacency? "We dedicated ourselves to a date night, once a week," Karl said. "We kept it up for about three months. It was great." Unfortunately, when school started for their oldest child, that was the end of date night for a while. How long is "a while?" Neither partner knows.

"There is some research that shows that the more involved a guy gets with his kids," says Schwartz, "the more it becomes helpful to and benefits the marriage." And yet, she adds, the ideal balance can be as elusive as ever, back in the real world. In that world, and very likely in yours, a millennium man/new dad may well ask, "What does it mean if I'm supposed to be the provider and protector, but you can earn more money than I do?" Schwartz answers the question directly: If both parties are "integrated adults," meaning that both can play the roles of protector/provider and can comfortably dance between the two roles, then there's likely to be more harmony within the home than many modern couples ever enjoy.

On the other hand, if they get hung up on the old roles, the new rules won't fit. "This is what leads to conflict and withdrawal," Schwartz says. "There's incredible stress on young folks now, and through it all, I try to convince them that their marriage is their primary relationship, not their kids. 'This is the relationship you chose,' I'll say. 'This is the relationship that is going to go on.'" This is not to suggest, in any way, that kids should be neglected. It instead is meant to serve as a reminder of what it is that will anchor a family through the inevitable swells that lie ahead.

Keeping Work in Perspective

He didn't exactly hear voices, but something was wrong. At about the time that his wife first told him he was talking to himself, which was in his early thirties, Tom S., a Los Angeles real estate developer and father of three—two girls and a boy—wondered if he was addicted to work. Not a workaholic, the term most people favor. But work addicted, because it sounded more severe. "Carol would find me in my office at home, punching numbers into a calculator. I was constantly thinking about a deal. I remember telling my friends at the time, and Carol, that I was addicted. Then I had the heart attack scare."

When something like a heart attack scare hits you squarely in your chest, "you never forget it," Tom said. "I was downtown, working out of our downtown office. I remember saying I wasn't feeling well, that I was going to take a walk. I was dizzy, nauseous. I felt like someone was standing on my chest. I couldn't walk right. My vision was blurry. I couldn't breathe or finish my sentences. There was pain in my left arm." Despite having the classic symptoms of a heart attack, Tom told a colleague he was going to take a walk and headed outside (as if the Los Angeles air would do him any good).

"There's this office plaza courtyard nearby in Century City," he explained, "but it was pretty empty. I remember telling myself, 'If I'm having a heart attack, this is a terrible place to be. I have to get back where people are walking.' A minute later, a colleague saw me. He was coming out of the building. He looked at me and said, 'Let's go to the hospital.'"

It wasn't a heart attack, fortunately. After quickly taking his medical history, the emergency room doctor asked Tom how old he was and what he did for a living. The first answer, 32 , wasn't surprising, but the real estate part was. "Usually it's traders," the doc said. Then he explained to Tom that, at 32, it was highly unlikely that he was having a heart attack. An anxiety attack was more like it. Although the proper tests and precautions would be taken, just to be safe, the doctor "told me a heart attack doesn't usually happen before 40 unless there's a defect," Tom said.

So a friend drove him home that afternoon. He remembers a few more things from that day. One, he didn't want to worry his wife. Two, Carol "wasn't as sympathetic as I thought she would've been." Finally, he remembers worrying about his kids' future. What if he wasn't around for it? Frightening thoughts for a 32-year-old dealmaker.

The next day, Carol drove Tom to work, and on the jammed-up Los Angeles freeway, Tom's symptoms started to recur. It was back to the doctor for more reassurance and maybe more tests. That day, he learned how to recognize symptoms of stress and anxiety, like sweating, knifelike pain, and a nauseated gut. He made his first commitment to working out after his doctor said he had to either exercise a lot more or work a lot less. Being a realistic guy, he chose the exercise. At the office, he worked about the same number of hours. But at home, he turned off the number-crunching as best he knew how.

"Over most of my career, I've arranged it so I could be home at night and not travel. "Because," he added, "you can change everything about your personal and business life with one exception: your kids. You only have one set of kids. And there's a defined period of time when they're going to live with you before they're young adults. A defined 20-year period. It's 100 percent predictable. So you either take advantage of that time or blow it. It wasn't until 4 or 5 years ago that I figured that out. That was about the time I was 35. There was a real estate depression that got me offtrack. When the smoke cleared, a lot of things became clear to me. One of the things I learned, one of the things I started to do at that age, is that I do not work at home. When I'm at the office, I'm going to give it 110 percent."

At 40, after a few heady years of land dealing (but not working at home, except for phone calls, he swears), Tom made plans for his family to move out of their half-million dollar home in Santa Monica and into the Holmby Hills section of town, not far from Beverly Hills. There, they set out to buy a seven-bedroom, five-bath, $2.2-million-dollar home in the old-money section of the community. They don't plan on moving for a good long while.

In addition, Tom has since sold part of his business, to be able to work what he calls normal hours, like 40 a week. As proof of his new emphasis on family time, Tom told me of a recent vacation they had made to Aspen after five years without having taken any vacations that involved flying. (Carol is afraid to fly, but she relented.) Clearly, he's settling in, not settling down. You might say he's getting to know his kids again after a long time, but he'll tell you he's just getting to know them better. For when he talks about Megan, Josh, and Erin, he slows down, as if to give them more time in conversation than he's perhaps given them before. Yet a question still lingers: With all those bedrooms in the new house, will he be able to resist the temptation of putting in a home office? There are only so many playrooms a 41-year-old man and his kids can design.

New Paths to Financial Security

Y ou don't often think of Michael Jordan, probably the greatest basketball player ever, as a failure. Yet Jordan, besides being an NBA idol, role model, pitchman, ambassador, and scratch golfer, readily concedes that he has been a failure more than a few times.

He was cut from his high school basketball team while growing up in North Carolina; in 1994, he tried with all his might to play professional baseball (at the minor league A-level) and failed to hit even a paltry .200 consistently. Then, too, in his memorable 1998 championship run against the Utah Jazz, though he did manage to steal the last game and glory for his team, Jordan shot with just 42.7 percent accuracy—a surprisingly low number for him—during the finals. Maybe now that he is approaching age 40, an offbeat poster of his will become even more popular. It features a photo of him clad in Chicago Bulls garb (sweat-soaked, as usual) with a quote at the bottom that reads, "I've missed more than 9,000 shots in my career. I've lost almost 300 games. Twenty-six times, I've been trusted to take the game-winning shot and missed. I've failed over and over and over again in my life, and that is why I succeed."

When I first saw the poster, displayed in the office of a 41-year-old Chicago investment broker, it seemed odd, because the man I was interviewing for this chapter told me he wasn't exactly an athlete or sports fan. Also, I thought brokers had to be cocky. It got me thinking, soon enough, about failure. It got me thinking about how men face up to it—or fail to—as they maneuver their careers and finances through what typically are the prime earning years of their lives. There are more than enough books on the market that promise to make you a corporate success in 7, 10, 12, or however many steps. This one won't. But it will provide you with forthright glimpses of how men in midlife have turned failures of the past into successes. From these and associated strategies, the hope is that you will be more likely to make meaningful career and money moves when they matter most.

The Stop-Out Exec

Call him the "Almost Millionaire." Or foolish. Either way, Joel C., 41, is the type of guy who thinks large, who was flying high in the computer software world in his late twenties and saw no reason to slow down. By age 31, he was named president of a major software-development firm, one of the youngest presidents in his elite circle of high-tech, high-flying entrepreneurs. At 33, he had the comfortable six-figure income, the glitzy New York/California lifestyle, the husky expense account, the future that looked golden. His love life was active, with a longtime girlfriend whom he loved. All cylinders were firing. Then, in his mid-thirties, the clincher came. After an acquisition, Joel was promoted within the company and was faced with a weighty decision that had to do with his future, with a pension-and-investment plan at work, and, most definitely, with his career arc.

"They had me sign a supplemental pension fund statement," he re-called of his first years at the firm, "which said that if I stayed with the company for 14 years, I would realize a seven-figure sum. (I already had several hundred thousand dollars saved in the pension plan.)" In other words, he was guaranteed a million-dollar payout for his long-term loyalty. And with fewer than five years left to go, he walked away from it.

"Logic says that what I did made no sense," Joel added, some seven years later. "But I had this ability to look far forward. And I wasn't happy in my job, in my life." Not happy with being able to cash out with a million dollars in fewer than five years?

"I had my midlife crisis at 32 and 33," he said. "I walked away from a golden parachute. People said I was crazy. But I wanted to get back to my life, and find my balance. It's just that the crisis was a lot earlier for me. It wasn't around 40, but after I quit the company, I felt at peace again."

When I asked him if he hated what he was doing at the time, he said no. But he also said his personal life had suffered during his go-go-go, bring-in-the-sales years. If there was any failure to correct, that was the part of his life that called for action. "The crisis was personal and professional," he said. "I didn't care for the company at the time. I was ill at ease after all those years. I was also living with someone a lot older than me back then, and I knew if the relationship couldn't go forward, it would feel like a dead end." Joel thought things over, more carefully than those around him might have imagined. And he pulled the plug.

"I felt that the only way to [rearrange things] was to remove myself for a while," Joel said. "I made so much money for a young guy—I felt in conflict about it. I felt my life was going down the wrong path. I was in a great relationship, too, but the timing was wrong. I was so busy in my twenties with [the firm]; I was so focused on the status, money, and power that one day I stopped and said, 'Huh? I don't have a family; I'm not married.' I just came to a stop. They (my mom, dad, everyone), said, 'How could you just walk away?' But I felt intuitively that I was doing the right thing." Most of his contemporaries didn't quite get it, either. It takes a confident soul, and a creative one, to turn this kind of career move into a low-risk proposition.

Joel's pullout makes more sense when you learn that he has a knack for creating business plans. He had a few squirreled away at home, it turns out, before he left his job. One involved a new company he later established, providing consulting services to businesses over the Internet. "I interviewed a lot of experts; helped them serve small businesses and charge them lower rates [than full-line consultants would charge]. It's a business resource institute—a virtual corporation made up of service departments—being put on the Web. I helped build that company, and I was so fascinated with new technology." Not only had he found a way to "add value"—the buzzphrase of the late 1990s—to customers' projects but he had also found a way to "create" value. A key lesson for someone to earn in his thirties, before setting out on his own.

His crisis was more about his career, it turns out, than his age. It wasn't truly a crisis at midlife; he even said as much. But it did turn Joel's world sideways for a few years, beginning with the breakup with his girlfriend after the better part of a decade. At the same time, he figured out a way to "stop out" for a while, live on his savings and get rid of a lot of credit card debt, and rearrange the important facets of his life, beginning with his family and relationships. (In the meantime, he developed his business plans vigorously, as ways of possibly providing for his future.) As for concerns about getting a job, he didn't let them dominate his mindset.

"I hope you know what you are doing," his boss wrote to him in a personal letter after Joel had left, ". . . but I understand very well that you have to feel excited and challenged by what you do."

Edward R. Koller, an executive recruiter and president of the Howard-Sloan-Koller Group in New York City, who has both placed Joel and socialized with him, says, "Joel is a very focused, driven person, who went out of his way to help others. It is rare to find someone who is a good manager, a good salesman, and a good trainer of people. Joel has all three skills. Normally, a [guy of his stature] might have two of the three."

So while Joel's colleagues and family members may have been alarmed by his actions, the oft-quoted psychologist Carl Jung likely would have understood. As the premier sage on life transitions in modern times, Jung was the first scholar, post-Freud, to propose a demarcation between the first and second half of life, with 40 as the midpoint. This point is when men (and women, we now know) begin to think more carefully about the various splits in their lives, such as how they can feel both young and old, how they view creation and destruction simultaneously (parents and family members die; they feel a need to create things or leave a legacy), and how they feel the pull of both attachment and separation (in love lives and within the family).

For Joel, the need to separate superceded all others for a time, until "the industry" came calling him back—literally. The last time we spoke, he had taken a new job in northern California with yet another high-tech start-up company, one that was heavily embedded in the emerging world of Internet business, or e-commerce. More important than the new job, though, is the fact that he got married at age 40 (to a woman 14 years younger) and that, by age 41, he was the father of his first child, a daughter.

"Any idea you have has validity," Joel said. "You just have to write it down and give it form. It starts like that, almost like art. It's a very powerful lesson, no matter what your age. This is what will give you energy; just writing it down in some ways helps you to complete it."

In Joel's case, leaving a great job with a great future was made a bit easier because he felt he had great ideas, all written down and filed, before he fled the nine-to-five. "I've been a modest risk-taker most of my life," he said. "But the time I walked away from a million dollars—that was my biggest risk. But it eventually gave me the love I was missing. And that's what was really irking me."

The Five-Year Plan

"Where will I be five years from now?"

When I first thought about the significance of that question—I mean really gave it some serious brain time—I was 31 years old and without a regular job. It resonated with me. I was an unmarried, underpaid freelance writer at the time, bouncing between magazine assignments and writing a book for men about women and their bodies. During my book research I happened upon a compelling book, *Intimate Partners*, by Maggie Scarf. Intimate it was: "I think Bruce believed, at that time, that the moment I was lubricated I was ready for intercourse," confided one of Scarf's subjects.

What does that have to do with a five-year plan? More than you might think. You see, when Scarf interviewed couples (and when psychotherapists do the same thing in private sessions), she had her subjects frame their futures figuratively. She asked them to envision an ideal situation five years down the road and to imagine a photograph of that situation. Who would be in it and why? What would it look like? Where would it be set? In this way, she was able to get a snapshot, of sorts, of the most important things roiling in the minds of couples who considered themselves frazzled, frustrated, and in many cases, sad. If a husband, wife, or partner, was not in that faux photo of the

REAL LIFE, REAL VOICES

It's a lot easier to say, "Take this job and shove it" when you're 25 and single than when you're a 40-year-old family man. So when conducting interviews with men across the United States, I made a point to ask subjects not just about their jobs but also about their goals and accomplishments. At this stage of life, more than half said they were satisfied with their careers, although more than 80 percent added that there was a lot more to accomplish in the decades ahead. Here's a brief sampling of respondents' voices.

• "I resigned from a heavy-duty, high-stress position after turning 40," one single, never-married communications exec told me. "I managed over 40 people at MCI. I had planned [to resign] for two years. It conveniently coincided with my 40th birthday. Just quitting my job opens the door to more career opportunity. I've already got a potential job offer with a newer company. Objectively, I'm satisfied. But there are all kinds of good things left. Like relationships, learning."

• "I left newspaper reporting to go into multimedia reporting," a 40-ish ex-journalist from the Midwest told me. "Eighteen months later, I was laid off. I took refuge in the corporate world of media relations in April of that year. It sucks, but it pays the bills, and the people aren't all bad." He added, "Now, to be relegated to being an assistant flack for a middling oil company is nearly shameful. I feel like I let myself down."

• "I've been putting together a business plan and funding to start a new company," said a recently divorced telecommunications exec from Colorado. "I've worked for large companies for the last 10 years and I'm ready to run my own show."

• "I'm less focused on my career than I used to be," said one 42-year-old from Baltimore. "This is probably the result of numerous disappointments. After a while, you realize you're not going to get what you want, so you redirect your energies elsewhere." He continued, "I'm not satisfied with my income, which should be twice as high as it is today."

future, there must be good reasons why. The question then begins to get a little more interesting, a little more powerful, than a simple prognostication. It's why Scarf continued to ask that question during research for her 1995 book *Intimate Worlds: Life inside the Family*, which is about family ties, family strife, family legacies, and how families thrive.

When I interviewed men about their jobs and careers, I asked about the future, but in a slightly different way. I asked them to envision a video—a highlight reel of themselves at work, spanning 10 or 20 years of the past and 5 years in the future. What snippets would be on that highlight reel? Let's go to the videotape.

Portrait of an Artist as a Young Internet Man

The highlight reel for Todd N., 40, a visual artist and Internet consultant, would open in 1988. He had just gotten married to a successful attorney, and his own career as a painter was taking off. "So there would be scenes of my paintings and of me having some one-man shows back then in Washington and New York," he said. It was a time, he explained, when he was painting prolifically, and those oversized cityscapes were selling for $4,000 to $8,000. And they were selling well.

The other thing that came to mind immediately, Todd said, "was that I had found a way to live; to support myself in a fun, fulfilling life. And to have both money and time to paint—that was a huge accomplishment—to have all that in New York City." The kicker? His Honda Nighthawk 750, on which he raced around the streets of the city. But as Todd's reel life unfolds, the bustling city fades into the tranquil suburbs. And his beloved bike turns into a Volvo station wagon.

The move to the suburbs was prompted by marriage and children. While Todd's wife, Gretchen, worked in New York City as an attorney during and after both pregnancies, she eventually switched to part-time legal work based in their home in White Plains. In his mid-thirties, Todd had to figure out how to paint himself out of a proverbial corner: His family couldn't live as comfortably once Gretchen worked at home and Todd had less time to paint. After all, he had taken over the child-rearing responsibilities for the first few years of his daughter's life. (His son came along three years later.)

The solution? For him, it was learning the new language of computer art. More specifically, learning how to adapt and present complex information visually. And just as important, learning how to teach what he learned to others—preferably large, innovative corporate clients.

Within a year and a half, Todd had fairly mastered the digital art part; the teaching would take a little bit longer (because that would also involve selling). And he certainly hadn't studied that in his four years of college at Parsons School of Design and nearby Cooper Union. Or maybe he had: His painting style was so striking, it had often sold itself. Or so gallery owners had learned. The key was not tricking people into thinking they were buying something of value. It was providing them with value in a medium they might not be familiar with. Same goes, Todd soon learned, with visual information created by computers and displayed and sent over the World Wide Web.

As with fine art, placing a monetary value on computer images can be tricky. But Todd isn't about to become modest in his early midlife years: "I am truly establishing myself as an expert in my field," he told me in a late-night interview. "There aren't a lot of people who do what I do. It's about combining different ways of communicating (Internet modeling/art/design); and it is a merging process—with language, with business, with art. It's creating digital business models."

Regarding a freelance project he was working on with a friend, he said, "It's the first time I've created something that's worth a million dollars. And I'm still in my first decade of purely financial motivation." He hadn't cashed in yet; that million was still speculation. Yet he did have a signed contract from a huge computing company in hand, in which he was slated to create a prototype of what might be called a new form of commercial art.

"I mean, right now my computer is turned on," he said, as midnight approached. "I have four proposals due at work, I'm working on the prototype project, and I just made a Web site sale today. Plus, I'm closing on the house [in a new hometown in North Carolina] tomorrow, and I'm going to go inside and caress my wife now." And with that, Todd was off to perhaps create a sensual video highlight of his life. If only someone were recording it.

The New Loyalty—To Yourself

You'd think that someone who thinks about structures and plans most every day would have designed airtight plans for his future. For Tim R., 39, a successful but frustrated Virginia architect, his failure to sketch an alternate career plan through his thirties forced him to reevaluate his behavior in a hurry as he neared 40. "At 30, I had this image of myself having a position in a group [of architects] that was successful, having a certain degree of success and notoriety. But the key expression would be 'within that group.' I didn't imagine myself being independent: I was working within that system. If you take architects, there's a little bit more ego than in other professions. In architecture school, you find a lot of guys who only imagine themselves getting out of school and being on their own. That's their plan."

Some 10 years ago, when Tim was working on a project at a less prestigious firm with a 26-year-old associate, he remembered the "kid" saying, "If I'm not successful and famous by 30, I'm going to kill myself." Tim found him to be arrogant—and also confident. "He had this idea that architecture was a singular pursuit. He wanted to have his own projects published in the magazines, and I, maybe because of my old Southern Protestant work ethic, had more of an employee mindset." It's not that Tim failed at his job or on a big project under tight deadline; it's more that he failed to put his personal future ahead of his firm's. In a sense, Tim was a throwback to the way so many of our fathers approached their careers 20 to 25 years ago. Loyalty came with the first big job and stuck. Today, jobs get unstuck and downsized all the time.

"At 30, I didn't imagine myself with a 'titled' position," he added, using a term akin to partner at a law firm. "I just imagined myself being a little precocious, ahead of myself, which I was. As I got into my thirties, my vision of myself expanded so that I was not just a member of a group any longer. I was going to be a leader." He was meticulous at work and in his off-hours. Maybe too steady, he thinks now, as he finds himself taken for granted at the office and still single, though he would prefer to be married.

When one of his colleagues left for a lengthy overseas job a few years ago, Tim was 37 and imagined stepping into the colleague's shoes—at least by age 40. "But now, at 40," he said, "I have a different vision. Looking ahead to 45, my vision is to be a principal. Not so much as Tim the architect, but as a partner." He also pointed out that at 38 or 39, his career took a subtle turn in how he began to view interdependence. He doesn't imagine working for someone for much longer. "I only imagine myself now working with people.

"My vision of the way I work with people has expanded," Tim stated. "I used to have myopic vision. A belief in the meritocracy. I figured if I did my job well, I would move forward." He has moved forward over the past nine years, but a bit haltingly. What might he have done differently to alter his prospective highlight reel? "I would have expanded my vision of how I worked with clients and people in the office. I was so focused on just doing good work that I neglected to work my relationships. I always thought the work would speak for itself. I never went out of my way to schmooze people. There's one guy I worked with who was always working on people as future clients. But I never operated that way. I had less patience for schmoozing than he did." Looking back, he now finds that the schmoozing was more than schmoozing—even in the sometimes rarefied world of architecture.

At 40, is it too late to alter his career path? Or to change careers altogether? "The closer I get to 40, the more I think about the possibilities to do other things," Tim said. "From 20 to 35, I was absolutely relentless. You have a vision and just go there. But as I get closer to 40, I see you can relax a little more. You can allow other things to enter the picture. I've gotten more comfortable financially and psychologically. I have also thought about bagging this whole thing and going to law school, also business school. Law school because people have told me I'm very rational and a cool thinker when there is conflict. Business school because I've gotten more interested in finance and my investment decisions and how they affect me.

"I started thinking about these things around 40," he continued. "But I have worked with guys who decide to start over at 33. They bag architecture, go to business school, try to make buckets of money over 10 to 12 years, and then come back and become gentlemen architects."

In describing these stop-outs of a different stripe, Tim sounded full of disdain. And perhaps a little envy. He has stuck with his chosen career and his current job for more years than most of his peers, in part out of insecurity. The fact is, most of the people in his office and profession come from wealthier families than Tim's. His father, for instance, was the lone child of nine in his family to have graduated from college. Continuing in that vein, Tim is the first of his family to have graduated with an advanced degree. "So," he concluded, "I'm not going to decide at 33 about going back to school and not know how to pay for it. At 40, I have enough money to pay for it without thinking about it."

This kind of defensive thinking and defensive career planning came in part from Tim's background. There weren't exactly artist/architect mentors in his family. "My grandparents were poor farmers from the South," he said, "Both sets of them. But my family had it a little better." As for tomorrow, though he can't count on it, Tim wants things to be a little better still.

The $200,000 Question

In order to plan properly for the future, a man has to stay ahead. There's so much that can go wrong when it comes to money. So it pays to act defensively in the first years of midlife. Before he even thinks about his big-time risk/reward savings plan, he has to cover the taxes. Only when those are out of the way can he start concentrating on the good stuff—the ease of winding down from the workforce, cashing in the 401(k), enjoying the proverbial 18 holes of golf after breakfast or the morning fly fishing jaunts that will appear, right on schedule, in the years 65 through 70. Ideally, a financially savvy man has been funding his retirement since about age 25. In reality, that's rarely the case.

"When my clients come in to do their taxes," says Mark Kornspan, 42, a New York City tax accountant who has numerous clients about his own age, "we talk a lot about career happiness—not about the physical aspects of the job, so much, but whether they are at the places in their careers where they expected to be at age 40. I know everybody's age," he adds. "It's right there in the computer when we fill out their forms—so we can track IRAs and such—and I'm curious to see how people are aging. I'll even say, 'Oh, you're turning 40 this year. I've been through it.' Or I'll say, 'Wow, we're having a special birthday this year.' It opens up the '40 conversation.'"

It gives Kornspan a way to delve deeper, but not as a voyeur. As a part-time financial planner. "I see 40 as being a real point of analyzing where you are and where you are going," he says. "It's not 30, when you can screw around and experiment. Now, you have to know where you are going." A lot of people don't really think about their assets

YOUR PIECE OF THE PIE

Joel Javer has a pie chart in his office that he'd like you to see. Whether you are 20, 40, or 75, this Denver-based radio talk show host and financial advisor with Sharkey, Howes, Wagner, and Javer financial consultants has a pie for you. Of course, you'll probably want to see all of the pies, for comparison's sake. In brief, they look like this.

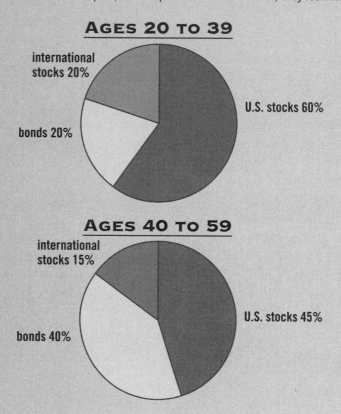

AGES 20 TO 39

international stocks 20%

bonds 20%

U.S. stocks 60%

AGES 40 TO 59

international stocks 15%

bonds 40%

U.S. stocks 45%

until they turn 40, Kornspan says. Then they shoot ahead (too quickly) and ask perhaps the wrong question: "What will I have at retirement?" That question should come later, at 50.

At the same time, Kornspan finds that it's actually rare for his clients to have thought in their early to mid-twenties about funding retirement, although he is well aware that simply living and working in New York City tends to drain countless dollars from potential savings, individual retirement accounts (IRAs), or other pension plans. This is true even of

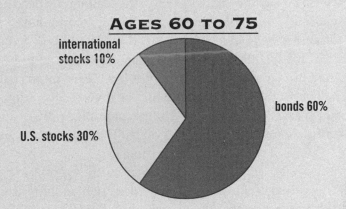

AGES 60 TO 75

international stocks 10%

bonds 60%

U.S. stocks 30%

The thinking goes something like this: When you're young, you may not have a lot of excess cash to invest, but what you have you'll likely have for a long while. You can afford higher risk in your twenties and thirties. (Or perhaps the better word is absorb.) By 40, there's still a long earnings curve ahead, but you've moved into a slightly more protective mode of investing—for your future and for your children or quite possibly your parents. Here's when you start moving toward a more even split between riskier stocks and predictable bonds. Between 40 and 45, financial experts add, you may see your earnings spike—and along with that, the chance to patch holes in your savings plans caused by unforeseen expenses. By the time you reach 60, you want to be able to get at your money in case the need arises (such as in the case of long-term care or illness). That translates into lowering your risk further.

people who are considered prudent. The key is to get a plan in place between the mid-twenties and mid-forties. Go ahead, start small, even if you've hardly started by age 39. But build it into your monthly budget and your lifestyle, Kornspan says. By 50, you'll be glad you did.

Okay, I'm thinking, I'm not in bad shape, with a couple of pension/savings plans firmly in place by age 40. Then I ask the question that hurts: What's a healthy number—in terms of total assets—for a 40-year-old to have socked away in savings?

"I don't like to give one number," Kornspan answers, in deference to many of his clients. Then he finally relents: "If they have $200,000 in assets by then, I'd say they're okay." (I do the math in my head and find that my wife and I fall short—uh-oh. Then again, I rationalize, *she's* not yet 40.) Of course, he points out that every household is different. And that most of his clients are in the $75,000 a year or higher income bracket. And that total assets at 40 in his mind means minus liabilities. At least half of that $200,000 target should be invested in various forms of long-range assets, including 401(k) pension plans, IRAs and Roth IRAs, securities, mutual funds, or bonds. The balance might be invested in a house, a condominium, or cars.

750 miles west of Kornspan's Lower Fifth Avenue Manhattan office, Howard Berger, 40, an agent with Metropolitan Life based in the Chicago suburbs, asks a slightly different question of his midlife clients. "I ask them what debt they have, and they may say, '$60,000.' I then ask, 'Is it mostly cars?' and they answer, 'Oh, do we include cars?'" Berger's first step, assuming taxes are clear and paid, is to help them ditch the debt. It's so much easier, we all know, to focus on assets. They are, after all, what we go to work for.

So there it is: $200,000. A nice round number. Divide it by 15 years, say, (the number of years you may have been working at a reasonable wage after high school or college), and you've been expected to save an average of $13,333 per year, including interest (compound, we hope) and bull markets (we also hope). The early years may have been $8,000, the later years $18,000. But that's the goal. It's a start.

Here's one more figure worth looking at as a reality check. According to *U.S. News and World Report* and a 1995 survey, more than half of all families headed by a person aged 35 to 44 had some savings set aside for retirement. The median amount: $25,000.

How to Retire in Your Sixties— And in Your Forties

Barry A. Shapiro, 42, has seen the future, and it *is* the future.

When he was 30, he had what he thought was a great job: an articles editor at *Sport* magazine in New York City. Then the magazine was sold and moved to California. Shapiro turned quickly to freelance writing and co-authoring innovative baseball front-office man Syd

SIX CAREER TENETS OF DR. JOB

When it comes to career advice, such as that doled out in *Dr. Job's Complete Career Guide*, sometimes Mother knows best. A note of self disclosure: Dr. Job's name is Sandra Pesmen; she happens to be my mother as well as a syndicated columnist in newspapers and online. After collecting hundreds of letters and queries from Americans who've had midcareer problems in the 1990s, Dr. Job saw fit to summarize a handful of her beliefs in the book, as follows.

1. Don't ever let others make you forget who and what you are.
2. It's far better to be known as a proven member of a good team through your own efforts than to count on promotions from a mentor.
3. Too few people realize they should begin to prepare for the next review five minutes after the last one.
4. No matter how pleasant any job is, there is no such thing as a career that is completely consuming and fulfilling.
5. There's no such thing as a small job or a small idea—only people who are content to think of themselves as small. Always consider that everything you do is a mission that matters.
6. Always view the crisis of termination as a challenge and an opportunity. The best revenge is rising to even greater heights.

Thrift's autobiography *The Game According to Syd*. Then, with freelance paychecks looking less-than-lavish and highly irregular, and with two small children, he turned to a less glamorous but seemingly more secure profession: selling life insurance.

Yet to rise above the stuffy image so many people have of insurance, and to get people to commit chunks of their salaries to the preretirement plans that he draws up for them, Shapiro has to get personal. That's one way his journalism training has served him well: He's very comfortable asking people about the intricacies of their lives. Such as, "Are your parents secretly supporting or helping to support you or your children? In your twenties or thirties, did you set aside any savings for the kids' educations? If you make $200,000 a year, do you think you can save more than $200 a month?"

"Most financial planning is uncomfortable," says Shapiro, a chartered life insurance underwriter and financial consultant based in Garden City, New York. "I have to, at some point, ask them questions no one else is asking. To present to them the best solutions, I have to pretend I'm them."

Another key question Shapiro and other agents pose to men arriving at midlife is: Are you covered in cases of disability or major health problems? This is the kind of thing that perpetual teenagers or financial stragglers often fail to address, and it is exactly the kind of thing that can raid a family of its financial assets. Remember: defense first.

"There's a question I often ask prospective clients," Shapiro says. "'What's important about money to you?' They'll think about it, and eventually they'll get to what it is that they want. It becomes, to them, 'What do I really want out of life?' When you come back to them later, you are able to say, 'Here are your goals; here's the reality.'

"And sometimes you get to say, 'You're right on track.' They're the type of people who, at 60, will walk away from their jobs and be fine. And other people will say, 'How did they do that?'" It's everyone's dream to be able to retire comfortably. The question remains, though, for how long?

Now that life expectancy is creeping up to the mid-seventies for men, you want to make certain that you don't "outlive your savings," as financial planners like to say. "A lot of times, people ask me, 'You see lots of people. Am I on track?' The best people for me to work with are those who are making money but who have problems with allocation," Shapiro says. Put another way, if you are 60 years old and want to retire a bit early, you'll actually be the chief executive officer of your own retirement "company." And, different from most companies, this one may not have any new revenue streams.

According to Shapiro, a quick way to check if you're on track is to take your gross income and divide by five. If you're saving 20 percent of that gross income, you're doing well. "People say to me, 'Are you nuts?' I then say, 'How much are you putting into your 401(k) plan at work?' They might say, 'I'm maxing out.' So I'll tell them, 'Well, that's 11 percent, so you only have 9 percent to go.'

"I'm not saying that you have to write me a check for 20 percent," Shapiro points out. "It's just that the government is doing a good job of warning people that they won't have checks coming in when they retire. Sometimes, I'll tell people, 'Let's just start: If you can't save that much now, maybe we'll set up an automatic overdraft into a money market account.' Then we'll look at it after three months, then six. It's like in a gym: 'Here's your baseline fitness; we'll build on that.' It's not about me having more sales. If people see themselves saving, they feel empowered."

It's not as if the kids won't go to camp next summer, Shapiro says. He just wants his clients to start moving forward. "I keep a diary," Shapiro says, "of everything I spend money on. Everything. I tell clients to do the same thing for a year. Simply be a reporter." What people start to find, he adds, is that there are usually a few thousand dollars each year that could be redirected. "One of my clients, who is at a major TV network, brown-bags his lunch," he says. "He figures that taking a turkey sandwich, a pickle, chips, and a soda, instead of buying them at a deli in midtown Manhattan, saves him $160 a month, or about $1,900 a year. I mean, you buy the food for home anyway. The same thing goes for cigarette smokers who quit or cut back. That's a little bit of change that adds up: $2, $3, $4 a day." Or another $1,200 or so a year.

When people feel that they are behind in their retirement planning, they may think they can apply only $50 a month or so to some "vague future account," says Shapiro. "I say, 'Fine.' The guy may be making $200,000 a year, and he wants to set aside $50, or even $200. But I have to ask him, 'What's that percentage-wise?'"

The Millionaires Club: An Inside Look

Being a millionaire is boring.

Well, maybe not the "being" part, but becoming a millionaire is boring. At least, that's the unforeseen message that readers got from the book *The Millionaire Next Door* by Thomas J. Stanley, Ph.D., and William D. Danko, Ph.D., when it showed up on the bestseller lists and hung out there for a long while in the late 1990s. "I'd like my million, too," tens of thousands of folks thought to themselves while flipping through the book from back to front in Barnes and Noble, wondering whether the advice was worth the cover price. After skimming a chapter or two, most of those readers made the next connection: "I'd like to be bored, if that's what it takes to make a million."

Of the dozens of surprising findings that Dr. Stanley and Dr. Danko offered up about America's richest, some key characteristics turned out to be anything but exciting. One trait of the prototypical millionaires dredged up by the marketing guru authors is that "many of the types of businesses [millionaires] are in could be classified as dull-normal." Millionaires also told the authors, "We live on less than 7 percent of our wealth." Still another millionaire revealed, "We live well below our means." Ho hum, ho hum, let's invest another $100,000 in another 22-percent-return no-load mutual fund. . . .

See what I mean? These folks are boring. They're also a lot wealthier than I am, or than most of my friends are, for that matter. But having reached 40 in a reasonably healthy financial state, I found that I was now thinking about having a million dollars a lot more often than I had at age 20 or 30 or even 35. And so, while waiting for my windfall, I decided to turn to a few men who already had passed the million mark by 40. I was curious about their strategies, spending habits, family lives, and frustrations. And I wanted to know what they did for fun. I wasn't looking for a financial blueprint; I was in search of a few lessons that I and other "hundred-thousandaires" might appreciate.

"How did you get there?" I asked. "What drives you now?" I asked later. It wasn't because I didn't trust the writers of *The Millionaire Next Door*, but I wanted to know what it felt like to reach a goal that's supposed to set you up for life. For the record, when Dr. Stanley and Dr. Danko surveyed more than 1,000 millionaires in 1995 and 1996 to get their results, they found out the following about the average American millionaire (although, with all due respect, is any millionaire really "average"?).

- He's male and 57 years old.
- He works between 45 and 55 hours each week.
- He lives well below his (and his family's) means.
- He knows how to target a market.
- He believes that achieving financial independence is more important than high-income status symbols such as luxury cars or designer suits.
- He didn't get a lot of financial help from his parents.
- He doesn't give a lot of financial help to his children.

In this chapter, you'll get to know three men who were not in that survey—three men who hit the big time and hit it early, compared with the average age of 57. I'd like to think that these guys are anything but boring.

Keeping the Faith—In Himself

It was not an auspicious beginning. In fact, it was so hapless that it would make a good scene in a movie. When Mike B. was 22 years old, he had a job interview that would change his life, although he hardly knew it then. All he knew was that he hated the job he was in, executive trainee (gofer) for a large men's clothing line, and that he'd gotten word about an opening with a new real estate firm that specialized in office space and large commercial buildings. So one day after work, Mike drove out to the suburbs of Boston to have at it.

Going in, he didn't know much about real estate. Mike was simply hoping for a break, a chance to ditch the apparel business and get into some kind of sales. He thought the interview went okay. Going for honesty points, he admitted he had no related experience. He didn't even try to pull the "classes in college" thing. That didn't bother the principals. But he didn't ace the interview, either. So as he left the office and headed out to his car, he wasn't cocky, especially when he realized he had locked his keys in the car.

Sure, he could have called a locksmith or tow truck right away. Problem was, he didn't want to jinx the job possibility by having the real estate guys come out just as his door was being jimmied. They'd think he was an asshole and dump him, with no need for a second interview. So Mike went next door to a *Cheers* type of bar, but where nobody knew his name. He had a beer, then two. The Realtors lights were still on. He had a third and a fourth beer, then thought, "God, these guys work long hours. Maybe I don't want to work there." It was after 11:00 P.M. when the execs finally came out, and, with his lousy luck, Mike was right there waiting for the locksmith. What he didn't know was that all the time he thought they were at work, they were playing basketball in the warehouse in the same building.

Luckily, they had a sense of humor. Two weeks later, they offered Mike a job as a leasing agent, with no salary but a decent commission. And to help him get going, they arranged for him to obtain a $5,000 loan. It was enough, he thought. Consider: He was five Gs in the hole, in a job without a regular paycheck, and he thought he was a tycoon.

Lesson 1: Focus on your abilities more than on your dreams.

"I always believed I was going to be a huge success," Mike said, "since I was four, five, six years old, even in an environment where I didn't feel that those around me believed that. When I was growing up I wanted to be a banker, architect, hotel builder; I wanted to be in sales, marketing, an engineer at one point, an inventor. All these things that were seemingly unrelated. I realized later, much later, that the real estate business allows you to do all those things every day. Plus, I realized that there was no limit to how much money you could make."

These realizations didn't come easily, of course. Mike made it through college at the state university as a C student—not exactly Dean's List fare. He graduated without a plan. Meanwhile, his older brother was getting some of the highest marks achievable and was cruising through Yale Law School, destined for the good life. Mike's father was a manufacturers' rep; his mother was a homemaker. When the time came to assess his potential strengths in business, Mike believed he could eventually do the best in sales. He wasn't the most popular kid in high school and college, but he had learned a few tricks about persuasiveness. He could plead a good case because he wasn't afraid to portray himself as in need yet also confident. That's a rare combination for a young man pumped up on testosterone to possess.

How did he acquire those skills? For lowly student council events in high school, he had somehow persuaded a few big-name Boston sports figures and politicians to appear at his school, gratis. In college, his dormitory unofficially elected him the leader of oh-so-serious party and special event planning. His trademark wheels on campus were suitably quirky, bordering on dorky: He drove, proudly, a 1955 Cadillac hardtop. The "Mike-mobile," his friends called it. From this, he learned another lesson: Shtick stuck.

Still, "At 21, I didn't know what I wanted to do career-wise, but I thought I wanted to get a job at the biggest, strongest company I could," Mike said, "because I figured they didn't get that big without a good training program. I wanted desperately to work for IBM. And I could've worked for them, but they were in St. Louis. I didn't want to move." When he thought back to his life at that time, Mike said he was looking for things to anchor him, with one obvious anchor being Boston. "I didn't want to take a risk to move where I had no friends or family," he said. "Once I did not get that position with IBM, I went from being totally secure to being totally lost. 'What would it be like to go on welfare?' I couldn't believe I was thinking that. I was totally ungrounded. I was rudderless."

So when an offer came from the big apparel maker, he didn't set his sights too high. It was just a first job, after all. He was, at best, a glorified gofer, cleaning clothing showrooms and, on cold days, going out to the parking lot to start the president's car. "My dream, going to work at a corporation, was supposed to be the ideal environment for me at the time," Mike recalled. "But I was a nonentity."

His self-esteem was shot. "I remember my roommate after college saying to me, 'If you don't quit that job, I won't be your roommate. You're miserable.' I left after about nine months. I didn't have any money saved up. At the time, our expenses were low. We had three guys living in a three-bedroom place; my share was $110 a month. All I needed was rent, food, and beer."

Soon he was off and running with the real estate firm, selling office space. Except nobody was buying. "I got off to the slowest start of anybody in the business," Mike said. "I had budgeted the $5,000 loan for six months; I stretched it out to about seven months. I went to my brother and borrowed another $1,000. And I still had not made a deal, hadn't closed a deal." It would be another six months and another loan from his company before Mike's luck changed. Interest rates were high. Companies were delaying moves and canceling building expansion plans. For commercial brokers, things looked, in a word, bleak.

"After 13 months, I made my first deal, but I was $10,000 in debt," Mike said. "The prime interest rate was up to 21 percent. The markets were terrible. Inflation was double digits. I remember that a friend was having a party, that day; I couldn't believe my 'luck.' I had signed a contract that day, sold my first building. That would've been 1980. I went 13 months. What it taught me about myself was that I don't give up. It goes back to this thing that I always believed when I was a kid— that I would be successful.

The tenacity that had carried him through his first 13 months of low rent, pizza slices, and cheap pitchers of beer with the boys sustained him over the next three years, as he got by on middling commissions. He made contacts, if not money, and took the time to get married while things were still lean.

"The first big deal I was involved in was one for a huge payroll company. We moved their headquarters from the city out to Route 128. I remember using the money from that deal to buy my first house. I did the same thing a few years later; I made another large transaction, which helped me buy my house in Cohasset. That was a huge fee, like $100,000."

"I put myself on a fictitious salary," Mike recounted about the days when things started to gel financially for him. "I would laugh and give myself a raise every year. It was as if I was on salary—about $7,000 a month. I would write a check from our money market account and put it in checking. It kept me out of trouble. Because, at a young age, a lot of people I know who were successful got in trouble."

Even after Mike and his wife, Katie, began having children, they kept their lifestyle and spending habits well below his earnings. One year, they told their two young kids that they were driving to Florida on vacation, but Mike and his wife had another plan: They actually drove only a few towns away, at night, to a Holiday Inn that had an indoor pool. The children, who woke up the next morning in a hotel and who got to play video games and splash in the pool all day, weren't the wiser.

At the same time, Mike had a hunch that he shared with Katie: "My career is about to blast off." It did, for one main reason and a few supporting reasons. First, Mike helped revolutionize corporate relocation office leasing by assigning one agent to each account. This meant that the agent would get to know the client's needs and then use that familiarity when helping the client to lease new offices around the country. This template approach was foreign to the industry at the time. In the traditional type of relocation service, an agent from the real estate firm's home office would handle the paperwork, retrain the firm's personnel, and parcel out the day-to-day leasing arrangements to a local agent at the new site.

The new setup meant tons more travel for Mike. But it was also a creative way for him and his partners to set their firm apart from the pack. "I began to see myself as separate from my peers," Mike told me, "in terms of my abilities and success."

The first discovery Mike made mid-career was that he had superior sales skills. Not only was he persuasive, he said, but he also found that he was able to think faster on his feet than most of his contemporaries were. We've all heard about how location, location, location is the answer in real estate. But instinct is a highly underrated asset. When there's potential trouble on a multimillion-dollar lease, a leasing agent needs an attractive alternative for the client, sooner rather than later. He also needs to know when to back off. And when companies are nervous about making huge decisions about office space (which they have a right to be, with 10- or 20-year commitments), they want to know that their move will add to profits years down the road, not merely a short-term, puffed-up corporate image.

Mike was able to do these things for companies, time and again, in healthy economies and skittish ones. After five years of amassing successes, he recalled, he went home one day and told Katie, "We have to realize how lucky we are, at such a young age. This is not normal. Do you realize we're earning more money than 99 percent of everyone else in this country?"

Lesson 2: Plan for the upside; react to the downside.

Looking back at age 30, when the money started streaming in, Mike realized that all was not perfect. "I was absolutely working at capacity," he told me. "I was totally stressed out. I was made a partner at 28; I had management responsibilities; and I was a straight commission broker trying to deal with success. Real estate markets were on fire. I was so driven," he added, "compared to my peers. Katie would always comment that I was always so distracted at home. I would disappear. Plus, I remember saying to myself that I wasn't maintaining relationships with my friends, which really bothered me. But I had to have that separation."

Once his children were old enough to go to school and his career was solid enough that he didn't worry so much about tomorrow's big deal, he started checking in with his friends more regularly. And most weren't put off by his temporary absence from their lives. They understood. A lot of them had done the same dance in their early thirties, but without as much material success to show for it.

"Absolutely, you've got to have plans and goals when you're working that hard," Mike said. "I wanted to be able to retire by the time I was 40. And I remember saying to one of our old college friends, before I started out, that I wanted to be able to do whatever I wanted by the age of 40. When we had a chance to sell our company a few years ago, that was one of the reasons I was in favor of selling." In the spring of 1997, in fact, Mike's company was sold for an undisclosed sum. It is safe to say that he pocketed at least a few million dollars as a result of the sale. He still has a job, just not as much pressure. "I have enough money now," he told me, "that I'm kind of borderline. If I didn't want to work anymore, we'd have to cut back a little on expenses, but we could do it.

"I'd like to have a second career," he added, "but I can't focus on what I'd ideally do in a second career." That's one thing, he's found out, that money can't buy.

I asked, finally, what he's learned about himself since he's turned 40. He had given the question some thought.

"There's a quote I like: 'Plan for the upside; react to the downside,' he said. "Now, I follow that. I used to do the opposite. It comes from confidence. I converted the worrying into thinking. That's made all the difference.

"What I've also come to think is that what drives me is fear of failure," he said. "And part of that comes from being broke at 22. It's a core feeling that drives me. After all, no one thought I was going to be successful: not my family, not my friends. But as a little kid, I thought I was going to be President of the United States or chief executive officer of the biggest company in the world, and the richest man in the world. Nobody thought I was going to be any of those things. I believed them." When you tie it all together, here was someone who had tremendous confidence in himself, but who, from time to time, was very confused because he wasn't getting reinforcement in his beliefs.

Sometimes, it seems, it's easier to prove things to others than it is to prove them to yourself. In that sense, the harsh realities of the business world can actually be tamer than pressures that build on you from other sources, like family and friends. It's the kind of realization a 30-year-old might not appreciate.

"I always did a reality check," Mike said. "I never thought I deserved it. And I've always kept perspective on how lucky I was. But I never assumed that I deserved it. There's a fine line—probably a gulf—between thinking that you deserved it and thinking that you earned it and are capable of doing it. If you confuse those, it leads to problems. You have to earn it, and you have to be fortunate."

Cultivating Financial Security—And Fun

On the near wall of the office that's farthest from the entrance of Multi-Market Search, there's a framed copy of an unsettling front page of the *Denver Post*, dated July 20, 1989. The oversized, 72-point headline reads, "178 Survive." It refers to a horrifying crash of a DC-10 plane, in which more than 100 Denver-bound passengers died. Beneath the clipped and matted copy of the article is an old United Airlines boarding pass, made out in the name of "Pete N.," with the exact flight number, date, and time of the flight that crashed that day. "When I'm having a really bad day," said Pete N., "I look over at the wall and think of how things really aren't so bad." He was supposed to be on that plane, seated in row 19.

To this man who travels an average of 180 to 200 days a year on business, the front page is also a reminder to get to the airport ahead of schedule and take an earlier flight when space is available. For that's what happened on July 19, 1989. Pete arrived at the airport early and got a standby seat on the flight before the ill-fated flight 232. He's anything but smug when I meet up with him nine years later in the president's office of the company he has since founded. He's a survivor, a fortunate guy who's more than willing to share a few principles of membership in the unofficial, unpretentious, understated millionaires club.

"I'm very different from a lot of these entrepreneurs you read about," Pete explained during a 90-minute morning interview in which he neither sipped a cup of coffee, juice, or bottled water nor offered me any of the above. "I never dreamed that I had to be my own boss. My drive was always to be economically independent. I thought if I worked hard early on, then if I didn't want to work after a while, I wouldn't have to." Now he doesn't have to, but he does anyway.

Lesson 3: Rethink retirement at 40.

Unlike most guys, Pete was already thinking about retirement in his mid-twenties. "Early on, I had this goal. I wanted to have nine different $90,000 certificates of deposit," he says. "Then I was going to give them names: Bob, Helen, whatever. And then they were going to generate enough income so that I didn't have to work." What a plan, I thought, taking notes and comparing my modest savings at midlife to what he had somehow planned, in detail, 15 years ago.

What was the reason Pete had his savings carved up in uneven, $90,000 increments? I asked. "So they'd be insured," he answered, as if I were asking a third-grade question. Pausing for a moment, I thought about how federal deposit insurance goes up to $100,000. Then I realized that for each and every one of his $90,000 certificates of deposit (CDs), he was building in some room for interest. The odd part of the formula, aside from the fact that he gave the CDs names, was that, in a way, he didn't trust the banks. Yet he often worked in the banking industry. Banks have been some of his major customers since the early 1980s. He set up short- and long-range marketing programs for savings and loans and commercial banks of various sizes nationwide. His onsite visits were all about making the banks trust him and his employer to make things better for the banks' profits.

Without hesitation, from his second job on (his first was as a low-paid political aide), he started socking away his commissions. "When I got married, I had $10,000," Pete said. "I remember my wife, Laurie, thinking that was a ton of money; I liked that." He lived like a married graduate student, shunning big vacations, never going out to dinner when he was at home—hell, that's what he did on the road. (Only he wouldn't say "hell." As an upstanding, observant member of the Mormon Church, swearing is not his style. Neither is drinking alcohol or ingesting caffeine.) "At 30," Pete said, "soon after my first kids were born, I remember taking time off from work to be with them and help Laurie out, but not nearly as much time as I would've liked. By that time, I was self-employed, and I'd heard about these guys who had paternity leave. I thought, 'Great, but I can't do it.'"

Lesson 4: Think like a CEO, work as an employee.

For Pete, a marketing man who logs some 100,000 flight miles each year, there is a correlation between his number of days on the road and the yearly income of his company. "I usually take about 100 flights a year," he explained, "and at some point, I looked at the cost of growth not in terms of dollars but in terms of 'nights out.'" It's a new statistic for frequent travelers, one that takes into account the toll on one's family. "At the end of the year, I save all of my calendars, and I look at how many nights out I had." Of course, his company could hire more people to cover some of the president's territory, but his corporate mission has always been to provide a hand-holding kind of marketing support. He's not in favor of diluting that and never has been.

I was impressed with how carefully Pete had logged his travel miles. His logbook looked like that of a flight student keeping track of "air hours" while training for a pilot's license. I was not impressed by his company's offices, but that made sense. The headquarters, subleased from a bank building that has four drive-in windows, measures some 1,400 square feet and is home to five full-time employees. That's it. Revenues now exceed $2 million a year, while the company is run as leanly as is seemingly possible. A few years ago, Pete's semi-retired father did some consulting for the company and wrote up a plan for the firm to reach $10 to $12 million a year in sales within five years. Pete thought about it and decided to stay "small." He also turned down a bid to buy the company. His wife was worried he'd get bored and so was he.

"In 1989, I had 200 nights out," Pete said. He wasn't about to do that again for a measly $3 to $4 million extra in net revenue. "To go to $6 million a year, I'd have to go up to 180 nights out." The math looks like this.

Income Statements

	1989	1996	1997
Sales	$45,000	$1,436,000	$3,000,000
Expenses	$12,000	$674,000	$1,250,000
Net Income	$33,000	$762,000	$1,750,000

These days, Pete says his wife views his travel as "financial security." She didn't at first. Neither did he.

The secrets to Pete's success aren't overwhelming. They are, however, effective. By keeping his firm small, his doubling and tripling revenues in the early years of operations were plowed right back into the company. The marketing services, including pesty phone solicitation surveys, provided by the company are smart and highly targeted, but they are also outsourced to contract firms. That means overhead remains small even as revenues and the value of jobs subcontracted out to other firms grow to impressive heights.

Pete has long turned his thrift into a game of sorts. In high school, he was the kind of guy who would cruise past a tollbooth without paying, slapping the toll-taker a high five. (This was before the days when tollgate arms were installed.) He was also the only student in his class to attend auctions of U.S. post office vehicles and consequently buy a Jeep for $300. Who cared if the steering wheel was on the wrong side? That made it cool. Plus, as there wasn't a seat next to the driver's, the better to store mail, he put a toilet fixture there for passengers. Ten or so years later, he turned to selling his frequent flier miles surreptitiously, partly as a game, partly as a source of income. He did this until the airline sleuths tracked him down, that is.

Pete also put his thrift to good use when he left a secure job to start his own firm. When he made this move, his goal was to make a mere $2,000 a month, gross. "I had weaseled my expenses so low that I didn't have much of a mortgage," Pete explained. "Laurie would just shake. She talked about $2,000 as if it were nothing, because I was making $75,000 a year at the time. Fortunately, within the first four months, I made $48,000."

Of course, looking down from a seat of wealth, it's not surprising for Pete to say that reports of male midlife crises are often exaggerated: "I don't think men have crises," he said. "I think they have cycles. In 1993, when we first reached $1 million a year, I had to make a decision about whether to grow this thing into a huge enterprise or try to spend more time with my family." He chose a family cycle, in part, due to his own upbringing; and in part, he said, due to his church's emphasis on family time.

"I am in a position now where it feels great. I'm where I had always hoped to be. I don't need to work for that $200,000 a year of interest income. But Laurie says that if I closed the doors of the firm, I'd be impossible to be with."

It's a joke, to be sure, but one that contains elements of truth. Money does funny things to people. Even if they have a lot of it, many won't live as if they do. "When I met that goal," Pete recalled of the nearly $900,000 in CD savings he socked away before age 33, "I was still working for somebody else. When I got that ninth CD funded, I went home and showed Laurie the deposit slip. She wasn't that excited. I thought she should have been. I asked her, 'What am I going to do now?' I was thinking of going back to school and getting a Ph.D. Laurie said no. 'You're going to do the same thing you did yesterday!' To her, the last $90,000 was security."

A MILLIONAIRE'S WHEELS: THE ANTI-LIMOUSINE

Unlike so many wealthy, middle-aged entrepreneurs, Pete N., 42, of Salt Lake City, doesn't get giddy over German-made sedans or brutish four-wheel-drive vehicles. As the father of five children, he's a minivan man, favoring the trusty Dodge Caravan as his family's workhorse vehicle.

"I bought this one used," he said of his $16,000 Caravan. "It was only a year old, and it had everything we needed." His previous minivan, a screechy number with worn shocks and upwards of 80,000 miles, could hardly have made it through another winter in the Rocky Mountains without major work. And even though he could afford any car or sport-utility vehicle on a Lexus lot, Pete, a self-made millionaire, has never seen a need to impress the neighbors. He's been too busy saving money for more important things, like his children's educations. And one recent summer, it was time to put his oldest son to work, to introduce him to the art of selling.

Out in the parking lot of the $2.5-million-a-year marketing company that Pete started in the mid-1980s, a forlorn-looking, 1991 Ford Escort station wagon sat with hand-lettered signs taped to the front windows. They read, "For Sale, 1991, air, 5-spd, one owner. Call 555-XXXX." Pete, a company president but a salesman first and foremost, had told a neighbor that he'd be glad to sell the car for her, as a way of teaching his son Kevin, 16, about business. The deal was: If Kevin wrote and placed the ads in the paper, took the phone calls, showed the car during test-drives, and kept the sale price above $1,500, he would earn a $100 commission. If he sold the car for less, the commission would drop to $15.

The first few times Kevin took phone calls from potential buyers, he was stony, in a teenage way. "Yeah, it's still for sale," he'd say, or "Uh, huh. 77,000 miles" or "Black." His voice was monotone. But as the first two weeks went by without a serious offer, Pete and Kevin decided to drop the price from $1,800 to $1,700. Then, Kevin became decidedly more animated when the phone rang. "I couldn't believe it," Pete said. In addition to bragging about the five-speed transmission, "he was telling people the air conditioner has five settings. I don't even know what that means. The air conditioner? But he was excited about it.

"I am really trying, as a father, to teach my kids how to work," Pete said. "If I can do that, I can view my sunset years a lot easier." Might there be an antique Escort in his sunset years? The last I heard, the car hadn't been sold. But the price had dropped once more, to $1,600.

Maybe it was also what gave Pete the security to go out on his own. Maybe that's why his company made it. Because it wasn't going to be a mere business. It was going to be at least a little bit fun. Or else, $4 to $6 million later, what would be the point?

Sowing His Wild Oats— And Striking It Rich

At first glance, Mike Gilliland doesn't look like a millionaire. When I met this chief executive officer of the 63-store, $400 million-a-year natural foods chain, he was wearing khaki hiking shorts, a sweaty gray polo shirt, a white baseball cap, a Timex Ironman watch, and well-worn sneakers. He was sitting on a fence, alongside his 21-speed bike, at 8:45 A.M., toward the end of his 12-mile bicycle commute from Longmont to Boulder, Colorado, two towns away. A Christmas tree pattern of sweat had formed on his back, and, some 10 weeks shy of his 40th birthday, Mike could easily have passed for a graduate student at the nearby University of Colorado. His shaggy red hair, youthful complexion, stocky build, and decidedly uncorporate clothes didn't say "executive" as much as they said "small-town grocery store manager." And Mike wouldn't have a problem with that.

As he arrived at headquarters, he wheeled his bike into the building to a chorus of hellos. Except something was odd: Employees called him by his first name. I also noticed that Mike, a husband, father of 10-year-old twins, and the head honcho of the second-largest chain of natural food stores in America, didn't wear a bicycle helmet. Not smart, I thought, for someone who rides 24 miles round-trip when he commutes. I wondered what the stockholders would think.

Lesson 5: Stay in touch (figuratively) with your customers.

When he handed me his business card, I saw once again that this businessman was different. Sure, the card had all the required information: phone, fax, and e-mail numbers and even a hip logo of proud grains embossed on the upper-left corner (probably printed in soy ink). But when I looked at the card more carefully, I saw that his home phone number was also there, betwixt his pager and cellular phone numbers.

This guy must be kidding, I thought. Or else he must be serious about groceries. He's long felt that if you're in a service business, you should be accountable to your customers. When he and his co-owner and wife, Libby Cook, first started out, they made a decision that was unheard of in the grocery business, be it old-line supermarket or natural food store. They printed their home phone number on each and every grocery bag that went out of the store.

It turns out that Mike and his wife don't get all that many calls from customers wondering why the White Wave chocolate soy milk, say, is so much more expensive than the standard dairy stuff. A few each month is more like it. Mike and his wife wanted to stand out; they wanted customers to become fiercely loyal to their stores. And they figured out one unique way to stoke that loyalty. That's staying in touch with your customers.

I wondered whether this philosophy of customer service carried down through the ranks, and I found some evidence in the staff handbook. "Smoking: If you smoke, please stop. But until you become so enlightened, smoke off-premises and without being seen by customers. Wash your hands, and mints are recommended. Many of our customers are very sensitive or allergic." It went on: "Telephone: Do not leave anyone on terminal hold. Bike Policy: We encourage staff members to ride their bikes to work." (I found no evidence of a helmet policy.)

Of course, by itself, accountability to customers won't make you a gazillion dollars. In fact, the first few years they were in business, Mike and Libby (a lawyer by training) were in danger of going out of business. They had amassed a mini-chain of three grocery stores, and things weren't looking good. They'd maxed out their credit cards, taken a second mortgage on their house, even borrowed $7,000 from his mom to try to stay afloat. "We were working some pretty serious hours," Mike said. "I was going seven days a week, going in on four hours of sleep, for one year. It was a stressful time. We were kiting register checks, then running to the bank to make deposits. It was all debt-financed."

But as he explained later, "Our business always has been our survival. It's never been a point of conflict for us." He added, "I'm the dysfunctional one of the family." He's also modest. When I asked about second homes his family has or "escapes" they make, he said that their home is their home and that there's no need for a vacation home. He likes living near where he works and on a plot of land that's big enough on which to grow crops. In addition, Mike explained that by the time he was 14 years old, his family had moved 14 times. "My dad had a government job," he said by way of explanation. "When we were teenagers, one day he just split."

That's another reason why Mike plans to stay put. Even when his company outgrew its headquarters in downtown Boulder, he found new space on the edge of town, but moved no farther. A sense of place is clearly important to him. After all, he could live most anywhere. And as owner of 15 percent of the common stock in the 11-year-old company, which does $400 million in annual sales, he could retire early—way early. But he's chosen not to. "Libby's goal a year ago was to get down to working 20 hours a week," he added, sounding as if she hasn't made it there yet.

Although their vision of natural food stores didn't click at first, Mike had a hunch about food service early on—and about making numbers work. One day when he was living in Paris for a time in his early twenties, after dropping out of the Air Force Academy, he spotted a man making crepes and was enthralled.

"You wouldn't happen to remember how many he was making, would you?" I asked, on a lark.

"Seventy-five crepes an hour," Mike answered. "And $2.50 a crepe seemed like pure profit to me, close to $200 an hour." Sure enough, when he returned Stateside, he went into entrepreneurial action by opening a crepe stand in New Orleans. It promptly bombed, as did his short-lived career as a parasailing-school proprietor in St. Croix, West Indies.

"We've messed up enough to realize that we're not infallible," Mike said. "Lately, I've been getting e-mail asking why the stock has been a little soft." That might be expected when a company doubles in size three years in a row, but Mike and company have a three-pronged plan for the long-term.

1. To keep the culture intact: great natural products and great customer service

2. To hit the financial targets they have provided to Wall Street analysts

3. To manage the strain of opening new stores relatively comfortably

When venture capitalists dangled $5 million in front of Mike and Libby, to help them grow the business, they were skeptical about losing control. "We had a line of $5 million and only took $2 million at first," he said. "We felt like we knew the business and wanted to minimize the interference from the banking community. It's only been in the last couple of years that we've realized we don't have to own 51 percent of the company to run the business." As the company has grown from 8 stores to 20, to 40, and now to more than 60, Mike and his officers have ceded some control to "the money people." He now owns some 15 percent of the company's stock, he told me, although that is more than enough to help keep the company's heart and affiliates "pure." It's also enough to cash out and go home to live on the farm. Instead, Mike, Libby, and their two children will continue to run the business while gearing up for a four-month sabbatical in Europe.

"I have a sister who's a classics major," he said. "She's going to be our tour guide through Greece and throughout. We're getting out as a family unit, which is getting tough to do. The way I see it, our kids are 10. We've got two or three years before they talk back to us, and one or two years later they'll hate us."

Lesson 6: Stay in touch (literally) with your customers.

Through all the ups and downs, the owners and managers of the natural food stores have tried to hold firm to the belief that they are in a "dignified" profession. That is Mike's term, and when he dons an apron in Columbus, Ohio, to help open a store, he isn't just playing Mr. Whipple. "I like my kids to see me in an apron," Mike says. "I want them to know what I do, even though retail is not everybody's favorite profession. It's a tough job, but we are selling great food and also supporting a cause. We are supporting an industry, and we are supporting local farmers. When we were reworking our mission statement the other day, someone in our company said, 'We've got to get people to fall in love with the company.'"

"Dignified," "supporting a cause," and "fall in love" are not words and phrases you'd associate with your basic corporate chain.

And there's one final lesson that Mike and his employees are

MIDLIFE-MILLIONAIRES' LESSONS

Of the many tips offered to me by the millionaires I interviewed, here are six that rose to the top and ways that you can make use of them in your business and personal life.

Lesson 1: Focus on your abilities more than on your dreams.

You have lots of dreams at 20, and a lesser number by 30, but by then you should have some strengths. By 40, get ready to put them into action, big-time, if you haven't already.

Lesson 2: Plan for the upside; react to the downside.

Don't be too aggressive, but you need to have a business and financial strategy for success, or else you may deplete too much earning power on defensive money moves.

Lesson 3: Rethink your retirement plan at 40.

The millionaire who passed this edict along had a plan for his retirement firmly in place before he was 30. No matter where you stand at 40, drawing up a plan for a retirement fund and committing to it over the next 10 years should set you up nicely for your sixties and beyond.

Lesson 4: Think like a CEO, work as an employee.

As an entrepreneur, when you meet with clients and customers, remember your company's mission. Think large. But when it comes to such things as office space and expenses, scale down—way down. It'll pay off a decade hence.

Lesson 5: Stay in touch (figuratively) with your customers.

Some (maybe only a few) successful executives list their home phone numbers on their business cards or on their companies' products. For the rest of us, an e-mail address might suffice.

Lesson 6: Stay in touch (literally) with your customers.

Mike Gilliland, president of Wild Oats Markets, recently found a way to give hands-on service to customers. He started a nonprofit health center adjacent to his natural food store, in which customers can make appointments for massages, yoga, and acupuncture. Brand extension and creative thinking may breed customer loyalty, if not big profits.

putting into action: They are finding new ways in which to become, literally, a hands-on company. In 1998, the company opened its first free-standing Wellness Center next to one of its grocery stores in Boulder. The goal is to provide customers and employees with massage, nutrition advice, acupuncture, and other healing modalities in a less clinical, more community-oriented setting.

Masseuses, chiropractors, and acupuncturists have donated time and cut their fees to introduce their services; Mike is a major financial backer. Money isn't important for now, the company says, as the centers will be run on a nonprofit basis. The plan is to provide interchange between local alternative medical providers and the community in an increasingly HMO-dominated world. The basic idea is that if you believe in organic lettuces, chances are you'll find something of value in shiatsu. And, of course, the hope is that you will feel better and remember the company name. Any way you look at it, the granola ethic is growing up, growing stronger, and growing richer.

CHAPTER 12

The View
from 50

If there is a single date to which we can attach the establishment of Stalin's power as absolute dictator, it is that of his 50th birthday on December 21, 1929.
> —RONALD HINGLEY, *JOSEPH STALIN: MAN AND LEGEND*, 1974

I am moving away from washboard abs and closer to washtub abs. Away from six-packs, more toward the keg look.
> —BILL GEIST, *THE BIG FIVE-OH!*, 1997

Long before golfer Leonard Thompson turned 50, he learned that his career might be in jeopardy. Had he been a salesman, accountant, or marketing manager, things wouldn't have been so dicey when he threw out his back mightily in 1993, at age 46. But Thompson is one of those few souls whose job consists largely of strolling over lush green fairways and swatting golf balls around. When I spoke with him, he was standing on the island of Maui, Hawaii, after just another day's toil as a competitor in the 1998 EMC^2 Kaanapali Classic, coming off a two-week stretch in which he'd won a total of $70,000 at just two California tournaments. His dark days seemed, for the moment, behind him.

Thompson, who turned professional in 1970, shortly after graduating from Wake Forest University in Winston-Salem, North Carolina, never really thought about getting a desk job. Fairways would be his way of making a living. Trouble was, after winning two tournaments (the Jackie Gleason–Inverrary Classic in 1974 and the 1977 Pensacola Open) in his first seven years as a pro, he hit a drought. A major drought. He didn't win again until the 1989 Buick Open, which meant he had gone winless on the PGA Tour for nearly 12 years. Although (thanks to the Buick win) he won $261,397 in 1989—by far his best year up to that point—his earnings in 1988, by comparison, weren't so pretty: He won just $84,659.

It didn't take an accountant to realize that $85,000 a year doesn't go a long way when one must pay to travel to 20 or 30 cities a year, with no guarantee of taking home a paycheck for the week. Plus, in this line of work, one's spine is quite literally the backbone of one's earnings. So when Thompson's first traumatic injury—diagnosed as severe strain in a sacroiliac joint—struck in 1993, it was only a matter of time before he would have to face the question of whether to have surgery. "It lingered on and on," he said of the pain. "I had almost a year of rehab, three hours a day, five days a week, for six months. Everything I know, I learned from physical therapists," he added.

Fortunately, he had a good friend who is an orthopedic surgeon, a friend who told him, "The last two things I want to hear from you are 'injections' and 'surgery.'" They both realized that even surgery couldn't guarantee pain-free golf swings with full flexion. Thompson never went under the knife. He worked his way back to health, back to the tour, and back into a frame of mind in which he could, at 47, start to think anew about his future.

On one hand, he was in the midst of a PGA career that would net him $1.8 million over 26 years (or an average of about $70,000 in winnings per year). On the other hand, even after his impressive rehab, he was on the downslope of his career. Except for the fact that the Senior

PGA Tour lately has become quite lucrative . . . and for the fact that players must be at least 50 years old to play on the Senior Tour. It's brought a lot of new life to midlife golfers—and a lot of fresh starts to those who've had tough seasons in their forties. (It also must be said, however, that the Senior Tour has doused the hopes of thousands of potential players who thought it would be relatively easy to earn a living with the "legends.")

"I really looked at the Senior Tour almost as a retirement plan," Thompson said over the phone from Hawaii. "That if you play well enough for four or five years, and you haven't made enough before, then this is an awfully good place to be." During an arduous rehab, the Senior Tour "was all I thought of . . . getting there."

"Were there any dark days back in the early '90s?" I asked, ingeniously.

"More than a couple," Thompson answered politely.

After turning 50 on New Year's Day 1997, it was time for the seasoned Leonard Thompson to "grow up." As such, he found himself in a unique position . . . someone who was simultaneously "playing" a game and working rather hard at setting himself up for retirement. For the record, in his first year on the Senior Tour, Leonard Thompson won some $385,000 in 30 events and tied for 40th on the tour's money list. Forget the bad back; he was back in fine form.

Greene with Envy, At 50

When I was 25, precisely half the age of the Senior PGA rookies, I worked for *Esquire* magazine as a fact-checker. It was not exactly a glamour job at a big-time magazine; in short, I did writers' dirty work, verifying an odd assortment of reported facts, spellings, and figures before they went into print. One morning, my job required me to check the facts of a story titled "Fifteen," written by Bob Greene of the *Chicago Tribune*. He was 35 or so at the time, writing about the exploits of a couple of 15-year-old boys who had nothing better to do one day than hang out at a suburban Midwestern mall. It was your basic fly-on-the-wall reporting job, in which Greene infiltrated their world and took you back, if only for a few minutes, to the Gap, to the record store, to your sophomore year of high school. Mall rat vérité.

Fifteen years after "Fifteen," I remember three things about that story: that the kids didn't buy much, except at the food court; that at one point, the mall security staff spotted reporter Greene trailing two male students, then intervened to make sure he wasn't some sort of creep; and third, that I'd wondered why a national columnist would spend one of his precious 12 "American Beat" columns a year on teenage guys skulking around a mall. Would it be compelling enough to older guys? Years later, I understood: It turns out that Greene, a four-time best-selling author, syndicated columnist, former *Nightline* correspondent, part-time performer in rock-and-roll bands, husband and father, wishes—at times—that he were back in high school. Two of his books, *Be True to Your School* and *All Summer Long*, are directly based on memories of his high school years. His most recent national bestseller, *The 50-Year Dash: The Feelings, Foibles, and Fears of Being Half a Century Old*, contains more than a dozen passages in which he looks back, fondly and longingly, upon his teenage years.

"At 50," Greene writes, "the people in your life you value the most are not the ones who promise they can make you rich; they are the ones who can make you laugh. If you're lucky, they're still the ones who could make you laugh when you were 17. They're the friends you want around you all the time."

I called Bob Greene's office soon after reading that passage, to ask him about being 50 versus being 15 or 40. We aren't exactly friends, but as an ex-colleague, he was amenable to an interview. Perhaps because I worked with him when his beat comprised the entire United States, I asked him first about travel. At 51, as a kind of Charles Kuralt for the newsprint world, wasn't he tired of the Hyatt-Hilton-Keep-your-seat-belts-fastened-till-we're-at-the-gate life yet? I mean, he chose to end one of his mid-career books with the lines: "The trip was still young, and here I was, already in the Twilight Zone. The road is long, but my patience is longer."

"When you're in your twenties, you think it's better than your salary," Greene said of business travel. "But after you've been to enough places, it starts taking more and more to make it memorable." New York and Los Angeles trips simply don't do it for him anymore. Predictably, though, Greene found a way to make travel at midlife memorable. In the early 1990s, on a whim, he accepted an invitation to travel, sing, and play with 1960s surf-music icons Jan and Dean. He turned out to be not half-bad, they said of Greene's singing and serviceable guitar skills. And so, partly in jest but mostly for kicks, he has traveled to county fairs and other wayward gigs every summer since, as a backup singer with the band.

"When you're 50, you've been on a lot of trips," Greene said. "It's hard to persuade yourself that there's that thrill that was there [when you were in your twenties]." Today, his reporting trips are business trips. Not that there's anything wrong with that. On the other hand, he said, when he travels with the band on his weekend time, the fact that he's carrying a guitar tends to invite questions from fellow travelers. He's not shy about answering them, either. "I know the same three chords I knew in high school," he said. "It's Jan and Dean and five backup guys. And it's the music I've always loved.

"This thing came out of nowhere," Greene said, adding that he doesn't often write about this other side of his life. It seems more charming to him when he doesn't draw attention to it. "We went to Worlds of Fun Amusement Park in Kansas City, Missouri; later, we played a convention of grocers and [Jan and Dean] gave me lead vocals on 'Dance, Dance, Dance' and 'Little Honda.'" These trips, he said, have given him "a freshness of eye" that he says he had when he first went on the road for the newspaper with steno pads and pens in hand. But, he added, as a backup singer in his "second" career, he realizes those trips aren't exactly his. They are booked and planned by Dean Torrance, not Bob Greene. Which is a new position for a guy who has long called his own shots on the road.

I was also curious about Greene's career goals at this stage of life, because, after all, he's had more than a few jobs in addition to newspaper man. In an era when Vietnam protests raged and heavy metal music hadn't yet surfaced, Greene put on makeup and leather and all sorts of rocker regalia and went on tour for six months with Alice Cooper. The result? *Billion Dollar Baby*, a hardcover book and journal about traveling across the land and playing amped-up rock with a male rocker named Alice who painted spiders about his eyes and wrapped snakes around his body. Not your average job description. "It was a reporting device," Greene said nonchalantly of his Alice Cooper year on the road.

The same went for the year he spent tracking Richard Nixon and George McGovern for his 1972 campaign journal. And the same went for the week in the early 1970s that he spent living in Hugh Hefner's Playboy mansion, along with 25 Bunnies and assorted others. A simple reporting device, indeed.

These days, in the midst of middle age, his goals have shifted. At 50, Greene says he is no longer driven by the mindset of "What more can I achieve?" Instead, he is more concerned with "What is the most fun I can have while working?" (At the same time, however, many of his columns in recent years have taken a serious turn, focusing on evocative child custody and legal issues.)

"To me—there's a place in *The 50-Year Dash* where I talk about this—the impulse is not to keep moving so fast. Instead it's about finding a 'backyard' to the soul. And it's not a static place. Instead of setting yourself a career goal at 50 . . . maybe the phrase 'Have fun' sounds too shallow . . . but if you can find something that puts a smile on your face," and that also has something to do with putting bread on the table, you will, Greene believes, be heading in a healthy direction. Of course, it almost goes without saying that it helps to have earned six-figure salaries for years, as Greene has, to have covered such middling concerns as college costs for the kids and retirement costs for your family.

One key difference between work life at 40 and work life at 50, then, is a subtle but striking move from proving things to others to proving things to yourself. As Greene told me, "When the world tells us being 50 is not the same for us as it was for other generations, well, there's no way you can say that 50 is young; you can't." Time to grow in different ways, gentlemen.

As noted life-stage psychologist Carl Jung put it, back in the early 1900s, 40 is the "noon" of life, while midlife is the period of "greatest unfolding." He believed quite strongly that the second half of life has a purpose very different from that of the first: Instead of making our impression on the world through career conquests and raising children, the post-40 and post-50 years should be marked by a contraction of sorts, marked by a lesser focus on getting ahead and an increasing focus on developing one's self.

This is very likely what Greene was alluding to with his quest for the "backyard of the soul." It's just that he's not the kind of guy to use the psychobabble of the therapist's office. That wouldn't jibe with the

CHANGES IN ATTITUDES

Jimmy Buffett, the perennially popular singer and cheeseburger-lover (who actually penned the paean "Cheeseburger in Paradise" to them) can now add "author" to his list of accomplishments: He wrote a bestselling book about his birthday, entitled *A Pirate Looks at Fifty*. Obviously not laced with psychological gleanings, Buffett's breezy journal/travelogue nonetheless contains a few nuggets of wisdom well-worth contemplating. Here are a few of the chart-toppers.

• The early bird gets to fish. "These days, I get up when I used to go to bed," he writes. "That's when you know you're getting older. Just to stay up until my birth hour, I had to have a two-hour nap this afternoon and a double espresso after dinner."

• When traveling for long stretches with your family, take a traveling partner who shares your interests. At least that's what 50th-birthday boy Buffett did in planning his 'round-the-Caribbean birthday and vacation tour. He and his wife, Jane, agreed, before they packed their seaplane, that each of them would take along a friend to pal around with on the three-week trip. This is not something a typical 30-ish or 40-ish couple would include in their travel prep. Yet Buffett explains, "Now, don't get me wrong. Jane and I truly enjoy each other's company . . . but we still are different people with different interests."

• Forget haggling, pay the price. "I have never been a bargainer, especially in foreign countries. It is not in my nature. Bargaining should not be a part of life after 50. By that time, you know whether you can afford something or not." Not a bad lesson to sock away.

kind of life lived by an Ohio native who wrote *Chevrolet Summers, Dairy Queen Nights*. He is, as he himself would tell you, much more comfortable at county fairs and county courthouses.

In Bob Greene's soulful backyard, there will, apparently, always be green grass, crickets, and surf music blaring through screened windows. "It's about getting your summer back," he said. "It's getting something back you never thought you'd get again." Sometimes it's experienced through family reunions or through the exploits of your children; other times it strikes without warning.

"It's like you're 17 again," Greene said of his unlikely return to singing the songs of his youth on stage with the same Jan and Dean he sang along with on that car radio in Bexley, Ohio, some 35 years ago. "What was so odd," he added, was that after singing those same songs with the band he grew up with, he ended up, one summer night, "eating cheeseburgers at 2:00 in the morning at Waffle House." One man's fantasy at 50, one man's reality. You want fries with that?

Bill Geist: New "Philosophies at Phive-Oh"

Truth be told, when I spoke with Bill Geist, resident funnyman/reporter for CBS News and author of *The Big Five-Oh!*, I expected wisecracks about hitting 50. But I was surprised to find a more serious side to Geist, one that emerged from behind the scenes of his public image as wry spokesguy for the 50-plus set.

Not surprisingly, he talked a lot in his book about his middle-age spread and the growing importance of food in a man's life once he exits his forties. "I talk about how food has become more important in our lives," Geist said, "and about how you drop the Playboy channel and pick up the Food Channel [from your cable TV 'menu']. About how you now get 'aroused' by buffets, even though you can't read the menu any more."

But when I pressed him a bit, he said his 50th year held meaning for him beyond the idea of a milestone or half-century marker. "I just didn't like the whole idea of turning 50," Geist said. "I really felt a lot older, suddenly. When I was 49, my mother passed away. It was terrible. It changed everything, as my father had passed away 20 years ago." While he was growing up in Illinois, Geist's parents ran a small newspaper in Champaign County, in the corn-and-soybean belt of the state. Geist the younger got into newspapering after college, working for a suburban paper at first and eventually "graduating" to columnist for the *New York Times*.

Then came his TV and nonfiction book years, his forties. Multiple bosses, multiple careers, multiple goals, most of which were fulfilled before 50. "The only good thing I can tell you about 50 is that you can be a lot more comfortable with yourself," Geist said. "You can be a lot

HANGOVER HELPER

He didn't want to party.

Although Bill Geist, resident funnyman/reporter for CBS News and author of *The Big Five-Oh!*, didn't want a big celebration for his 50th birthday, one of the reasons why may lie in his observation that "age and alcohol don't mix." In fact, he has constructed a helpful scale for people who drink too much too often over the years—a veritable hangover age gauge.

To figure your approximate Hangover Recovery Time, Geist says in his book, simply multiply your age by your alcohol consumption by the morning hour at which you fell sloppily asleep. That equals your hangover longevity in "waking minutes."

An example is a 21-year-old guy who drinks six beers and flops down in his Jeep at 2:00 A.M. Sunday morning: Hangover Recovery Time = $21 \times 6 \times 2 = 252$ waking minutes. Or put another way: He'll feel fuzzy-headed for 4 hours and 12 minutes after he awakens.

Consider, then, a 50-year-old who sips six beers and takes a cab home at 2:00 A.M.: Hangover Recovery Time = $50 \times 6 \times 2 = 600$ waking minutes. Or translated: He'll feel like hell 10 hours after he gets up, so if it's a noon wakeup, you can pretty much write off all of Sunday.

Readers'/Guzzlers' Note: When I quizzed Geist about the accuracy of these figures, he didn't hesitate to come clean. "Some of it's theoretical," he said. "It wasn't actually tested in a lab." He was semi-serious. I was semi-kidding.

Cheers.

more honest about things. Your career is either made or not; you know who your friends are. So there's no need to waste time, anymore, going out with people you think you ought to be with. You'll feel more free to be yourself."

In the "old" days, according to Geist, he or his colleagues often would go out for dinner with certain people because they felt that they should or because certain people "might be able to help you get into a nightclub—not that I ever got into a club. It was networking for social reasons." These days Geist avoids that type of lockstep corporate ascent. "You can see the top," Geist said. "And how miserable they might be, and how awful their lives are," although they are healthy and wealthy. Not the obvious answer, perhaps, from someone who has a good gig at CBS and who cashes substantial paychecks, on cue, from the network, every two weeks. But a refreshingly honest one.

"You do start to look ahead," Geist said. "I still have all my faculties, and so I start thinking it is time." In Geist's case, that means time to prepare to write a novel, which is something he simply hadn't done in more than 25 years of writing nonfiction. "Although," he quipped, flinging one last crack, "writing a book about 50 is a lot more lucrative than writing a novel."

Lessons from a Lifelong "Coach"

When Michael "Mickey" Hoffman turned 50, life was literally the pits. As a commodities broker in the financial markets of Chicago, he spends his working days within shouting distance of the cacophonous Chicago Mercantile Exchange, one of the largest financial markets in the United States. He is successful, but not wildly so. Consider his predicament: Some people go through life as gym teachers; others become assistant principals at high schools. Some sell life insurance for a living; others earn Ph.D.'s from prestigious universities, then try to market their knowledge in and out of educational settings. Still other men take a risk or three and delve into "life in the pit," as traders call the Merc Exchange. (The pit is where the world goes to shop for tomorrow's and next year's orange juice, coffee, sugar, cotton, cocoa, even Eurodollars; it is also where Hoffman started his career anew in midlife.) In fact, he has had all these careers, from teaching through trading, from his twenties through age 50.

Teaching and counseling were in Hoffman's blood. In the 1970s, after many years as a coach, he became a counselor at Glenbrook North High School. "I remember, in my earlier years, my grandfather said, 'Get as much education as you can, because nobody can take that away from you.' Hoffman had studied for three years to get his Ph.D. in order to become a principal, but that was not destined to happen soon for him at Glenbrook North. "I just wasn't willing to wait 20 years for a principal to retire; and I wasn't willing to go to Wisconsin or Iowa."

So in his early forties, Hoffman logged a few financially secure but ultimately unfulfilling years as an insurance salesman. Besides security, what initially appealed to Hoffman about his move from education to insurance was that he got to be a counselor again. "I was in the insurance industry for three years," he said, "and it felt good meeting with people and learning about their endeavors. It also felt good to take part, in a way, in other people's successes. Almost all of them were doing well, and it was shocking to learn that so many people I had known in high school and college had made it that far. I mean, there were dentists earning a million dollars. In college, I was the token athlete of the house, the 'athlete-face guy' brought in to bring prestige to the fraternity." His fraternity brothers, it seems, never expected him to be a financial hotshot. It wasn't his role.

Neither, it turned out, was insurance sales. While it was lucrative and proved to be a steady job at a time in his life when he craved stability, eventually he became uncomfortable with the job. "The sales part of it wasn't me." He also realized his company wanted him to hawk plans he didn't believe his customers truly needed. "They wanted me to sell whole-life [long-term, investment-type insurance plans], when what these people actually needed was [less expensive, fixed-rate] term insurance." Nonetheless, "the first contract I sold was for a million-dollar life insurance policy for one family," Hoffman recalled. "The second was a 78-man group policy for a business." His prospects were good, plus his two kids probably wouldn't have to worry about going to college 5 to 10 years hence.

Soon after Hoffman turned 40, he decided to take a shot at making his big bucks well before 50, when a friend offered to usher him into the trading business, with guidance and a seat on the exchange. Yet Hoffman felt, for the first time in his multifaceted business career, unprepared. A respected athlete all his life, he hit the ground walking, not running. He didn't score a million-dollar payoff his first, second, or third year in the pit, as he thought he might, though he didn't do badly, either. He plateaued.

"I went into pit trading making an assumption I could or would make a million. I didn't. I was unprepared." While he points out that he was far more mature at age 40 than 30, Hoffman concedes that his move was more impulsive than reasoned. "I probably would have been better off staying in insurance—definitely for the family, if not for me personally," he said. But those are the kinds of decisions you have to make at 40 sometimes, because you feel, as Hoffman did, that it might be too late to make such a drastic switch at age 50. (Not everybody gets to go on the road with Jan and Dean like Bob Greene.) Hoffman assured me he enjoyed support from his wife, Shari, but that she was merely "half" supportive. He did not hide the fact, either, that she enjoyed the steady income and security he was providing; whereas commodities was a kind of crapshoot.

"I mean, I had doubled my earnings," he said of insurance sales. "Now I'm going to go into commodities? I thought, 'The sky is the limit,' but there was no formal education on how to do it. Day one, I walked into the pit knowing nothing. What a friggin' idiot I was. My mentality was, 'I'm going to beat up these guys.' But in truth, I didn't want to beat them up. I wanted to compete."

The upshot? It wasn't his 40th or 50th birthday that derailed him. It was the thought that so many guys around him were younger and perhaps hungrier. Not smarter, mind you. But it was a shock of recognition that stayed with him a couple years into his early fifties, when I asked him to reflect on his biggest birthday.

"I felt more at home in the pit. It made more sense to me to be there, instead of all the other places I'd worked. I guess that was because I always felt more comfortable as an athlete, and that competitive environment was comfortable from that standpoint." As he moved into the life of a trader, where men crowd each other chest to back to chest in human sandwich formation to shout trades, he was forced to bring back the person he once was—"an athlete and a street fighter"—as opposed to reinventing himself. Still, it wasn't easy. "I hadn't been that person for a long time," he said. "I didn't want to be that person again. But I wanted more money, and the freedom to do what I wanted, when I wanted."

He has learned enough, over the years, to compete in a way that's both tolerable and profitable. So much so that both of his daughters are involved in the commodities business; so is a son-in-law.

He has also learned enough to know that his maximum value in life will likely be in some form of teaching. He no longer jostles for position in the pits. Over the past six years, Hoffman has moved into a recruiting role at USA Trading, a job he describes as a sort of "rainmaker." "I've been able to teach people to trade," he says, "and to the young people, I've always been a teacher."

There is one new twist on his life at midlife, however: motivational speaking. It's a bug he caught in his late forties, and he has since built a small business offering training tips and doing such speaking. In other words, the coach has found a way to coach once more. "I can say this," he said of his checkered career, "the earlier someone can determine who they are and what their strengths and weaknesses are . . . It's vital that he be happy with himself. I was happy selling and it helped me pay for college and weddings; it helped me [learn to] do what I want to do. Trouble was, Hoffman didn't realize until rather late in his career path that "it's not a particular happy experience doing what people tell you to do. I am an entrepreneur now; I own my own business. But you still develop relationships—you still have to suck it up. When I grew up, people in my parents' generation stayed in the same jobs their whole lives. They always tried to make someone else happy. That's a bunch of bull."

Now that he knows what he knows, now that he's coaching again, does it make him feel young? "In my fifties, I feel much older," he said. "In my forties, I still felt really young. I don't really believe that I've 'made it,' in many ways, while many of my contemporaries say they've made it and now they're 'finished.' It may be erroneous thinking, but I'm not finished. I don't want to be. I wouldn't want to be part of that golfing-everyday crowd, without looking ahead.

"I want to be, somehow, contributing to other people's lives. I feel really good about that, too. Some of my old fraternity brothers; they're sort of lost. They don't have anything to do. I'm probably the happiest I have ever been, in my fifties, in terms of fulfillment of what I believe. I don't know if it has anything to do with money. Because that hasn't kept me young."

A Men's Group Leader Looks at 50

You don't have to have a Ph.D. in psychology to know that many men never grow up. But Tom Fiester, a Boulder, Colorado, psychologist, has both a Ph.D. and the intimate knowledge of scores of midlife men's lives. He helped found the Boulder Men's Center in the mid-1980s, and during many of the past 15 years, he has led men's groups and related therapy sessions in which men have complained far and wide about

BOX SCORE

FIVE THINGS TO DO AT 50

If you haven't taken stock of yourself at 40 or 45, relax. Here's a short course—an extremely short course—in midlife self-improvement, as suggested by Neil Rosenthal, Ph.D., a Denver marital and family therapist and syndicated newspaper columnist who turned 50 himself not long ago.

1. Be physically active, making a point to include rigorous activities in your weekly mix—not just for the faux youthful feelings but also to feel vital for hours at a time.
2. Treat yourself to healthful pleasures. If you don't reward yourself in this way, you'll likely seek unhealthful alternatives.
3. Settle the troubling issues of your past; make a point to keep growing.
4. Live (more) honestly. It's time to open up with people at home, with family, and on the job. Even if some people get hurt. Don't be mean, however; use both tact and guile.
5. Make a vow to maximize your life. Not just with money or toys. And not all at once, but set a course. Then, over time, allow your passions to play out and eventually make an imprint upon you.

"It's taken us half a lifetime to figure out that contentment comes from personal growth," Dr. Rosenthal says. The sooner you get started, then, at 41, 45, or 50, the better off you'll be.

the lot of their lives. Fiester has done some complaining himself. You can call him a straight shooter.

"Midlife is when the faulty socialization of men really shows up," says Fiester. He adds, "You don't get the meaning of connection, as a man, by age 40." He believes it typically takes longer. "And if you don't eventually get that, you'll be missing out on security, a sense of belonging in the world." The "connection" he is addressing goes beyond career talk and neighborly wrangling.

"Marriages don't have to be happy," Fiester suggests. "What's important is that they are meaningful." Can't they be both? I wonder. I've been married fewer than five years and I want badly to believe there's a future in our future. Of course they can, Fiester allows. But they don't have to be. He was just being honest, more honest than I can perhaps imagine in my psychologically adolescent state. This makes me feel young, at least for a minute.

"We go through more changes in our lives from 40 to 50 than we ever do in the rest of our lives," Fiester concludes. "Being 'happy' in life is not a worthy goal," he adds, from the comfortable perch of being both 55 and, finally, happily married. "It must be meaningful."

As a man who conceived this book at age 39, who planned to have it written by age 40½, and who shunned a large celebration for his 40th birthday, I understood where Fiester was coming from. The big birthdays are big for reasons other than having a "0" attached to them. They signify more than we as men can comfortably handle on one boozy day. But that's all right. When you think of it, we've got 10 years or so to make sense of them. When you think of it, there's no rush.

Afterword

The kid in me just couldn't keep quiet: "Go, bitch, go! Go, bitch, go!" On a hot, bright, blue-sky summer day in northern Colorado, along the Front Range of the Rockies, at approximately 7,100 feet of altitude, I found myself short of breath, yelling it again, at no one in particular: "Go, bitch, go!"

Actually, I was yelling at my Cannondale mountain bike, while trying to ascend a steep pitch of uneven trail in the Walker Ranch Open Space area of Boulder County—and I wasn't about to give in. No matter how limited my lung and leg power might have been at the moment, I was not about to dismount the bike and walk it up the rest of the rise. That was unacceptable. I'd been training for this relatively technical ride all summer, the first summer of semi-serious bike riding I had done in my life. (And that includes 15 years of on-and-off bicycle commuting that I had survived in New York City.) So I kept on screaming, adding four or five more "Go-bitch-go's," and kept on grinding—to the consternation of my riding mates. Within three minutes, tops, in granny gear still, I reached the top of the crest and pulled over in some shade to catch my breath.

"I wondered who you were yelling at," said a hardbodied 39-year-old female friend, who earlier had passed me by a quarter-mile.

"Just me," I replied.

I realized then, or maybe a few hours later, that I had graduated. I had made it up the grade, excuse the pun. I may not have been "elite," but I was an authentic mountain biker, after a year of acclimating my 40-year-old body to the mountains, trails, and altitude, to the obstacles involved in singletrack and kinder trail riding—in sum, the kind of riding that's so often encountered in the off-road areas of the Rockies.

Which, I should add, is the general region I now call my home. Although the Walker Ranch views from the saddle of a mountain bike rivaled those I had seen in such areas of Vail and Keystone, Colorado, they happened to be located less than 15 miles from my home, where my wife, Paula, and I moved just a couple of years before. As I was 38 at the time, some might call it a midlife crisis: I mean, leaving New York City and a bunch of good friends and a great job and a six-figure income and a clean, affordable, not-yet-roach-infested apartment and all. For what exactly? So-called open space and astounding views? Not quite.

It was more than that. It was time for us to make a move, figuratively and literally. We had played the commuter-marrieds coast-to-coast airport shuffle for too long. In two-plus years of marriage, we had rarely lived in the same home together for more than four months at a time. Job demands kept calling. More to the point, it was time for me not to start over, but to start anew. New jobs, new house (my first), new car (also my first, non-rental), new friends, new family plans, and yes, some old issues.

Paula and I still spend too much time apart, we believe, and neither of us has the next two or three years of salary guaranteed. (That's the price we both pay for working in creative industries—she's an associate film producer.) And after four years of marriage, we still don't have the child we'd hoped to have had by now—at least, not at the time of this writing. But we most definitely have a future. And, thankfully, we have our health. And wonderful families to reach out to for love and support.

Nowadays, I guess, when I yell, "Go, bitch, go," I'm not just yelling at my knobby wheels to keep turning. I'm celebrating a challenge, releasing years of pent-up stress, and becoming more engaged (however embarrassing it may be to my wife or other riding partners) in a new kind of life. And much as I'd like to say I have all the answers, the truth is that I'm still climbing.

This is another way of saying that you don't have to make a huge move at age 38, 39, or 40 to find your own version of what I didn't quite know I was looking for at 38½. It doesn't have to be a move to the country, the mountains, the big city, or even to a different suburb. If I've learned anything from all the people who talked with me about turning 40—who make up the bulk of this book—it is that the early forties are an opportune time to make sound moves, not wild ones.

To hear some 42-year-olds tell it, it doesn't even have to be a major career move. A minor one may be sufficient to right your course, if it's accompanied by changes in your family life, churchgoing, or socializing habits. I mean, when was the last time you heard that a lateral move in business was a step up? I've now heard it time and again from some thoughtful midlife cohorts.

Midlife, as the sage psychologist Carl Jung stated so presciently, long ago, is a time in which to try to remain connected. He summarized a particularly rough patch in his own life, saying, "It was most essential for me to have a normal life in the real world. My family and my profession remained the base to which I could always return, assuring me that I was an actually existing, ordinary person. The unconscious contents could have driven me out of my wits. No matter how deeply absorbed or how blown about I was, I always knew that everything I was experiencing was ultimately directed at this real life of mine. I meant to meet its obligations and fulfill its meanings."

Obligations and meanings—that's hard and soft, simultaneously sharp and fuzzy. And appropriately so, for that's what being 40, and beyond, is ultimately about. As well as a couple of throaty "Go, bitch's." Truth be told, life at this point may not be completely open-ended. But it is far, far from over. For one thing is certain: When a man turns 40, there's no turning back.

Acknowledgments

With all due respect to the women who helped shape these pages, I'd like to first thank men for helping this book come to life. From the guys who sat for interviews in their offices, at their homes, on their computers, and over the phone, to those who spoke with me on golf courses, on bike trails, in restaurants, in bars, and on too many airplanes, my 40-ish male compatriots contributed more to this work than perhaps I had a right to expect. Generosity comes in many forms; I'm grateful to have had such time with such a wide variety of men. I'm also grateful to the countless women in their lives.

Similar thanks go out to the dozens of medical professionals and other experts who pitched in along the way. In particular, I'd like to thank Tom Fiester, Ph.D.; Ken Goldberg, M.D.; Jed C. Kaminetsky, M.D.; Neil Rosenthal, Ph.D.; David Schnarch, Ph.D.; Olga Silverstein, Ph.D.; George Thomas, M.D.; Patrick C. Walsh, M.D.; Elizabeth Yow; Steve Antonopulos of the Denver Broncos; Leonard Thompson of the Senior PGA Tour; Michael Korda of Simon and Schuster; Philippa Brophy and Nicki Britton at Sterling Lord Literistic; and Jack Croft of Rodale Press.

Closer to home, I'm grateful to my friends and family for supporting my habit—my fascination with one year in the lives of so many men—for the better part of two years. Most of all, I thank my amazing wife, Paula, for making me feel, always, young.

Index

Underscored page references indicate boxed text. *Italic* page references indicate illustrations.